BOOK OF ABRAHAM APOLOGETICS

BOOK OF ABRAHAM APOLOGETICS
A REVIEW AND CRITIQUE

DAN VOGEL

SIGNATURE BOOKS | 2021 | SALT LAKE CITY

To Brent Lee Metcalfe
and H. Michael Marquardt

The opinions expressed in this book are not necessarily those of the publisher.

Cover design by Jason Francis.

FIRST EDITION | 2021

LIBRARY OF CONGRESS CATALOGING-IN-PUBLICATION DATA

Names:	Vogel, Dan, 1955- author.
Title:	Book of Abraham apologetics : a review and critique / Dan Vogel.
Description:	First edition.	Salt Lake City : Signature Books, 2021.	Includes index.	Summary: "Said to have been dictated by Joseph Smith as a translation of an ancient Egyptian scroll purchased in Kirtland, Ohio, in 1835, the Book of Abraham may be Mormonism's most controversial scripture. Decades of impassioned discussion began when about a dozen fragments of Smith's Egyptian papyri, including a facsimile from the Book of Abraham, were found in the New York Metropolitan Museum in 1966. The discovery solved a mystery about the origin of the Egyptian characters that appear in the various manuscript copies of the Book of Abraham from 1835, reproduced from one of the fragments. Some LDS scholars devised arguments to explain what seemed to be clear evidence of Smith's inability to translate Egyptian. In this book, Dan Vogel not only highlights the problems with these apologetic arguments but explains the underlying source documents in revealing detail and clarity" — Provided by publisher.
Identifiers:	LCCN 2020056911 (print)	LCCN 2020056912 (ebook)	ISBN 9781560852902 (paperback)	ISBN 9781560853954 (ebook)
Subjects:	LCSH: Church of Jesus Christ of Latter-day Saints—Apologetic works—History and criticism.	Pearl of Great Price. Book of Abraham—Authorship.	Pearl of Great Price. Book of Abraham—Controversial literature.	Pearl of Great Price. Book of Abraham—Criticism, interpretation, etc.	Mormon Church—Apologetic works—History and criticism.
Classification:	LCC BX8629.P53 V64 2021 (print)	LCC BX8629.P53 (ebook)	DDC 289.3/24—dc23

LC record available at https://lccn.loc.gov/2020056911
LC ebook record available at https://lccn.loc.gov/2020056912

CONTENTS

Introduction vii

Abbreviations xix

Chronology xxiii

1 Documents and Timeline 1

2 Princess Katumin 33

3 The Pure Language 59

4 Race 95

5 The Cosmos 119

6 A Student of Hebrew 145

7 The Lost Papyrus and Catalyst Theories . . 179

8 Nineteenth-Century Sources 215

Conclusion 243

Index 251

Scripture Index 259

About the Author 263

Introduction

In early July 1835, twenty-nine-year-old Mormon prophet Joseph Smith arranged for the purchase of four Egyptian mummies and a number of writings on papyrus for $2,400, a considerable sum at the time. Five years earlier, Smith had founded the Church of Christ, later Church of the Latter Day Saints, and eventually Church of Jesus Christ of Latter-day Saints. According to assistant church president Oliver Cowdery, the 1835 acquisition included "two rolls of papyrus ... [and] two or three other small pieces of papyrus, with astronomical calculations, epitaphs, &c."[1] These items were purchased from a man named Michael Chandler, who said he had inherited them from his recently deceased uncle, the celebrated French traveler Antonio Lebolo.[2] After exhibiting and selling some of his Egyptian artifacts in several major cities, including Baltimore, Pittsburgh, and New Orleans, Chandler heard that Smith had translated the Book of Mormon from "Reformed Egyptian," published in 1830, so he traveled to Kirtland, Ohio, hoping to make another sale.

When Chandler showed up with his mummies and papyri, Smith saw an opportunity to translate an ancient text that would confirm some of his recent doctrinal developments as well as be available for public inspection, unlike the golden plates from which he said he had translated the Book of Mormon. Smith began immediately to exploit Chandler's documents by comparing

---

1. "Egyptian Mummies—Ancient Records," *LDS Messenger and Advocate* 2 (Dec. 1835): 234. This article includes an extract from a lengthy letter from Cowdery to William Frye (see Cowdery, Letter, Kirtland, Ohio, to Frye, Lebanon, Calhoun County, Illinois, 22 Dec. 1835, Oliver Cowdery Letterbook, 68–74, Henry E. Huntington Library, San Marino, California). Today, $2,400 is roughly the equivalent of $70,000-plus.

2. "Egyptian Mummies," 234. Chandler's claim that Lebolo was his uncle has never been verified. See H. Donl Peterson, *The Story of the Book of Abraham: Mummies, Manuscripts, and Mormons* (Salt Lake City: Deseret Book Co., 1995), 88.

the hieratic Egyptian characters to the so-called Reformed Egyptian characters that he said he had copied from the golden plates in 1828. According to Cowdery, "The morning Mr. Chandler first presented his papyrus to bro. Smith, he was shown, by the latter, a number of characters like those upon the writings of Mr. C[handler]. which were previously copied from the plates, containing the history of the Nephites, or book of Mormon."[3]

At Chandler's request, Cowdery reported, "bro. S[mith]. gave him the interpretation of some few [characters] for his satisfaction."[4] Cowdery then reproduced a certificate that Chandler supplied "unsolicited" attesting to Smith's ability as a translator.

> Kirtland, July 6th, 1835.
>
> This is to make known to all who may be desirous, concerning the knowledge of Mr. Joseph Smith, jr. in deciphering the ancient Egyptian hieroglyphic characters, in my possession, which I have, in many eminent cities, shown to the most learned: And, from the information that I could even learn, or meet with, I find that of Mr. Joseph Smith, jr. to correspond in the most minute matters.
>
> (signed) Michael H. Chandler.[5]

How seriously Chandler's statement may be taken is a fair question since he stood to make a great deal of money. As LDS scholar Terryl Givens observes, "Given Chandler's desire to unload his inherited mummies and papyri on a prospective buyer, his ignorance of ancient languages, and the unlikelihood that strangers in New York and Philadelphia would refer him to the presumed charlatan Joseph Smith, we do well to see in Chandler more flattery than sincerity."[6] Yet it is possible that Smith could have made some general observations about the papyri that might have coincided with what the learned had told Chandler. Concerning this matter, Cowdery said, "While Mr. Chandler was in Philadelphia, he used every exertion to

---

3. "Egyptian Mummies," 235.

4. Ibid.

5. Ibid. See also Michael Chandler, Certificate, Kirtland Township, Geauga County, Ohio, to Joseph Smith, Kirtland Township, Geauga County, Ohio, 6 July 1835, Oliver Cowdery Letterbook, 72.

6. Terryl Givens with Brian M. Hauglid, *The Pearl of Greatest Price: Mormonism's Most Controversial Scripture* (New York: Oxford University Press, 2019), 120.

find some one who could give him the translation of his papyrus, but could not, satisfactorily, though from some few men of the first eminence, he obtained in a small degree, the translation of a few characters."[7]

Since the details of François Champollion's decipherment of the Rosetta Stone were not yet widely disseminated in the United States, it is unlikely that the learned could decipher the Egyptian characters.[8] LDS scholars Robin Scott Jensen and Brian Hauglid agree that "neither Chandler nor any other American at that time would likely have been able to make such an attestation authoritatively."[9] Cowdery also said, "While yet in the custom house [in New York], that there was no man in that city who could translate his roll; but was referred by the same gentleman, (a stranger) to Mr. Joseph Smith, junior, who, continued he, possesses some kind of power or gifts, by which he had previously translated similar characters."[10]

Whatever Smith said to convince Chandler, it had nothing to do with Hebrew Bible patriarch Abraham. One point of possible agreement could have been the circular-shaped hypocephalus (now Book of Abraham, Fac. 2), which may have reminded Smith and his contemporaries of magic amulets, the zodiac, and astronomy, for which Egyptians were well known.[11] In December 1835, Cowdery reported that Chandler had sold some of his artifacts prior to his arrival at Kirtland, including "a small quantity of papyrus, similar, (as he says,) to the astronomical representation, contained with the present two rolls"[12]—referring to the circular hypocephalus. Although Smith had obtained a statement from

---

7. "Egyptian Mummies," 235.

8. See R. B. Parkinson et al., *Cracking Codes: The Rosetta Stone and Decipherment* (Berkeley: University of California Press, 1999), 41.

9. *JSP*, R4:xx.

10. "Egyptian Mummies," 235.

11. Examples of magic circles may be found in Francis Barrett, *The Magus, or Celestial Intelligencer; Being A Complete System of Occult Philosophy*, 2 vols. in 1 (London: Lackington, Allen, 1801), Book 1, between 174–75, as shown in fig. 1. A comprehensive collection of these circles is in Fred Gettings's *Dictionary of Occult, Hermetic and Alchemical Sigils* (London: Routledge and Kegan Paul, 1981).

12. "Egyptian Mummies," 236.

Figure 1. Plate from Francis Barrett's *The Magus* (1801), between pages 174 and 175, showing magic seals and talismans.

Chandler that ostensibly confirmed his abilities as a translator, he had nevertheless learned from this stranger from the East that any translation he would eventually offer to the public could not be confirmed or rejected by the learned.

Translation

Soon Smith announced that one of the scrolls contained the writings of Abraham and another scroll the record of the ancient patriarch Joseph (son of Jacob/Israel)—the two Old Testament characters, besides Moses, who had dealings with the Egyptians. On 19 July 1835, church member W. W. Phelps wrote a letter to his wife, Sally, in Missouri and told her: "As no one could translate these writings they were presented to President [Joseph] Smith. He soon knew what they were and said that the rolls of papyrus contained the sacred record kept by Joseph in Pharoah's court in Egypt and the teachings of Father Abraham."[13]

Working with scribes over the next several months, Smith produced among other things:

- Two small notebooks containing copies of now-missing fragmentary Egyptian texts and some preliminary translation. Though these notebooks contain similar content and nearly identical translations of some hieratic characters, one in the handwriting of Phelps and the other in Cowdery's, only Cowdery's notebook includes an inscription on the cover in the handwriting of church member Frederick G. Williams, which reads "Valuable Discovery of hiden reccords that have been obtained from ancient buring place of the Egiyptians," and Smith's signature.

- Three nearly identical "Egyptian Alphabets" in the handwritings of Phelps, Smith, and Cowdery containing individual characters and their translations or definitions in columns.

- A bound "Grammar and Alphabet of the Egyptian Language" (GAEL), mostly in the handwriting of Phelps with a small part in scribe Warren Parrish's handwriting, containing an expansion of the Alphabets into five degrees of meaning.

- Three translation documents in the handwritings of Phelps, Williams, and Parrish consisting of several pages each containing characters in the left margin and to the right the text of what Smith called the "Book of Abraham" (now Abr. 1:1–2:18).

In 1842 in Nauvoo, Illinois, where his church had settled three years earlier, Smith produced additional documents related to the Book of Abraham, some of which have survived in fragmentary form only.

- A printer's copy of the Kirtland translation documents in the handwriting of church apostle and scribe Willard Richards containing

---

13. William W. Phelps, Letter, Kirtland, Ohio, to Sally Waterman Phelps, Liberty, Missouri, 19 July 1835, partial transcription in Historian's Office, Journal History of the Church, 20 July 1835, CHL. Another partial transcription with some variant readings is also available in Leah Y. Phelps, "Letters of Faith from Kirtland," *Improvement Era* 45 (Aug. 1942): 529.

some revisions but with no characters in the margins, which was published in the 1 March 1842 issue of the *Times and Seasons*, the church's official magazine, under the heading: "A translation of some ancient Records that have fallen into our hands, from the Catacombs of Egypt, purporting to be the writings of Abraham, while he was in Egypt, called the Book of Abraham, written by his own hand, upon papyrus."[14]

- The text of twelve points of explanation for what is termed Facsimile 1 in the handwriting of Richards, which appears on the back of page 2 of the printer's copy of the first installment of the Book of Abraham. Facsimile 1 was also published in the 1 March 1842 issue of the *Times and Seasons*.

- A one-page fragment containing the text of Abraham 3:18–26 in the handwriting of Richards, which was part of what was published in the 15 March 1842 issue of the *Times and Seasons*.

- The text of twenty-three points of explanation for what is termed Facsimile 2 in the handwriting of Richards, which was published in the 15 March 1842 issue of the *Times and Seasons* with the second installment of the Book of Abraham.

Understanding these documents and correctly interpreting them is the key to understanding what occurred.

BOOK OF ABRAHAM AND RELATED DOCUMENTS[15]

Title	Contents/Source	Scribe	Date
"Valuable Discovery"	Amenhotep papyrus and translations	Cowdery	ca. early July 1835
Notebook of copied characters	Amenhotep papyrus and translations	Phelps	ca. early July 1835
Copies of Egyptian characters-A	Ta-sherit-Min papyrus	unknown	ca. July 1835
Copies of Egyptian characters-B	Ta-sherit-Min papyrus	unknown	ca. July 1835

---

14. "A Translation," *Times and Seasons* 3 (1 Mar. 1842): 704.
15. This chart follows the labeling of the documents in *JSP*, R4.

Title	Contents/Source	Scribe	Date
Copies of Egyptian characters-C	Ta-sherit-Min papyrus	unknown	ca. July 1835
Copy of hypocephalus	Hypocephalus of Sheshonq	unknown	July 1835–Mar. 1842
Egyptian Alphabet-A	Amenhotep papyrus pure language JSP I, cols. 3, 4, 5	Smith additions by Cowdery and Phelps	ca. July–Nov. 1835
Egyptian Alphabet-B	Amenhotep papyrus pure language JSP I, cols. 3, 4, 5	Cowdery	ca. July–Nov. 1835
Egyptian Alphabet-C	Amenhotep papyrus pure language JSP I, cols. 3, 4, 5	Phelps additions by Parrish	ca. July 1835 ca. Nov. 1835
Egyptian Counting	source of characters unknown	Phelps	ca. July–Nov. 1835
Grammar and Alphabet of Egyptian Language	Amenhotep papyrus pure language JSP I, cols. 3, 4, 5	Phelps additions by Parrish	ca. July–Nov. 1835
Book of Abraham Manuscript-A	Abr. 1:4–2:6	Williams	Nov. 1835
Book of Abraham Manuscript-B	Abr. 1:4–2:2	Parrish	Nov. 1835
Book of Abraham Manuscript-C	Abr. 1:1–2:18	Phelps Parrish	ca. July/Nov. 1835
Book of Abraham Manuscript and Explanation of Facsimile 1	Abr. 1:1–2:18	Richards	ca. Feb. 1842
Explanation of Facsimile 2		Richards	ca. Mar. 1842
Book of Abraham Manuscript Fragment, pp. 7–8	Abr. 3:18–26	Richards	ca. Mar. 1842

Loss and (Re)Discovery of the Papyri

After Smith's death in mid-1844, the mummies and papyri were sold by his widow, Emma, to Abel Combs in 1856. Combs immediately sold a large portion of the collection to the St. Louis Museum, which then sold it to the Woods Museum in Chicago, where the materials were evidently destroyed in the Great Fire of 1871. It was assumed that the source of Smith's Book of Abraham had been destroyed, but Combs had retained a portion of the papyri that he eventually sold to Edward and Alice Heusser.

Many were surprised when about a dozen fragments of Smith's Egyptian papyri were discovered in the New York Metropolitan Museum in 1966 and transferred to the LDS Church in 1967. Many believers anticipated that Smith's translation would be verified by Egyptologists, who in the interim had discovered how to decipher the three Egyptian writing systems: hieroglyphic, hieratic, and demotic. However, the discovery of the papyri only confirmed what Egyptologists already suspected from the published facsimiles:[16] Smith had purchased fairly commonplace Egyptian funerary texts known as the Book of the Dead and the Book of Breathings.

EGYPTIAN PAPYRI IN SMITH'S POSSESSION

Papyrus	Contents	Fragment/Copy	Date
Papyrus of Hôr (Horos)	Book of Breathings	JSP I, XI, X, part of IV	ca. 238–153 BCE
Papyrus of Ta-sherit-Min (Semminis)	Book of the Dead	JSP VII, VIII, V, VI, IV, II, part of IX; copies of Egyptian characters-A, copies of Egyptian characters-B	ca. 300–100 BCE
Papyrus of Nefer-ir-nebu (Noufianoub)	Book of the Dead	JSP III A–III B	ca. 300–100 BCE

16. See F. S. Spalding, *Joseph Smith, Jr., As a Translator* (Salt Lake City: Arrow Press, [1912]), Chapter 7: "Opinion of Scholars upon the Book of Abraham," 23–31; Samuel A. B. Mercer, "Joseph Smith As an Interpreter and Translator of Egyptian," *Utah Survey* 1/1 (Sept. 1913): 4–36.

Papyrus	Contents	Fragment/Copy	Date
Papyrus of Amenhotep (Amenophis)	Book of the Dead	"Valuable Discovery," 1, 2; Notebook of copied characters, 2	unknown
Hypocephalus of Sheshonq	Fac. 2	Copy of hypocephalus	unknown

The scroll that Smith identified as the text of the Book of Abraham was found on the breast of the only male mummy he purchased in early July 1835. Three months before selling the four mummies to the Mormons in Kirtland, Chandler exhibited them in nearby Cleveland, where the male mummy was soon after described by one resident as being 4 feet 4½ inches tall and about eighty years of age with its "arms crossing on the breast, each hand on its opposite shoulder" holding "a roll of writing."[17] This writing was actually an ordinary Egyptian funerary text dating to the Ptolemaic period, about 150 to 250 years BCE, known as the Book of Breathings or Breathing Permit, which allowed the owner, a priest by the name of Hôr (or Horos), to regain the ability to breathe in the afterlife. University of Chicago Egyptologist Robert K. Ritner recently stated that the now-lost mummy "must be identified with the corpse of Hôr,"[18] but, as I discuss in chapter one, Smith proposed something different.

It was also discovered that the group of documents from the New York Metropolitan Museum not only included Facsimile 1 of the Book of Abraham but that one of the fragments contained the same hieratic characters that appear in the margins of the three Kirtland translation documents, that the characters had been copied sequentially from the first four lines of what scholars have now designated as Joseph Smith Papyrus XI, except where a few characters had been invented to fill in gaps in the papyrus where the papyrus had been damaged. It was obvious to many observers that the source of Smith's Book of Abraham had been found. The problem was that none of Smith's translations bore

---

17. "Mummies," *Painesville Telegraph*, 27 Mar. 1835.

18. Robert K. Ritner, *The Joseph Smith Egyptian Papyri: A Complete Edition* (Salt Lake City: Smith–Pettit Foundation, 2011), 86.

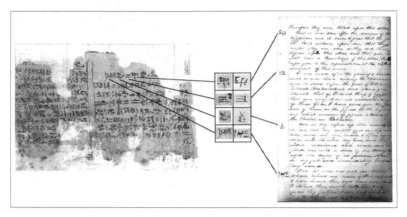

Figure 2. Joseph Smith Papyrus XI and page 3 of Book of Abraham Manuscript-C in the handwriting of Warren Parrish.

the slightest resemblance to what the characters actually meant. When Egyptologists translated the characters, they said nothing about Abraham but instead gave instructions on how the mummy was to be wrapped.[19]

Abraham's Apologists

Defenders of the Book of Abraham's antiquity began immediately to propose alternate interpretations to explain away what seemed to be clear evidence that Smith could not translate Egyptian. Brigham Young University professor of ancient scripture Hugh Nibley led the way in the 1970s, and others soon followed. In the present study, I am primarily concerned with the more recent writings of Brian Hauglid, a professor of Middle Eastern studies at BYU (now retired), as well as Egyptologists John Gee and Kerry Muhlestein, also at BYU. While I respond to some of Hauglid's published statements, Hauglid has since changed his mind and now tends to agree with many of my interpretations.[20] Never-

---

19. See ibid., 99–101.

20. Brian Hauglid, Facebook post to Dan Vogel, 8 Nov. 2018 (www.facebook.com/dan.vogel.35/posts/1398006876998582?hc_location=ufi; accessed 12 Aug. 2019); also in Jeff Lindsay, "A Precious Resource with Some Gaps," *Interpreter: A Journal of Latter-day Saint Faith and Scholarship* 33 [2019]: 19 (www.journal.interpreterfoundation.org/a-precious-resource-with-some-gaps). See Brian M. Hauglid, "'Translating an Alphabet to the Book of Abraham': Joseph Smith's Study of the Egyptian Language and His Translation of the Book of Abraham," in *Producing Ancient Scripture: Joseph Smith's*

theless, because Hauglid's writings remain representative and are used by defenders of the Book of Abraham, I occasionally respond to his earlier arguments.

One of the major arguments put forth by defenders is to claim that the characters in the left margins of the Abraham English translation manuscripts were added as mere decoration or as a method of organizing the English paragraphs.

Another tactic is to claim that the entire text of the Book of Abraham as we have it and probably more was dictated by Smith within the first month of his acquiring the papyri and that the Egyptian Alphabets and bound Grammar were actually the work of Smith's scribes, not Smith himself.

Another assertion is to claim that the source of the Book of Abraham is still lost and was probably destroyed in the 1871 Chicago fire.

I believe that each of these claims is demonstrably false.

As a biographer of Joseph Smith, I hope to preserve an accurate chronology of Smith's life and events and to prevent the perpetuation of error, distortion, and misinformation. I also am interested in exploring Smith's interaction with the Egyptian papyri and the creation of the English text of the Book of Abraham.[21]

The study that follows is a work of history. While I see the Book of Abraham as a product of the nineteenth century, my approach and conclusions are based entirely on a dispassionate, balanced analysis of the relevant historical documents. I believe that what is required in any treatment of the Book of Abraham is not fluency in hieroglyphics or a belief in Joseph Smith's prophetic calling, but a firm, clear-headed understanding of the methods of history and of the relevant nineteenth-century historical sources. Anything else is counterproductive.

Finally, in transcribing manuscript sources, I indicate interlinear insertions with the customary angled brackets ("<word>"), and

---

Translation Projects in the Development of Mormon Christianity, ed. Michael Hubbard MacKay, Mark Ashurst-McGee, and Brian M. Hauglid (Salt Lake City: University of Utah Press, 2020), 363–89, for an essay that closely comports with my findings.

21. In 2018–19 I posted a series of videos on my YouTube channel *Mormon Origins Explained* dealing with the Book of Abraham. The present study adds considerable new material to this discussion, which, I hope, helps to raise the dialogue to a more productive level.

I generally produce the texts in their final form, ignoring minor or insignificant erasures and written-over letters or words. Strikeouts are indicated.

Special thanks to H. Michael Marquardt and Brent Lee Metcalfe, two thoughtful, trenchant scholars of the Book of Abraham, for their insights and suggestions. Of course, I alone am responsible for all facts and interpretations presented in this book.

This work assumes on the part of readers a basic familiarity with the sources, arguments, and personalities regarding the Book of Abraham. For a helpful introduction to these and other relevant matters, I refer readers to the following treatments: Robin Scott Jensen and Brian M. Hauglid, eds., *Book of Abraham and Related Manuscripts* (2018), for a scholarly presentation of the relevant documents; and Terryl Givens with Brian M. Hauglid, *The Pearl of Greatest Price: Mormonism's Most Controversial Scripture* (2019), for an overview of the controversies and debates associated with the Book of Abraham.

Also, because of the sometimes close scrutiny I employ to explain the various intricacies of the Book of Abraham, the Egyptian papyri, the Egyptian-related documents that Joseph Smith and his colleagues produced, as well as apologetic treatments of these materials, I strongly encourage readers to refer as needed to the figures, charts, and illustrations that accompany my analysis.

Abbreviations

Abr.	The Book of Abraham. In The Pearl of Great Price. Salt Lake City: Deseret Book Co., for the Church, 1981.
BYU	L. Tom Perry Special Collections, Harold B. Lee Library, Brigham Young University, Provo, Utah.
CCLA	Community of Christ Library-Archives, Independence, Missouri.
CHL	Church History Library, Church of Jesus Christ of Latter-day Saints, Salt Lake City.
D&C	[Joseph Smith Jr. et al.] *Doctrine and Covenants of the Church of Jesus Christ of Latter-day Saints: Containing Revelations Given to Joseph Smith the Prophet, with Some Additions by His Successors in the Presidency of the Church.* Salt Lake City: Deseret Book Co., for the Church, 1981.
D&C, 1835 ed.	[Joseph Smith, et al.] *Doctrine and Covenants of the Church of the Latter Day Satins: Carefully Selected from the Revelations of God.* Kirtland, Ohio: F. G. Williams and Co., 1835.
DHC	Documentary History of the Church / Joseph Smith Jr. et al. *History of the Church of Jesus Christ of Latter-day Saints,* edited by B. H. Roberts, 2nd ed. rev. ,7 vols. Salt Lake City: Deseret Book, 1977 printing.
GAEL	"Grammar & A[l]phabet of the Egyptian Language," [ca. July–Nov. 1835], Kirtland Egyptian Papers. CHL.
JS History	Joseph Smith et al. History, 1838–56. Vols. A-1–F-1. CHL.
JSP	Joseph Smith Papyrus, accompanied by fragment numbers I–XI.
JSP, D2	Matthew C. Godfrey, Mark Ashurst-McGee, Grant Underwood, Robert J. Woodford, and William G. Hartley, eds. *Documents, Volume 2: July 1831–January*

1833. Vol. 2 of the Documents series of *The Joseph Smith Papers,* edited by Dean C. Jessee, Ronald K. Esplin, Richard Lyman Bushman, and Matthew J. Grow. Salt Lake City: Church Historian's Press, 2013.

JSP, D3 Gerrit J. Dirkmaat, Brent M. Rogers, Grant Underwood, Robert J. Woodford, and William G. Hartley, eds. *Documents, Volume 3: February 1833–March 1834.* Vol. 3 of the Documents series of *The Joseph Smith Papers,* edited by Ronald K. Esplin and Matthew J. Grow. Salt Lake City: Church Historian's Press, 2014.

JSP, D4 Matthew C. Godfrey, Brenden W. Rensink, Alex D. Smith, Max H Parkin, and Alexander L. Baugh, eds. *Documents, Volume 4: April 1834–September 1835.* Vol. 4 of the Documents series of *The Joseph Smith Papers,* edited by Ronald K. Esplin and Matthew J. Grow. Salt Lake City: Church Historian's Press, 2016.

JSP, D5 Brent M. Rogers, Elizabeth A. Kuehn, Christian K. Heimburger, Max H Parkin, Alexander L. Baugh, and Steven C. Harper, eds. *Documents, Volume 5: October 1835–January 1838.* Vol. 5 of the Documents series of *The Joseph Smith Papers,* edited by Ronald K. Esplin, Matthew J. Grow, and Matthew C. Godfrey. Salt Lake City: Church Historian's Press, 2017.

JSP, D6 Mark Ashurst-McGee, David W. Grua, Elizabeth Kuehn, Alexander L. Baugh, and Brenden W. Rensink, eds. *Documents, Volume 6: February 1838–August 1839.* Vol. 6 of the Documents series of *The Joseph Smith Papers,* edited by Ronald K. Esplin, Matthew J. Grow, and Matthew C. Godfrey. Salt Lake City: Church Historian's Press, 2017.

JSP, H1 Karen Lynn Davidson, David J. Whittaker, Mark Ashurst-McGee, and Richard L. Jensen, eds. *Histories, Volume 1: Joseph Smith Histories, 1832–1844.* Vol. 1 of the Histories series of *The Joseph Smith Papers,* edited by Dean C. Jessee, Ronald K. Esplin, and Richard Lyman Bushman. Salt Lake City: Church Historian's Press, 2012.

JSP, H2 Karen Lynn Davidson, Richard L. Jensen, and David J. Whittaker, eds. *Histories, Volume 2: Assigned Historical Writings, 1831–1847.* Vol. 2 of the Histories series of

The Joseph Smith Papers, edited by Dean C. Jessee, Ronald K. Esplin, and Richard Lyman Bushman. Salt Lake City: Church Historian's Press, 2012.

JSP, J1   Dean C. Jessee, Mark Ashurst-McGee, and Richard L. Jensen, eds. *Journals, Volume 1: 1832–1839.* Vol. 1 of the Journals series of *The Joseph Smith Papers,* edited by Dean C. Jessee, Ronald K. Esplin, and Richard Lyman Bushman. Salt Lake City: Church Historian's Press, 2008.

JSP, J2   Andrew H. Hedges, Alex D. Smith, and Richard Lloyd Anderson, eds. *Journals, Volume 2: December 1841–April 1843.* Vol. 2 of the Journals series of *The Joseph Smith Papers,* edited by Dean C. Jessee, Ronald K. Esplin, and Richard Lyman Bushman. Salt Lake City: Church Historian's Press, 2011.

JSP, J3   Andrew H. Hedges, Alex D. Smith, and Brent M. Rogers, eds. *Journals, Volume 3: May 1843–June 1844.* Vol. 3 of the Journals series of *The Joseph Smith Papers,* edited by Ronald K. Esplin and Matthew J. Grow. Salt Lake City: Church Historian's Press, 2015.

JSP, MRB   Robin Scott Jensen, Robert J. Woodford, and Steven C. Harper, eds. *Manuscript Revelation Books.* Facsimile edition. Vol. 1 of the Revelations and Translations series of *The Joseph Smith Papers,* edited by Dean C. Jessee, Ronald K. Esplin, and Richard Lyman Bushman. Salt Lake City: Church Historian's Press, 2009.

JSP, R4   Robin Scott Jensen and Brian M. Hauglid, eds. *Revelations and Translations, Volume 4: Book of Abraham and Related Manuscripts.* Vol. 4 of the Revelations and Translations series of *The Joseph Smith Papers,* edited by Ronald K. Esplin, Matthew J. Grow, Matthew C. Godfrey, and R. Eric Smith. Salt Lake City: Church Historian's Press, 2018.

Chronology

1835

late June	Michael Chandler arrives in Kirtland, Ohio, with four Egyptian mummies, two scrolls, and several fragments.
3 July	Joseph Smith views the mummies and papyri.
early July	Smith purchases the mummies and papyri from Chandler.
6–8 July	Smith, with W. W. Phelps and Oliver Cowdery as scribes, translates some of the characters and identifies the authors of the two scrolls as Abraham and Joseph. This may include Smith's dictation of Abr. 1:1–3.
early July	Phelps and Cowdery copy hieratic Egyptian texts from fragments of the Book of the Dead owned anciently by Amenhotep into two small notebooks (one of which is titled "Valuable Discovery of hiden reccords"); Smith translates a portion as the epitaph of princess Katumin.
17–31 July	Smith translates an "Egyptian alphabet," three versions of which appear in the handwritings of Smith, Phelps, and Cowdery. This information is transferred from three small notebooks into a bound volume by Phelps and expanded by Smith into five degrees of a "Grammar and Alphabet of the Egyptian Language."
1 October	After a break of about two months, Smith resumes work on the bound Grammar with Phelps and Cowdery. At this time, the system of Abrahamic astronomy is revealed, indicating that Smith is working near the end of the bound Grammar.
7 October	Smith resumes translating, probably near the end of the bound Grammar.
19 November	After inspecting the Kirtland House of the Lord edifice with scribes Frederick G. Williams and Warren Parrish,

	Smith returns home (presumably with his scribes) and begins dictating at Abr. 1:4.
20 November	Smith's dictation continues to Abr. 2:2, when Parrish leaves and Williams continues writing to Abr. 2:6.
24–25 November	Smith dictates Abr. 2:7–18 to Parrish.
26 November	Smith and his scribes spend the day "transcribing Egyptian characters from the papyrus," probably referring to copying the hieratic characters from damaged fragments into blank pages in the Valuable Discovery notebooks and/or onto single sheets of paper.

1842

1 March	First installment, containing Abr. 1:1–2:18 and Fac. 1, appears in *Times and Seasons*. Actual release date is after 15 March.
8–9 March	Smith dictates to Willard Richards Abr. 2:19–5:21.
15 March	Second installment, containing Abr. 2:19–5:21 and Fac. 2, appears in *Times and Seasons*. Actual release date is after 19 March.
16 May	Fac. 3 and explanation published in *Times and Seasons*.

1   Documents and Timeline

The discovery of Joseph Smith's Egyptian papyri in the New York Metropolitan Museum in the mid-1960s not only failed to confirm the accuracy Smith's English translation of the Book of Abraham, but it was soon discovered that one of the papyri fragments had provided the hieratic characters in the margins of Smith's three Kirtland, Ohio, hieratic-to-English translation documents. Because these hieratic characters had been copied sequentially from the first four lines of the papyrus now known as Joseph Smith Papyrus XI, except where other hieratic-looking characters had been created to fill in gaps where the papyrus had been damaged, the placement of the Egyptian characters next to the English text in the translation documents implies a process of translation. (The various pieces of Smith Papyri are hereafter cited as JSP followed by the number of the piece.) Some Book of Abraham defenders questioned the assumption regarding translation, citing the disproportion of the text between the Egyptian characters and English translation text—the English text seemed to be too voluminous to have come from the Egyptian characters.[1] In 1971, Hugh Nibley, a professor of religion at LDS Church-owned BYU, remarked:

> The position of the [Egyptian] symbols raises more doubts than confidence: there are not nearly enough of them; they are much too far apart. Much capital has been made of the ridiculous disproportion between the eighteen brief hieratic symbols, which take up just two short lines of the Book of Breathings, and the long and involved history of Abraham which is supposedly derived from them.[2]

---

1. Hugh W. Nibley, "The Meaning of the Kirtland Egyptian Papers," *BYU Studies* 11 (Summer 1971): 371–72; Brian M. Hauglid, "Thoughts on the Book of Abraham," in *No Weapon Shall Prosper: New Light on Sensitive Issues*, ed. Robert L. Millet (Provo, Utah: Religious Studies Center, Brigham Young University; Salt Lake City: Deseret Book Co., 2011), 255.
2. Nibley, "Meaning of the Kirtland Egyptian Papers," 370.

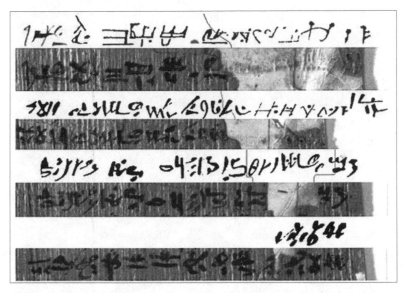

Figure 1.1. Comparison of characters from the margins of the Book of Abraham Manuscript-C and the first four lines of Joseph Smith Papyrus XI. Courtesy of Christopher C. Smith, with some modifications.

Nibley's description, though it expresses an oft-repeated complaint of Book of Abraham defenders, is an inaccurate exaggeration. There are not eighteen characters taken from two lines of the Book of Breathings, but twenty-seven groupings of characters taken from four lines of JSP XI.

"Comprehensiveness of the Language"

Despite Nibley's skepticism, the expansion of individual hieratic characters into many words of English text is entirely consistent with Smith's and his followers' understanding of the Egyptian language. In an article describing the Egyptian papyri published in the *Latter Day Saints' Messenger and Advocate* in December 1835, Oliver Cowdery said:

> The language in which this record is written is very comprehensive, and many of the hieroglyphics exceedingly striking. ... When the translation of these valuable documents will be completed, I am unable to say; neither can I give you a probable idea how large volumes they will make; but judging from their size, and the comprehensiveness of the language, one might reasonably expect to see a sufficient to

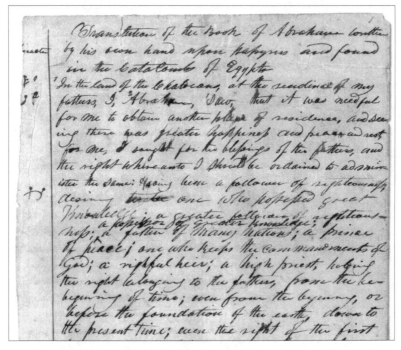

Figure 1.2. Book of Abraham Manuscript-A in the handwriting of W. W. Phelps. The first two characters were taken from Joseph Smith Papyrus XI, now damaged. The third character was taken from column 2 of Joseph Smith Papyrus I.

develop much upon the mighty acts of the ancient men of God, and of his dealing with the children of men when they saw him face to face.[3]

The first three pages of Smith's bound Egyptian Grammar explain how this "comprehensiveness" works using the first three characters from Book of Abraham Manuscript-A. The third character in the margin would have appeared in the missing portion of JSP XI, but was one character Smith did not create but instead took from column 2 of JSP I, which was originally attached to JSP XI. The character in the column has been slightly damaged, but from copies in each of the Egyptian Alphabets it may be seen that the character is a man holding a staff, although Smith

---

3. "Egyptian Mummies—Ancient Records," *LDS Messenger and Advocate* 2 (Dec. 1835): 236 (see Oliver Cowdery, Letter, Kirtland, Ohio, to William Frye, Lebanon, Calhoun County, Illinois, 22 Dec. 1835, Oliver Cowdery Letterbook, 72, 74, Henry E. Huntington Library, San Marino, California).

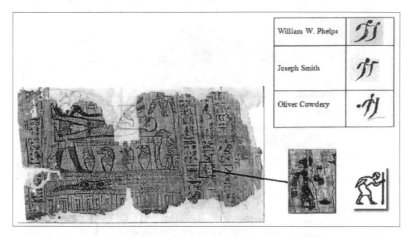

Figure 1.3. Comparison of a hieratic Egyptian character in Joseph Smith Papyrus I (left) and the three Egyptian Alphabets (top right). The character is of a man holding a staff representing "great" (bottom right).

and his scribes did not recognize it as such. It is the hieratic sign for "great," and together with the sign next to it representing the god Osiris, becomes the name "Osorwer," which was the name of Hôr's father.[4]

On page 3 of the Grammar, this character is given the name "Kiah broam = Kiah brah oam = zub zool oan." Below this, W. W. Phelps wrote, "This character shown dissected," and in the left margin the character is, in fact, drawn with each line and dot separated.[5] The Grammar assigns a name and meaning to each part of the character. On the previous page of the Grammar, the prefix "Ki" is defined as "<the compound of iota> see saw = seeing or having seen." On the same page, "Ah brah-oam" is defined as: "Ah brah-oam—a father of many nations a prince of peace, & one who keeps the commandments of God. A patriarch a rightful heir, a highpriest."[6]

Ah brah-oam was created from the name Abraham, and giving a meaning to the name would be similar to Adam Clarke's explaining in his influential early nineteenth-century Bible commentary

---

4. "The individuals named in the 'Breathing Permit' include the priest Hôr, his father Osorwer and his mother Taikhibit" (Robert K. Ritner, *The Joseph Smith Egyptian Papyri: A Complete Edition* [Salt Lake City: Smith–Pettit Foundation, 2011], 88).

5. GAEL, 3 (*JSP*, R4:121).

6. GAEL, 2 (*JSP*, R4:119).

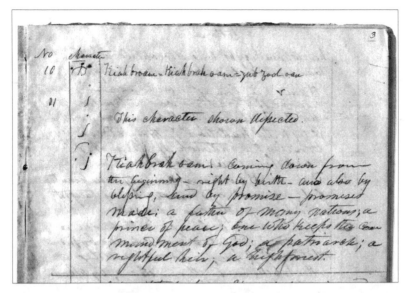

Figure 1.4. Page 3 of the Grammar and Alphabet of the Egyptian Language, showing the character "Kiah broam = Kiah brah oam = zub zool oan" dissected.

that Abraham in Hebrew means "the father of a multitude" or "great multitude."[7] On the same page of the Grammar, "Zub zool-oan" is defined as "The first born, or the first man or fathers or fathers." On page 3, the combination of Ki and ah brah oam is defined as "Coming down from the beginning– right by birth– and also by blessing, and by promise– promises made; a father of many nations; a prince of peace; one who keeps the commandment of God; a patriarch; a rightful heir; a high priest."[8]

Thus one character may yield many sentences. Before criticizing the "absurd disproportion" between Egyptian characters and English translation, defenders of the Book of Abraham should at least understand what was being claimed. The idea that Egyptian was a comprehensive language goes back in Smith's thinking to 1829, when Moroni, a character in the Book of Mormon and later an angel, declared that he wrote his record in "reformed Egyptian," explaining that "if our plates had been sufficiently large we

7. Adam Clarke, *The Holy Bible … With a Commentary and Critical Notes*, vol. 1 (New York: N. Bangs and J. Emory, for the Methodist Episcopal Church, 1825), 90, 109; s.v. Gen. 12:2 and 17:5.

8. GAEL, 3 (*JSP*, R4:121).

5

should have written in Hebrew," clearly implying that Egyptian is more economical than Hebrew (Morm. 9:32–33). During an 1881 interview, David Whitmer, one of the Book of Mormon's three witnesses, reportedly said of the Book of Mormon translation process that "frequently one character would make two lines of manuscript, while others made but a word or two words."[9] According to W. W. Phelps, Martin Harris, another Book of Mormon witness, represented noted linguist Charles Anthon as allegedly identifying the Book of Mormon characters as "shorthand Egyptian."[10]

At the time Smith worked on his "Grammar and Alphabet of the Egyptian Language," he does not appear to be aware of the significance of François Champollion's contribution to Egyptology, as was the case for most Americans. When Champollion died in 1832, his work on the Rosetta Stone was incomplete and his "decipherment remained a speculative hypothesis to many scholars." As late as 1854, orientalist Gustavus Seyffarth was still arguing in New York against Champollion's system. Not until 1858 would a complete translation of the Rosetta Stone come off an American press.[11] LDS scholar Samuel Brown has noted that "Champollion's phonetic Egyptian was slow to find traction because hieroglyphs had so long been understood to function as secret pictographic codes,"[12] and historian John Irwin has observed that "Champollion's discoveries did not, however, topple the metaphysical school of interpretation ... and the tension between these two kinds of interpretation was to have a significant

---

9. "The Last Man. Of the Men Who Attested to the Truth of the 'Book of Mormon,' David Whitmer Only Is Left. In the Sunset of Life He Bases His Hopes of Heaven on the Records of the Lost Tribe. And Solemnly Reiterates All that He Has Ever Said Regarding Them," *Chicago Times*, 17 Oct. 1881, in Dan Vogel, *Early Mormon Documents*, 5 vols. (Salt Lake City: Signature Books, 1996–2003), 5:86.

10. W. W. Phelps, Letter, Canandaigua, New York, to E. D. Howe, Painesville, Ohio, 15 Jan. 1831, in E. D. Howe, *Mormonism Unvailed* (Painesville, OH: by the author, 1834), 273.

11. See R. B. Parkinson et al., *Cracking Codes: The Rosetta Stone and Decipherment* (Berkeley: University of California Press, 1999), 41; John T. Irwin, *American Hieroglyphics: The Symbol of the Egyptian Hieroglyphics in the American Renaissance* (New Haven, Connecticut: Yale University Press, 1980), 8–9.

12. Samuel Brown, "Joseph (Smith) in Egypt: Babel, Hieroglyphics, and the Pure Language of Eden," *Church History* 78/1 (Mar. 2009): 44.

influence on the literature of the American Renaissance."[13] After reviewing this subject, Terryl Givens, another LDS intellectual, recently suggested that "Smith or those working to assemble the grammar and alphabet appear to have been operating within the existing cultural assumptions of the time about how hieroglyphs concisely embedded substantial discursive meaning."[14]

This gave Smith freedom to imagine whatever he wished about Egyptian grammar. His Egyptian-language project began as a relatively simple alphabet and the five-degree amplification of Egyptian meanings came later, which helps to explain evolving definitions. It also provided more flexibility when he later dictated his translation.

Inventing History

In 1971, Nibley argued that the characters in the margins of Smith's translation documents did not imply a translation and that the Grammar and Alphabet project was actually the work of Smith's scribe W. W. Phelps and others trying to retrofit Smith's Book of Abraham translation to the Egyptian papyri in an attempt to learn to translate on their own.[15] Without any evidence, Nibley dated the production of the extant translation manuscripts, three Alphabets, and bound Grammar to 1837—when Smith experienced fallout from the failure of his anti-banking society—instead of July 1835, as Smith's own history indicates.[16] In 1975, Nibley changed the date to 1835 but asserted the same theory:

> The brethren at Kirtland [Ohio] were invited to try their skill at translation; in 1835 the Prophet's associates, miffed by his superior knowledge and determined to show him up, made determined efforts to match up the finished text of the Book of Abraham with characters from the J.S. Papyrus No. XI; but they never got beyond the second

---

13. John T. Irwin, *American Hieroglyphics: The Symbol of the Egyptian Hieroglyphics in the American Renaissance* (New Haven, Connecticut: Yale University Press, 1980), 6.

14. Terryl Givens with Brian M. Hauglid, *The Pearl of Greatest Price: Mormonism's Most Controversial Scripture* (New York: Oxford University Press, 2019), 188.

15. Nibley, "Meaning of the Kirtland Egyptian Papers," 351, 391–97.

16. JS History, vol. B-1, 597 (DHC 2:238). This is discussed in more detail in chapter two.

line of characters—if they were really trying to translate, they soon demonstrated that it simply didn't work.[17]

There is no evidence that such an event ever took place. Nibley's explanation requires that Smith's translation of Abraham precede his scribes' speculations about Egyptian grammar, which, as I show in the following pages and chapters, is the opposite from what the evidence actually shows. Yet Nibley's apologetic has been recently adopted by a new generation of defenders. BYU Egyptologist John Gee, for example, asserted in 2017 that

> the grammar seems to have been produced from the Book of Abraham and not the other way round. … A decipherer comes up with a translation first, recording insights along the way. Later, scholars … systematize them into a grammar book from which others will learn the language. Phelps and his associates seem to have envisioned the same process with the Book of Abraham: Joseph Smith's translation coming first and any grammar coming later.[18]

Earlier, Gee wrote in 2000,

> The Kirtland Egyptian Papers that have been connected with the papyri appear to be a later attempt to match up the translation of the Book of Abraham with some of the Egyptian characters … If one assumes that the Book of Abraham was the second text on the papyrus of Hor, a possible scenario is that having the translation of the Book of Abraham, the brethren at Kirtland tried to match the Egyptian characters with the translation but chose the characters from the first text. Yet it is not certain that this is what they thought they were doing.[19]

Here Gee leaves open other possible explanations for the characters in the margins, which I explore shortly. He also alludes to the theory that the Book of Abraham was written at the end of the same papyrus scroll that contained the Book of Breathings owned by Hôr, another theory that I examine in detail in chapter

---

17. Hugh W. Nibley, *The Message of the Joseph Smith Papyri: An Egyptian Endowment* (Salt Lake City: Deseret Book Co., 1975), 2.

18. John Gee, *An Introduction to the Book of Abraham* (Provo, Utah: Religious Studies Center, Brigham Young University; Salt Lake City: Deseret Book Co., 2017), 37, 39.

19. John Gee, *A Guide to the Joseph Smith Papyri* (Provo, Utah: Foundation for Ancient Research and Mormon Studies, 2000), 23.

seven. At present, I merely point out that the most glaring problem with this theory is that Smith supposedly allowed his scribes to mistakenly believe that his translation came from the Book of Breathings. Nevertheless, the idea that the scribes accidentally copied the wrong characters is mistaken. Phelps had been present from the start of the translation project and would have observed from where Smith derived his translation. Warren Parrish, who scribed two of the translation documents, said, "I have set by his [Joseph Smith's] side and penned down the translation of the Egyptian Hieroglyphicks as he claimed to receive it by direct inspiration of heaven."[20] Without Smith's help, how would Phelps and Parrish know which characters went with which text? There would have been no need to guess since Smith was there with them—in charge of the whole operation.

A 26 November 1835 entry in Smith's journal mentions that he and Parrish "spent the day in transcribing Egyptian characters from the papyrus."[21] Some defenders have noted the difference between *transcribing* and *translating*. Brian Hauglid, formerly an associate professor of ancient scripture at BYU and editor of *Studies in the Book of Abraham* series, has suggested that the 26 November 1835 entry refers to "the drawing of hieratic characters" into the margins of the translation documents.[22] While this is not necessarily the case, Hauglid's suggestion would make Smith responsible for the choice of characters. Nevertheless, considering that there are at least six groupings of invented characters, partially constructed from characters appearing in the Alphabets and bound Grammar, Smith would have had to have been involved.[23]

---

20. Warren Parrish, Letter, Kirtland, Ohio, to the editor of the *Painesville Republican*, Painesville, Ohio, 5 Feb. 1838, *Painesville Republican*, 15 Feb. 1838.

21. Joseph Smith, Journal, 26 Nov. 1835, Joseph Smith Collection, CHL (*JSP*, J1:110–11).

22. Brian Hauglid, *A Textual History of the Book of Abraham: Manuscripts and Editions* (Provo, Utah: Neal A. Maxwell Institute for Religious Scholarship, Brigham Young University, 2010), 216n21.

23. The three groups of invented characters associated with Abr. 1:23–28 were later added to all three Kirtland-era Book of Abraham manuscripts in different ink. See Robin Scott Jensen and Brian M. Hauglid, *The Joseph Smith Papers. Revelations and Translations, Volume 4: Book of Abraham and Related Materials* (Salt Lake City: Church Historian's Press, 2018), 199, 240n83; 211, 241n143; 227, 242n171.

Meanings of the Characters in the Margins

Because defenders argue that the papyrus from which Smith translated Abraham is still missing and probably destroyed in the 1871 Chicago fire, they must explain the relationship of the hieratic characters in the margins of the translation documents and the English text as something other than a translation. Some defenders have argued that the relationship of the characters and English text is unknown. In his discussion of one of the Kirtland translation documents in the handwriting of Frederick G. Williams, who was Smith's secretary and counselor in the First Presidency, Hauglid observed, "Based on the present available information, it is difficult to determine definitively why these characters are in this manuscript."[24] The editors of the multi-volume *Joseph Smith Papers*, published by the LDS Church, make a similar statement in volume 5 of the documents series, "Though the juxtaposition of the characters and Book of Abraham text implies a relationship between the two, the exact nature of that relationship is not stated."[25]

Though not stated, the relationship is obvious. The editors of the *Joseph Smith Papers* published what they believe is the earliest manuscript of the Book of Abraham, which is in the handwriting of Williams, but they excluded the most complete text, which was begun by Phelps and completed by Parrish. The Phelps/Parrish document bears the heading: "Translation of the Book of Abraham written by his own hand upon papyrus and found in the CataCombs of Egypts"; and the left margin is labeled: "[Ch]aracter". With one column labeled *character* and the other essentially labeled *translation*, the relationship between the two is unmistakable. Phelps makes the connection even clearer by numbering the first two Egyptian characters and keying them to specific English words in the text: the first is keyed to "land of the Chaldeans" and to the act of seeing, the second is keyed to the name Abraham.

Commenting on this, Nibley admitted, "There cannot be the slightest doubt that the writer here intends to relate *specific* Egyptian characters to specific English words and ideas. Now ... this is the sort of demonstration for which we have been looking,

---

24. Hauglid, *A Textual History of the Book of Abraham*, 64. See also p. 84.
25. Historical Introduction, *JSP*, D5:75.

in which things are properly pinned down."[26] Nibley then tried to dismiss this evidence because Parrish did not continue this method when, months later in 1835, he copied the translation and characters onto this document. Granted, Parrish did not continue this method, but, at the same time, there is no indication that the purpose for the characters in the margins suddenly changed from the precedent Phelps had established. Even Phelps did not attempt to identify his third character with specific English words in the text. As previously discussed, this character—Kiah broam = Kiah brah oam = zub zool oan—is a compound character and therefore cannot be attached to any specific word or phrase. Again, defenders of the Book of Abraham seem not to understand what was being claimed.

Some defenders have offered alternative explanations for the characters to avoid the most obvious conclusion. Nibley suggested that "what we have therefore is either mere eyewash or coordinating their work, or both."[27] In other words, Nibley suggested that the characters were simple ornamentation or an exotic way to organize the paragraphs in the different documents instead of simply numbering them. Although Gee speculated that the scribes accidentally copied the wrong characters, which implies a translation scenario, he also suggested that the characters were added "perhaps to decorate the beginnings of paragraphs."[28] In 2000, Gee tried to discredit the theory that "the text to the right is the translation of the Egyptian characters to the left" by asserting:

> Unfortunately for this theory, the Egyptian characters were added after the entire English text was written (as evidenced by the use of different inks, Egyptian characters that do not always line up with the English text, and the Egyptian characters that sometimes overrun the English text). Thus it was not a matter of writing the character and then the translation but of someone later adding the characters in the margin at the beginning of paragraphs of text without explicitly stating the reason for doing so.[29]

---

26. Nibley, "Meaning of the Kirtland Egyptian Papers," 384; emphasis in original.
27. Ibid., 385.
28. Gee, *A Guide to the Joseph Smith Papyri*, 22.
29. Ibid., 21.

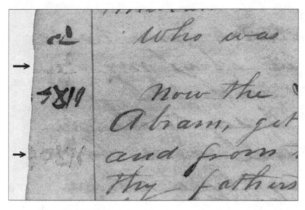

Figure 1.5. Page 7 of Book of Abraham Manuscript-C in the handwriting of Warren Parrish showing the repositioning of two groups of characters. The identical scraped-off characters are very light but still visible beneath the replacements.

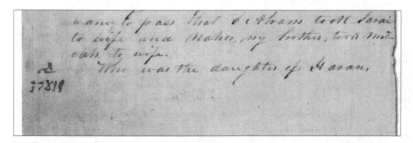

Figure 1.6. Page 6 of Book of Abraham Manuscript-B in the handwriting of Warren Parrish showing a character in the left margin without accompanying English text.

The situation is more complex than Gee represents. On page 7 of Parrish's longer text, there is clear indication that sometimes the characters were written in the margin before the English text was added. At the top of this page, two characters had to be scraped off the paper and repositioned at the beginning of the paragraphs. This particular portion of the document was copied from a text already containing characters and Parrish had miscalculated the number of lines the English text would occupy. One source for Parrish's longer document was his shorter document, which concluded with a character and no text. This clearly implies that some of the characters were written before the English text.

Whether the characters were written before, after, or simultaneously with the English text is ultimately irrelevant since it is also

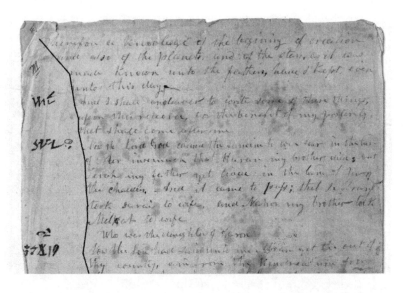

Figure 1.7. Page 4 of Book of Abraham Manuscript-A in the hand writing of Frederick G. Williams, with line added to show the text curving around the characters in the left margin.

clear that the text was being arranged in such a way as to accommodate the characters. In other words, the Egyptian characters were not an afterthought as additions, either to decorate or to organize the three manuscripts, but were integral to the creation of the English documents.

On the last page of the Williams document, the text curves in anticipation of the characters. Also on this page, as with the other two manuscripts, the second to last character is aligned with a sentence fragment: "who was the daughter of Haran." Regardless of when the character was drawn, isolating this phrase on a line by itself and juxtaposing a character would have taken some planning. The assertion that the characters were simply added after the English text was written as a means of decorating or organizing does not explain this observation. It only makes sense in a translation scenario. Another example of this occurs right in the middle of a sentence:

Character   *Translation*

    my fathers having turned from their righteousness, and from the holy commandments, which the Lord their God had given unto them, unto the worshiping of the gods of the heathens.

 utterly refused to hearken to my voice ...[30]

Dividing the paragraph abruptly and incorrectly is certain indication that the characters are not superfluous. The fact that the characters exceed the margin, as Gee has pointed out, implies that the scribe was being particular about which characters accompanied which text, which is best explained by a translation scenario. If the characters were decorations or an exotic method of organizing paragraphs, there would be no need to exceed the margin by making groups of several characters.

The presence of at least six groupings of invented characters is another reason to reject the suggestion that the characters were added to decorate or organize the translation. Concerning these characters, Chicago University Egyptologist Klaus Baer observed in 1968 that they "are clearly proposed restorations that bear no resemblance to the signs that certainly were on the papyrus before it was damaged; note also the difference in general appearance of style."[31] Who besides Joseph Smith could fill the lacunae or gap with invented characters? Smith's mother, Lucy, reportedly said that "when Joseph was reading the papyrus, he closed his eyes, and held a hat over his face, and that the revelation came to him; and that where the papyrus was torn, he could read the parts that were destroyed equally as well as those that were there."[32] As early as 1837, William West reported: "These records were torn by being taken from the roll of embalming salve which contained them, and some parts entirely lost; but Smith is to translate the whole by divine inspiration, and that which is lost, like Nebuchadnezzar's dream, can be interpreted as well as that which is preserved; and a larger volume than the Bible will be required to contain them."[33]

---

30. Book of Abraham Manuscript-B, 1 (*JSP*, R4:205).

31. Klaus Baer, "The Breathing Permit of Hôr: A Translation of the Apparent Source of the Book of Abraham," *Dialogue: A Journal of Mormon Thought* 3/3 (Autumn 1968): 129–30.

32. *Friends' Weekly Intelligencer*, 3 Oct. 1846, 211.

33. William S. West, *A Few Interesting Facts Respecting the Rise Progress and Pretentions of the Mormons* ([Warren? Ohio]: published by author, 1837), 5.

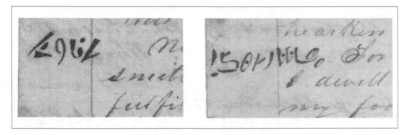

Figure 1.8. Pages 6 and 8 of Book of Abraham Manuscript-C in the handwriting of Warren Parrish, showing characters running over the left margin.

Obviously, decorating or organizing the paragraphs does not require—as Nibley and Gee would have readers believe—the invention of missing characters.

The Three Translation Documents and the Missing Source

Some defenders of the Book of Abraham claim that the three Kirtland translation documents are all partial copies of a missing original document that Smith dictated in July 1835. Gee, for example, has asserted: "Most of the extant Book of Abraham manuscripts seem to have been personal copies of portions of the Book of Abraham made for their owners."[34] However, if Smith's scribes had access to a complete text and were making copies for personal use, there would be no reason to begin their copies abruptly by skipping the first three verses, which is where Phelps's text just happened to have stopped. Obviously, they considered their work a continuation of Phelps's document, which is why Parrish later copied the text that Williams and he recorded into the translation book following Phelps's entry. We know that Phelps and Parrish originally recorded their texts into a ledger book and that the five sheets containing them were subsequently cut out with a straight razor because an examination of the inside edges of the sheets reveals an identical uneven cut, which damaged some of the characters and words. Evidently, Phelps had prepared a companion volume to the bound Grammar in which to record the final translation.

There is no evidence to support the existence of a now-lost original text from which the Parrish and Williams documents were

---

34. Gee, *Introduction to the Book of Abraham*, 31.

copied, although defenders' motivation for asserting such is the case is clear. If defenders want to maintain that the Alphabets and bound Grammar are reverse translations of the Book of Abraham, they must also maintain that the translation preceded creation of the Grammar and Alphabets. Since Parrish was not engaged as Smith's scribe until 29 October 1835,[35] defenders must, of necessity, conclude the document bearing his handwriting is a copy of a now-lost original manuscript dating to July 1835. Hence, Gee stated in 2000: "Joseph Smith began translating the papyri in early July 1835. The current text of the Book of Abraham was translated by the end of the month."[36] More recently, Gee similarly stated: "The current published text of the Book of Abraham, and probably more, seems to have been translated by the end of July 1835; the Book of Abraham appears to have been longer than the current text."[37] In 2016, Kerry Muhlestein, also a BYU Egyptologist, and Megan Hansen made similar assertions: "Three manuscripts created in 1835 still survive … None are the original translation manuscript … it seems likely Joseph Smith translated all of the text of the Book of Abraham we now have, and perhaps even more, by 1835."[38]

These claims are not supported by the documentation but, instead, result from defenders' need to make the facts fit their theory. As they see it, the hypothesized missing Abraham text needs to be longer than the current Abraham text for two important reasons:

1. If the Alphabets and bound Grammar were derived from Smith's translation of Abraham, defenders need to explain the presence of material in the Alphabets and bound Grammar that is not represented in Smith's translation.
2. If the translation of Abraham as we have it today was completed by the end of July 1835, defenders need to explain entries in Smith's journals that mention him translating in November 1835 and March 1842.

---

35. Joseph Smith, Journal, 29 Oct. 1835 (*JSP*, J1:76).

36. Gee, *Guide to the Joseph Smith Papyri*, 4.

37. Gee, *Introduction to the Book of Abraham*, 14.

38. Kerry Muhlestein and Megan Hansen, "'The Work of Translating': The Book of Abraham's Translation Chronology," in J. Spencer Fluhman and Brent L. Top, eds., *Let Us Reason Together: Essays in Honor of the Life's Work of Robert L. Millet* (Provo, Utah: Brigham Young University, 2016), 142, 157.

As will become apparent, defenders of the Book of Abraham, to maintain their central thesis, are forced to invent other equally weak theories to support it.

Relationship among the
Three Kirtland Translation Manuscripts

The strongest evidence against the missing-source theory is the Williams and Parrish documents themselves. While some defenders believe the Williams document is probably the earliest copy, and that Parrish simply copied the Williams document, a more careful analysis shows that Williams and Parrish wrote simultaneously as Smith dictated. This is apparent from the very first lines of these documents:

ABRAHAM 1:4

Williams	*Parrish*
I sought for ~~the~~ <mine> appointment ~~whereunto~~ unto the priesthood according to the appointment of God unto the fathers concerning the seed	I sought for ~~the~~ <mine> appointment ~~whereunto~~ unto the priesthood according to the appointment of God unto the fathers concerning the seed

Here, in Abraham 1:4, both Williams and Parrish wrote "whereunto" then cancelled it and instead wrote "unto" on the line immediately following the cancellation. This shows that one scribe was not simply copying the other; nor were they copying a now missing document. The simplest way to explain how the same in-line emendation occurred in two documents is that both scribes were writing from dictation at the same time and that Smith made an immediate correction which both scribes noted. There are other examples:

ABRAHAM 1:26

Williams	*Parrish*
... And also Noah his father. ~~For in his days~~ who blessed him with the blessings of the earth ...	... and also Noah his father, ~~for in his days~~, who blessed him, with the blessings of the earth ...

Here, in Abraham 1:26, Smith evidently changed the direction of his narrative after both Williams and Parrish recorded four words. The correction of this error is definitive evidence that both Parrish and Williams were writing as Smith was dictating. Another example of this kind of emendation includes evidence of oral dictation:

ABRAHAM 1:17

Williams	*Parrish*
… and this because ~~their hearts are turned~~ they have turned their hearts away from me to worship the god of Elk Kee-nah …	… and this because ~~their harts are turn~~ they have turned their hearts away from me, to worship the god of Elkkener, …

Here, in Abraham 1:17, Smith dictated "their hearts are turned" and immediately changed it to "they have turned their hearts." This emendation disproves any assertion that Williams and Parrish were copying from a now missing document, or that Parrish was simply copying Williams's document. Note that Parrish stopped writing before he completed the word "turned," but wrote "turn" before crossing it out. This suggests that the two men wrote at different speeds when Smith made a correction. This is most reasonably explained as the result of oral dictation.

Note also the difference in the name of the god "Elk-Kee-nah" versus "Ekkener." This difference provides evidence that Parrish and Williams sometimes misheard Smith's dictation, rather than mistranscribing while supposedly copying another document. Parrish consistently spelled the name "Elkkener," except once when he first wrote "Elkkenah," then quickly wipe-erased the terminal "ah" and overwrote "er". Williams, on the other hand, wrote "Elk-kener" for the first two occurrences of the name, but then started writing the word phonetically "Elk-Keenah," with an "ah" ending. The confusion was likely due to Smith's New England non-rhotic accent, which could either drop or add a terminal "r" sound. It is like pronouncing "watah" for "water" or "idear" for "idea." A similar error occurred on page 34 in the bound Grammar when Smith said that the planet Kolob had been "discovered by *Methuselah* and also by Abraham" but Parrish wrote "Methuselar." There are also instances where Parrish and Williams mistake "thee" for "the" and "son" for "sun." These kinds of errors are consistent with a dictated manuscript.

Comparison of Williams's and Parrish's
Spellings of Elkenah/Elkener

Verse	Williams	Parrish
1:6	1. Elk=Kener	Elkkener
1:7	2. Elk=Kener	Elkken[text damaged]
1:7	3. Elk=keenah	Elkkener
1:13	4. Elk-keenah	Elkkener
1:17	5. Elk Kee-nah	Elkkener
1:20	6. Elk-Keenah	Elkken{ah|er}
1:29	7. Elk keenah	Elkkener

In their publication of the *Book of Abraham and Related Materials*, Robin Jensen and Brian Hauglid observe that the Williams and Parrish documents were inscribed on "two halves of a single sheet"; that "one large sheet was separated in two, and the halves were used by Williams and Parrish as the first leaves of their respective documents"; and that "the same process was repeated with a second large sheet, the halves of which then served as the second leaves of the two manuscripts." They also acknowledge: "Given the similarities between the text of the two manuscripts and the revision process for both, JS [Joseph Smith] may have dictated some or most of the text to both scribes at the same time. In that case, these two manuscripts would likely be the earliest dictated copies of the Book of Abraham."[39]

Jensen and Hauglid then attempt to appease defenders of the Book of Abraham by suggesting that Smith "may have read aloud to Williams and Parrish from an earlier, nonextant text, making corrections as he went."[40] The problem with this suggestion is that the corrections in the Williams and Parrish documents are not simple rewordings of isolated phrases but a change in narrative direction that is typical when new text is being created orally. Besides, there is no evidence for a previous document and, as I will

---

39. Jensen and Hauglid, *Book of Abraham and Related Materials*, 192. This is a more careful analysis of the Williams and Perrish documents than Hauglid's previous offering. See Brian M. Hauglid, *A Textual History of the Book of Abraham: Manuscripts and Editions* (Provo, Utah: Neal A. Maxwell Institute for Religious Scholarship, Brigham Young University, 2010), 65, 85.

40. Jensen and Hauglid, *Book of Abraham and Related Materials*, 192.

show, no need to postulate the existence of one. Indeed, the only reason to assert the existence of a complete text of Abraham dating to July 1835 is to maintain the reverse-translation theory (the Alphabets and Grammar followed the text of the Book of Abraham), which also has no evidence to support it but, more importantly, is contradicted by the close examination of the documents.

The suggestion that Smith made emendations as he read the text of Abraham to Williams and Parrish is unprecedented, even though Jensen and Hauglid suggest that Smith "followed a similar process in his work in the Bible revision project."[41] The possibility that Smith made emendations in the existing King James Bible text as he read to a scribe, which was the most practical procedure in producing Smith's revision of the Bible, is not the same as making emendations while reading his own Abraham text to two scribes.[42] The purpose of having two scribes was to insure the accurate capture of a text as it was being created. This fits with Parrish's claim that he "penned down the translation of the Egyptian Hieroglyphicks" as Smith dictated.[43]

What This Means for the Reverse-Translation Theory

The evidence for Williams and Parrish writing from Smith's dictation contradicts the defenders' reverse-translation theory. We have the original dictated texts of the Book of Abraham from the Kirtland era, and there simply is no justification to theorize about a missing source. It is clear that the Williams and Parrish documents date to after the creation of the bound Grammar since both manuscripts begin with a character and reference to the Alphabet and Grammar.

---

41. Ibid.

42. In his largely hostile review of the Jensen and Hauglid volume, LDS apologist Jeffrey Dean Lindsay argued that "the most likely source of dictation was *not* Joseph Smith but one of the two scribes who was initially reading aloud for the benefit of the other," and that the "most plausible scenario to account for these documents is that Warren Parrish was dictating for the benefit of his fellow scribe Frederick Williams as they both made copies of an existing text" ("A Precious Resource with Some Gaps," *Interpreter: A Journal of Latter-day Saint Faith and Scholarship* 33 [2019]: 64; https://journal.interpreterfoundation.org/a-precious-resource-with-some-gaps/). This theory, however, runs into trouble when implausibly arguing that the identical emendations in both manuscripts were accidental misreadings by Parrish.

43. Warren Parrish, Letter, Kirtland, Ohio, to the editor of the *Painesville Republican*, Painesville, Ohio, 5 Feb. 1838, *Painesville Republican*, 15 Feb. 1838.

Williams	*Parrish*
Sign of the fifth degree of the ~~first~~ <Seceond> part	sign of the fifth degree of the ~~first~~ <second> part

Because Parrish and Williams were writing simultaneously, both documents must date to after 29 October 1835 when Smith hired Parrish as a scribe.[44] Two entries in Smith's journal for 19 and 20 November 1835 in the handwriting of Parrish mark the probable time when Parrish and Williams began to serve as scribes for Smith's dictation of Abraham 1:4–2:2, which is where Parrish's shorter document ends. The entry for the 19th states: "[Joseph Smith] went in company with Doct. [Frederick G.] Williams & my scribe [Warren Parrish] to see how the workmen prospered in finishing the house [of the Lord]; ... I returned home and spent the day in translating the Egyptian records."[45]

On the following day, Parrish recorded that Smith "spent the day in translating, and made rapid progress."[46] This is likely the exact time that Parrish referred to when he reported in 1838 that he "set by his [Joseph Smith's] side and penned down the translation of the Egyptian Hieroglyphicks as he claimed to receive it by direct inspiration of heaven."[47] From the preceding analysis, it is clear that four months had elapsed between procuring the papyri and Smith's dictating the bulk of the translation and that the Alphabets and bound Grammar were created in the interim.

Flawed Analysis

Jensen and Hauglid's suggestion that Smith "may have read aloud to Williams and Parrish from an earlier, nonextant text, making corrections as he went,"[48] although attempting to keep the theory of an earlier document alive, nevertheless damages some of the arguments upon which that theory had previously rested. The editors of the *Joseph Smith Papers*, for instance, have followed Gee in

---

44. Joseph Smith, Journal, 29 Oct. 1835 (*JSP*, J1:76).

45. Joseph Smith, Journal, 19 Nov. 1835 (*JSP*, J1:107).

46. Joseph Smith, Journal, 20 Nov. 1835 (*JSP*, J1:107).

47. Warren Parrish, Letter, Kirtland, Ohio, to the editor of the *Painesville Republican*, Painesville, Ohio, 5 Feb. 1838, *Painesville Republican*, 15 Feb. 1838.

48. Jensen and Hauglid, *Book of Abraham and Related Materials*, 192.

asserting: "Textual evidence suggests that these Book of Abraham texts were based on an earlier manuscript that is no longer extant."[49]

These scholars have relied on Hauglid's 2010 book, *A Textual History of the Book of Abraham*.[50] In a subsequent publication, Hauglid claimed that "all of the surviving manuscripts containing text of the Book of Abraham represent copies of earlier documents" and that "unlike the Book of Mormon, we have no originally dictated manuscripts for the Book of Abraham."[51] While Hauglid's book was useful for providing transcriptions of the Abraham manuscripts, its analysis of their contents and relationship to one another is inaccurate. On page 85, for example, he states that Parrish's document "also contains about a half dozen similar emendations" to Williams's document, but he neither explains the significance of these emendations nor lists their locations as he does for those emendations that tend to support his theory.[52] Instead, Hauglid asserts that the Williams document was "copied from an earlier exemplar" and that Parrish copied the Williams document.[53]

To support his conclusion, Hauglid observes that the Williams document "is paragraphed with some original punctuation, which could suggest that [it] is more developed than a dictated text of Joseph Smith, such as the Book of Mormon, which contained no paragraphing or original punctuation."[54] Concerning Parrish's document, he states that it too "is paragraphed and contains numerous punctuation marks, suggesting that the text was developed beyond Ab2 [i.e., the Williams document] and also well beyond the dictation phase."[55] Hauglid has since acknowledged that there is strong evidence supporting simultaneous recording from oral

---

49. *JSP*, D5:74.

50. Brian Hauglid, *A Textual History of the Book of Abraham: Manuscripts and Editions* (Provo, Utah: Neal A. Maxwell Institute for Religious Scholarship, Brigham Young University, 2010).

51. Hauglid, "Thoughts on the Book of Abraham," 250.

52. Hauglid, *Textual History of the Book of Abraham*, 85.

53. Ibid., 65, 85.

54. Ibid., 65.

55. Ibid., 85. Of course this is a subjective evaluation and difficult to controvert since any manuscript one might bring forward as an example of a dictated manuscript with punctuation would simply be declared a copy by apologists by virtue of its having punctuation.

dictation and, presumably, has abandoned his previous arguments based on punctuation and paragraphing.

LDS apologist Jeffrey Dean Lindsay criticizes Jensen and Hauglid because they did not mention the evidence of punctuation and paragraphing, but then asserts that it was Parrish, not Smith, who read aloud a pre-existing text as Williams and he recorded, presumably unaware of the contradiction.[56]

In fact, the argument based on punctuation and paragraphing never made good sense. When critically assessing a document, the presence or absence of punctuation is not a determinant of whether or not it was written from dictation. Instead, the determinant is whether the punctuation is inconsistent and confused, which is exactly what we find in the Williams and Parrish documents.[57] As Edward Ashment noted years ago, "Punctuation in both [the Williams and Parrish documents] is sparse, resulting in numerous run-on sentences."[58] Commas also appear where there should be none. Parrish especially overused the comma, sometimes dividing the subject from its verb, which he sometimes corrected when he copied his document into the translation book. He also changed some commas into periods. Thus the sparse and inconsistent punctuation in the Williams and Parrish documents is consistent with the evidence for simultaneous dictation.

We have already seen that the paragraphing was created to align the English text with the hieratic characters in the margins. There are only two paragraph breaks in the Parrish document that are not preceded by characters. The first was removed when Parrish copied the text into the translation book; and the second occurs

---

56. Lindsay, "A Precious Resource with Some Gaps," 63–64.

57. Just because Cowdery chose not to punctuate when Joseph Smith dictated the Book of Mormon in 1829 does not mean another scribe in a similar situation would choose to do the same. To be meaningful, one would have to know what Williams typically did when transcribing from dictation, and we do not have that kind of documentation. However, we do know that when Williams copied revelations into the Kirtland Revelations Book, he rarely inserted punctuation. So it is hardly a salient point.

58. Edward H. Ashment, "Reducing Dissonance: The Book of Abraham as a Case Study," in *The Word of God*, ed. Dan Vogel (Salt Lake City: Signature, 1990), 226. Ashment also noted: "and the existing punctuation is not consistent between Phelps's [Williams's] and Parrish's manuscripts, indicating that each was trying as best he could to punctuate as he wrote. This evidence contradicts Nibley's affirmation that … [they] represent 'the finished or nearly-finished text of the Book of Abraham.'"

in the middle of a sentence. Such ambiguous evidence cannot be used to support Hauglid's earlier assertion that Parrish's document is developed "well beyond the dictation phase," and therefore defenders would do well to abandon this argument because it provides no evidence that the Williams and Parrish documents were copied from a pre-existing document.

Other evidence Hauglid had previously articulated that apologists should now also abandon may be found in a 2011 essay, in which Hauglid explained what kind of scribal errors he thought demonstrated the Parrish and Williams documents were visual copies, although he provided no examples: "Once in a while the crossed-out or erased word or phrase will show that the scribe saw the word or phrase ahead of where the scribe actually was in the text. When this happened, the scribe would generally quickly catch it, cross it out, and put the word or phrase in its proper place."[59] However, in 1998, BYU linguist Royal Skousen listed this kind of scribal error as evidence that the scribe was writing from dictation and gave Alma 56:41 as an example: "& it came to pass that again we saw the Lamani[tes when the light] of the morning came *we saw the Lamanites* upon [us]."[60] From this, Skousen argued:

> This example suggests that Joseph [Smith] and Oliver [Cowdery] started out together, but by the time Oliver finished writing "& it came to pass that again," Joseph had moved along far enough that he was then dictating "we saw the Lamanites upon us" and Oliver started to write that down when he realized he had skipped the intervening text ("when the light of the morning came"), so he immediately crossed out "we saw the Lamanites" and wrote the correct sequence, possibly with Joseph repeating the correct text for him.[61]

Skousen called this kind of error "scribal anticipation," where "the scribe, in attempting to keep up with Joseph's dictation, jumped ahead of the actual text." While Skousen blames the scribe

---

59. Hauglid, "Thoughts on the Book of Abraham," 251.

60. Book of Mormon, Original Manuscript [Alma 56:41], CHL; emphasis added. See Royal Skousen, ed., *The Original Manuscript of the Book of Mormon: Typographical Facsimile of the Extant Text* (Provo, Utah: Foundation for Ancient Research and Mormon Studies, 2001), 446.

61. Royal Skousen, "How Joseph Smith Translated the Book of Mormon: Evidence from the Original Manuscript," *Journal of Book of Mormon Studies* 7/1 (1998): 25–27.

for this correction, which fits his belief in the inspired translation of a preexisting ancient text,[62] it may be more likely that Smith backed up in his dictation to add something to clarify his narrative—in this instance, to avoid a problematic reading that the Lamanites were seen in the dark.[63] Regardless, this type of error is best explained as the result of oral dictation, not visual copying. Certainly, it is a much more likely explanation than Hauglid's improbable suggestion that the scribe's eye skipped ahead.

There are no examples of this type of error in either the Williams document or Parrish's shorter document, but there are two possible instances in the text Parrish recorded in the translation book. After Parrish copied his shorter document into the translation book, he evidently began taking dictation from Smith and recording it directly into the book. While his copied text is relatively free of emendation, the new material begins with a number of corrections that are best explained as the result of oral dictation:

> ... the Lord appeared unto me, and said unto me, ... for I have purposed to take thee away out of Haran, and to make of the[e] <a> minister to bear my name ~~unto a people which I will~~ give in a Strange land *which I will give* unto thy seed after thee, for an ~~eternal memorial~~ everlasting possession ~~if~~ <when> they hearken to my voice.[64]

In 2010, Hauglid listed the cancellation of "which I will give" and its subsequent repetition as evidence that Parrish copied another document and that his eye accidently skipped ahead, but a more likely explanation is that Smith dictated "unto a people which I will give" and realized that it was the land that would be given to Abraham's seed, not the people, and so he had those words

---

62. Skousen is anxious to explain: "The clear majority of changes in the original manuscript were made immediately; that is, the scribe caught the error during Joseph Smith's initial dictation" (Ibid., 27).

63. Joseph Smith sometimes found it necessary to backtrack in his dictation to clarify or avoid a difficult reading without crossing out words. Examples of this are: "and thus we see that they buried their weapons of peace, or they buried the weapons of war, for peace" (Alma 24:19). "And now, my son, this was the ministry unto which ye were called, to declare these glad tidings unto this people, to prepare their minds; or rather that salvation might come unto them, that they may prepare the minds of their children to hear the word at the time of his coming" (Alma 39:16).

64. Book of Abraham Manuscript-C, 7–8 [Abr. 2:6] (*JSP*, R4:231–33); emphasis added.

cancelled and then clarified the text by dictating that Abraham would preach "in a Strange land which I will give unto thy seed." Hauglid skips the cancellation of "eternal memorial" and in-line correction to "everlasting possession," which is a sure indication that Parrish was writing from Smith's dictation. The confusion between "the" and "thee" is also a possible hearing mistake.

On the next page of the translation book is another example of what Hauglid believes is evidence of Parrish's eye skipping ahead: "... my name is Jehovah, and I know ~~the beginning~~ the end from *the beginning*, therefore my hand shall be over thee ..."[65] Again, a more likely explanation is that in dictating Smith got ahead of himself and quickly corrected it.

Dittography

Another kind of visual copying error described by Hauglid is called dittography, which happens "when a scribe would copy text from an earlier manuscript to another sheet, the eye would see the same word twice and accidentally rewrite it."[66] An example of this kind of error appears in 3 Nephi 22:4 in the 1837 edition of the Book of Mormon. By comparing the 1830 and 1837 editions of the Book of Mormon, we see that after typesetting the words "of thy," the typesetter's eye skipped up and slightly to the right at the same words *of thy*, which caused him to repeat the phrase "youth, and shalt not remember the reproach of thy."

3 NEPHI 22:4/ISAIAH 54:4

1830   "... for thou shalt forget the shame *of thy* youth, and shalt not remember the reproach *of thy* widowhood any more" (1830 Book of Mormon, p. 501).

1837   "... for thou shalt forget the shame of thy youth, and shalt not remember the reproach of thy *youth, and shalt not remember the reproach of thy* widowhood any more" (1837 Book of Mormon, p. 529).

Concerning this error, textual scholar Stan Larson has noted:

The probable reason these words appeared in the text in 1837 can be traced to the particular arrangement of the words on the lines of the

---

65. Book of Abraham Manuscript-C, 8 [Abr. 2:8] (*JSP*, R4:233); emphasis added.
66. Hauglid, "Thoughts on the Book of Abraham," 251.

1830 edition. While reading from an 1830 edition to set type for the 1837 edition, the typesetter's eye skipped up and slightly to the right at the words *of thy* and thus repeated the phrase *of thy youth*, and shalt not remember the reproach. It has not been detected as an instance of accidental dittography of a line because the doubled words do fit into a readable pattern.[67]

Hauglid found nothing like this order of dittography in the Abraham manuscripts, but instead pointed to two very unusual dittographs. One is a repetition of two words, which occurs when Parrish turned over the sheet to begin a new page of his shorter document and repeated the words "and my" from the previous page, which at some point was cancelled: "... I will take thee, to put upon thee my name even the priesthood of thy Father, ~~and my~~ [p. 3] and my power shall be over thee ..."[68]

In such a situation, a scribe writing from dictation could easily lose his place and accidentally repeat a word or two when turning over the page, and therefore this example does not provide definitive evidence that Parrish was copying another document.

The other repetition is also unusual in that it is a paragraph-long dittograph, which appears at the end of the Williams document. The bottom half of the page reads:

 Who was the daughter of Haron

 Now the Lord had said unto me Abram get the[e] out of
thy country, and from thy kindred and from
thy fathers house, unto a land that I will shew
thee: Therefore I left the land of Ur of the chaldees
to go into the land of canaan; and I took Lot
my brothers son, and his wife, and Sarai my
wife; and also my father followed after me
unto the land which we denominated Haran. And the
famine abated, and my father tarried in
Haran and dwelt there, as there were many
flocks in Haran; And my father turned again
unto his idolitry: Therefore he continued in
Haran

---

67. Stan Larson, "Early Book of Mormon Texts—Textual Changes to the Book of Mormon in 1837 and 1840," *Sunstone* 1/4 (Fall 1976): 51–52.

68. Book of Abraham Manuscript-B, 3–4 [Abr. 1:18] (*JSP*, R4:209–10).

> *Now the Lord had said unto <me> Abram get thee*
> *out of thy country and from thy kindred and from thy*
> *fathers house unto a land that I will shew thee. Therefore I left*
> *the land of Ur of the chaldees to go into the land of canaan, and I took Lot*
> *my bro[ther] son and his wife and sarah my wife and also my father follo[wed]*
> *me unto the land which we denominated Haran and the famine*
> *abated, and my father tarried in Haran and dwelt there as there were*
> *<many> flock in Haran, and my father turned again unto his idolitry*
> *Therefore he continued in Haran* but <I> Abram and
> and Lot my brothers son prayed unto the Lord, and the Lord appeared
> [*page 4 ends*][69]

The first thing to notice is that the Williams document ends abruptly, implying that it is not complete. Next, the repeated (italicized) paragraph is without characters and discontinues maintaining the left margin after three lines. Finally, the repeated paragraph continues beyond the repetition without creating a new paragraph as Parrish's longer document from the translation book does. This last observation is additional evidence that the paragraphing Hauglid emphasizes was indeed created to align the English text with the hieratic characters.

Because Williams changed his method of recording at the point where the repeated paragraph appears, it would be a mistake to conclude the entire document is a visual copy based on this unusual dittograph at the end. Yet Gee makes this very assertion: "Toward the end of the manuscript is a long dittography, which repeats part of the Book of Abraham, indicating that this manuscript is a copy of an even earlier manuscript, which unfortunately has not survived."[70]

There is a reconstruction of the events that best explains how the dittograph occurred, and once understood, it becomes clear that this repetition in no way threatens the oral dictation theory.

When Parrish and Williams recorded from Smith's dictation, probably on 19 and 20 November 1835, Williams wrote one more paragraph than Parrish. Parrish drew the last hieratic character, but left the remainder of the page blank.

69. Book of Abraham Manuscript-A, 4 [Abr. 2:2–6] (*JSP*, R4:201); repeated material italicized.
70. Gee, *Introduction to the Book of Abraham*, 30.

Figure 1.9. Bottom half of page 7 of Book of Abraham Manuscript-A, showing the paragraph-long dittography.

Next, Parrish copied the English text onto seven pages of the translation book following the half page Phelps had previously scribed, making some slight changes. After skipping a line, Parrish then copied the paragraph that had been dictated in his absence from the Williams document. At this point, Parrish again began writing from Smith's dictation directly into the book, which, as previously discussed, is evident from the in-line corrections made in his new English text. This possibly occurred on 24 and/or 25 November 1835, which are the last two entries in Smith's Kirtland journal in which translation is mentioned.[71]

---

71. On 24 November, Joseph Smith "translated some of the Egyptian records," and on the 25th he "spent the day in Translating" the papyri (Joseph Smith, Journal, 24–25 Nov. 1835; *JSP*, J1:109, 110).

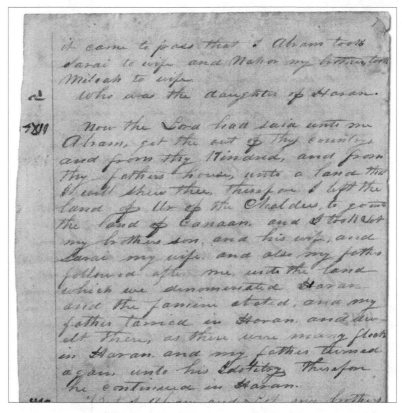

Figure 1.10. Top half of page 7 of Book of Abraham Manuscript-C, showing the first occurrence of the name "Haran" at the end of a paragraph, followed by a blank line between paragraphs, and evidence of the scraped off characters in the left margin.

Later, Williams wanted to copy the new text from the translation book into his manuscript to make it complete. The paragraph that Williams last wrote ended with the word "Haran" on a line by itself. As he turned the pages of the translation book looking for a paragraph that ended with that word, Williams would first have come to the top of page 7 and would have accidentally began copying the paragraph that he had already recorded from Smith's dictation. He was apparently unaware that the next paragraph also ended on the following page with "Haran".

What may have added to Williams's confusion was the blank line before the paragraph and the possibility that either Parrish's or Williams's document or both did not have the characters in the margin next to the paragraph. As previously mentioned, Parrish had evidently copied the characters into the margin before copying the English text but, having miscalculated the number of lines, found it necessary to scrape off two groups of characters on page 7, precisely where the dittograph occurs.

Because he was no longer a scribe recording from oral dictation and was merely recording a second copy of a text that had already been entered into the translation book, Williams saw no need to copy the characters or to maintain the margins and paragraphing.

We may not know exactly how Williams introduced a paragraph-long dittograph into his document, but the scenario I have proposed explains more of the evidence and facts than Gee's assertion that the entire document is a copy based on a repeated paragraph at the end. Gee's explanation cannot explain the presence of clear evidence of simultaneous recording from dictation that appears in the document prior to the dittograph. Nor can it explain the change in Williams's method of recording that occurs at the point of the dittograph.

Conclusion

After dictating three verses of the Book of Abraham to Phelps, probably in early July 1835, Smith began immediately to work on his Alphabets and bound Grammar of the Egyptian language. Then, the following November, he dictated forty-eight verses of Abraham to Williams and Parrish. Nothing in Gee's and Hauglid's discussions of the evidence compels us to abandon the simultaneous-recording-from-dictation theory, a theory that is supported by strong, compelling evidence and explains the majority of historical facts. Recognizing that the Parrish and Williams documents are the original records of Smith's dictation of Abraham and that they date to November 1835 means the theory that the Alphabets and bound Grammar were created *after* the translation must be abandoned. It also means that the missing document theory is both unnecessary and unsupported. Instead, these documents—the Joseph Smith Egyptian Papers—relating to the Egyptian language should be seen as Smith's preliminary efforts to understand his newly acquired papyri and to convince followers that his translation was derived from the papyri.[72]

In chapter two, I look more closely at the first phase of Smith's work with the papyri. I also continue to evaluate the theories of Abraham's defenders.

---

72. Although the general practice has been to follow Hugh Nibley's labeling and refer to the collection of papers dealing with the translation of some of the Egyptian papyri in Joseph Smith's possession as the Kirtland Egyptian Papers, which is inaccurate since some of the materials were created in Nauvoo, I have adopted the term Joseph Smith Egyptian Papers. I include under this designation the Book of Abraham Manuscripts, which some may wish to view as a distinct collection but are actually inextricably tied to Smith's Egyptian project.

2   Princess Katumin

In December 1835, responding to rumors that the Mormons claimed that they were in possession of the actual bodies of "Abraham, Abimelech, the king of the Philistines, Joseph, who was sold into Egypt, &c.," John Whitmer editorialized in the *Latter Day Saints' Messenger and Advocate*: "Who these ancient inhabitants of Egypt are, we do not pretend to say, neither does it matter to us."[1] Whitmer was evidently unaware that shortly after procuring the mummies and papyri, Joseph Smith had identified the male mummy as King Onitas and one of the female mummies as his daughter, Princess Katumin.

As noted in chapter one, the theory that W. W. Phelps and others used Smith's English translation of the Book of Abraham to create the Egyptian Alphabets and bound Grammar was proposed by Hugh Nibley as early as 1971. More recently, the theory was defended by BYU Egyptologists Kerry Muhlestein and John Gee. In this chapter, I look closely at the first phase of Smith's work with the Egyptian papyri in July 1835 and show that a more complete understanding of the content of the Alphabets and bound Grammar renders Nibley's reverse-translation theory even less feasible. More importantly, we get a view of the inner-workings of Smith's attempt to secure the confidence of his followers.

Phase One: Kirtland, Early July 1835

Smith's official history includes an account of when he began working on his translation of Abraham. This account, which appears between the 5 and 9 July 1835 entries, reads:

> I, with W. W. Phelps and O[liver]. Cowdery, as scribes, commenced the translation of some of the characters or hieroglyphics, and much to

---

1. "Egyptian Mummies—Ancient Records," *LDS Messenger and Advocate* 2 (Dec. 1835): 233.

our joy found that one of the rolls contained the writings of Abraham; another the writings of Joseph of Egypt, &c. a more full account of which will appear in its place, as I proceed to examine or unfold them.[2]

This entry in Smith's history was composed by LDS Apostle Willard Richards on 15 September 1843, as noted in Richards's own journal.[3] Since Richards had not joined the church until December 1836, he probably composed the July 1835 account with the help of Smith and/or Phelps, the latter of who also worked on Smith's history. Moreover, the history was read to Smith and approved by him on a regular basis.[4] The information that Richards included therefore likely came from one or both of the participants eight years after the event. However, the text should not be read as a statement that Smith began a formal translation of Abraham and that it continued without interruption until he had dictated at least the five chapters that we today possess, as John Gee has asserted. The wording of the entry is significant, stating that only "some of the characters or hieroglyphics" were translated to identify the authors of the two scrolls. On 19 July 1835, Phelps wrote to his wife, Sally, who was in Missouri, and told her: "As no one could translate these writings they were presented to President [Joseph] Smith. He soon knew what they were and said that the rolls of papyrus contained the sacred record kept by Joseph in Pharoah's court in Egypt and the teachings of Father Abraham."[5]

About this time, Smith may have dictated a rough draft of Abraham 1:1–3 to Phelps or Oliver Cowdery or both, which Phelps later copied into the translation book.[6] As previously mentioned,

---

2. JS History, vol. B-1, 596 (DHC 2:236).

3. Willard Richards, Journal, 15 Sept. 1843, 9:49, CHL.

4. On 8 November 1843, "from 9 to 11½ <A.M.–> Interv[ie]w with Phelp[s] an[d] Richa[r]ds clerks—read & hea[r]d read the history" (Joseph Smith, Journal, 8 Nov. 1843; *JSP*, J3:127). The previous day Richards and Phelps had reached page 729 in volume B-1, which recounts the events of April 1836 (Richards, Journal, 7–8 Nov. 1843).

5. William W. Phelps, Kirtland, Ohio, to Sally Waterman Phelps, Liberty, Missouri, 19 July 1835, partial transcription in Historian's Office, Journal History of the Church, 20 July 1835, CHL. Another partial transcription with some variant readings also available in Leah Y. Phelps, "Letters of Faith from Kirtland," *Improvement Era* 45 (Aug. 1942): 529.

6. Book of Abraham Manuscript-C, 1 (*JSP*, R4:219).

the five sheets comprising this document were subsequently removed from the book, and the document itself is the only manuscript—out of the three translation manuscripts produced in Kirtland—to contain a rough version of the first three verses of the Book of Abraham. The rest of this document, the longest of the three Kirtland documents, is in the handwriting of Warren Parrish, who did not become a scribe until late October 1835. The three verses penned by Phelps explicitly identified the writer of one of the scrolls as Abraham (fig. 1.2):

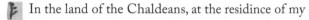 In the land of the Chaldeans, at the residince of my

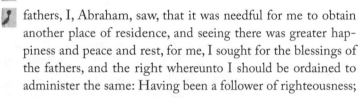 fathers, I, Abraham, saw, that it was needful for me to obtain another place of residence, and seeing there was greater happiness and peace and rest, for me, I sought for the blessings of the fathers, and the right whereunto I should be ordained to administer the same: Having been a follower of righteousness;

desiring ~~one~~ <to be> one who possessed great Knowledge; a greater follower of righteousness; <a possessor of greater Knowledge;> a father of many nations; a prince of peace; one who keeps the commandments of God; a rightful heir; a high priest, holding the right belonging to the fathers, from the begining of time; even from the begining, or before the foundation of the earth, down to the present time; even the right of the first born, or the first man, who is Adam, or first father, through <the> fathers, unto me.[7]

The first two hieratic characters in the left margin were taken from column 1, line 1, of JSP XI, reading from right to left (fig. 2.1). Smith evidently guessed, correctly, that Egyptian, like Hebrew, is read right to left. These characters can no longer be seen due to damage to the papyri, but the text can be restored from the Book of Breathings at the Louvre in Paris, France (call number Louvre 3284).[8] The origin of the third character, which would have appeared in the missing portion of the papyrus, is column 2

---

7. Book of Abraham Manuscript-C, 1 (*JSP*, R4:219).

8. See Robert K. Ritner, *The Joseph Smith Egyptian Papyri: A Complete Edition* (Salt Lake City: Smith–Pettit Foundation, 2011), 99, and Fig. 1 on p. 84; Brian Hauglid, *A Textual History of the Book of Abraham: Manuscripts and Editions* (Provo, Utah: Neal A. Maxwell Institute for Religious Scholarship, Brigham Young University, 2010), 58n3,

Figure 2.1. Joseph Smith Papyrus XI and page 1 of Book of Abraham Manuscript-C, showing the source of the first two characters and proposed position of the third.

of JSP I (fig. 1.3), and the meaning as explained in the Grammar and Alphabet of the Egyptian Language (p. 3) comports with the claimed translation given here, as does the translation of the previous two characters.

The first three verses of Abraham are Phelps's only contribution to the translation texts. At this point Smith's method changed when he discontinued a character-by-character translation and began to compile an Egyptian Alphabet, where he could give random interpretations. When the translation resumed in November 1835, Parrish was Smith's main scribe.

Phase Two: Kirtland, Circa 17–31 July 1835

The second chronological clue also comes from Smith's official history, which, following the entry for 17 July 1835, reads: "The remainder of this month, I was continually engaged in translating an alphabet to the Book of Abraham, and arrangeing a grammar of the Egyptian language as practiced by the ancients."[9]

Like the first statement, this entry was also composed by Willard Richards, on 16 September 1843,[10] no doubt with the help of Smith and/or Phelps. This passage alludes to three small nearly identical booklets containing the "Egyptian alphabet" in the

---

mentions parallel characters in Louvre 3284; see also Nibley, *The Message of the Joseph Smith Papyri: An Egyptian Endowment* (Salt Lake City: Deseret Book Co., 1975), 64.

9. JS History, vol. B-1, 597 (DHC 2:238).

10. Richards, Journal, 16 Sept. 1843, 9:50.

handwritings of Smith, Cowdery, and Phelps, as well as a bound "Grammar and Alphabet of the Egyptian Language" (GAEL), the greater portion of which is in the handwriting of Phelps.

The first thing to notice about Richards's 1843 description is that the Alphabets and bound Grammar were considered translations, which defenders typically ignore. However, the term alphabet is misleading since the Alphabets function more as dictionaries, recording a sign in the left margin, then in the next column a name, and finally the explanation or definition. How the Alphabets relate to the Book of Abraham is not stated, but it would be a mistake to assume that the Alphabets deal exclusively with the Book of Abraham.

The same characters in the Alphabets were later copied into the bound Grammar and their definitions were expanded in each of the five degrees of meaning. Three of the degrees are prefaced by short lectures on Egyptian grammar, mostly explaining the degree system and comprehensiveness of the language. The Grammar is discussed in detail in chapters four and five, although I occasionally draw on its content.

In his *Introduction to the Book of Abraham*, John Gee dated the Egyptian Alphabets to 1 October 1835 because an entry in Smith's journal states: "This after noon labored on the Egyptian alphabet, in company with brsr. O[liver]. Cowdery and W. W. Phelps: The system of astronomy was unfolded."[11] As I discuss in chapter five, this actually refers to the bound "Grammar and Alphabet of the Egyptian Language"—the only document dating to 1835 that includes a discussion of the "system of astronomy." Gee also seemed to ignore Smith's history and dated the bound Grammar to "Between January and April 1836."[12] As discussed in chapter six, this is without foundation.

Gee gave no reason for why he seemingly ignored the statement in Smith's history, which is our best source for both the time and authorship of the Alphabets and bound Grammar. Yet he relied on the same history for the July 1835 date for translating the Book of

---

11. Smith, Journal, 1 Oct. 1835 (*JSP*, J1:67).

12. John Gee, *An Introduction to the Book of Abraham* (Provo, Utah: Religious Studies Center, Brigham Young University/Salt Lake City: Deseret Book Co., 2017), 34.

Abraham, although he did not provide a footnote for this date.[13] On page 14 of his *Introduction,* Gee states that "Joseph Smith began translating the papyri in early July 1835, with Oliver Cowdery and William W. Phelps serving as his scribes," which clearly relies on Smith's history. Again, in his timeline on page 16, Gee lists July 1835 as the beginning of Smith's translating Abraham and skips the part mentioning the Alphabets and bound Grammar. Thus Gee repeatedly failed to give the source for the July 1835 date, although he included footnotes for nearly everything else. Gee's decisions for using Smith's history are puzzling, at best.

The two entries in Smith's history are important for understanding the initial phase of Smith's work on the papyri, and the participation of Smith and Phelps in both projects makes the entries impossible to ignore. As early as June 1842, Phelps wrote to LDS Apostle Parley P. Pratt: "I am now on the largest amount of business that I have ever undertaken, since I have been in the church: It is to write and compile the History of br. Joseph, embracing the entire history of the church. It will occupy my time and talents for a long time, should nothing intervene."[14] Phelps's handwriting appears on pages 75–130 and 135–57 of volume A-1 of Smith's history—seventy-seven pages in all. On 1 December 1842, Smith "Called on W. W. Phelps to get the historical documents &c. After which he commenced reading and revising history."[15] On 19 January 1843, Phelps wrote in his journal, "I recommenced writing on the history of the Church for B[r]. Joseph."[16] On the following day, Willard Richards recorded in Smith's journal, "[Joseph Smith] Returned at 10 o'clock and gave some instructions about Phelps and Richards uniting in writing the history of the church."[17] The two men were still working together on 22 March 1843, when Richards wrote to his brother Levi: "I am writing the

---

13. Gee dates the translation to July 1835 without giving a source, but Smith's history is the only documentary evidence (Gee, *An Introduction to the Book of Abraham,* 14, 15, and 26).

14. W. W. Phelps, Letter to Parley P. Pratt, 16 June 1842, Parley P. Pratt Correspondence, CHL, cited in *PJS* J2:495n3.

15. Smith, Journal, 1 Dec. 1842 (*PJS* 2:495).

16. William W. Phelps, Journal, 19 Jan. 1843, CHL.

17. Smith, Journal, 20 Jan. 1843 (*JSP,* J2:246–47).

History of the Church in Joseph's office, in connection with W. W. Phelps."[18] On the backs of sheets containing reproduction-print-ings of Facsimile 2 of the Book of Abraham, Phelps drafted an account of activities in Liberty, Missouri, in June 1834, which Richards copied on 1 August 1843 onto pages 494 and 495 of volume A-1 of Smith's Manuscript History.[19] Two weeks later, Richards recorded the entries dealing with the Book of Abraham on pages 596 and 597 of volume B-1.[20]

The details of Smith's participation in the creation of his own history are not as well known, but apparently Richards and Phelps worked under Smith's direct supervision. On 8 November 1843, Smith's journal records: "from 9 to 11 ½ <A.M.–> Interv[ie]w with Phelp[s] an[d] Richa[r]ds clerks—read & hea[r]d read the history."[21] The previous day Richards and Phelps had reached page 729 in Book B-1, which recounts the events of April 1836.[22] Pre-sumably this procedure involving Richards and Phelps had been followed for the previous portions of the history.

In his 2010 book, *A Textual History of the Book of Abraham*, Brian Hauglid acknowledged that both entries in Smith's history were likely the result of Phelps's contribution. Of the passage dat-ing the Alphabets and Grammar to the latter part of July 1835, Hauglid wrote, "W. W. Phelps likely inserted this entry in 1843."[23] Kerry Muhlestein and Megan Hansen have also noted that the entries in Smith's history "seem to be written by Willard Richards,

---

18. Willard Richards, Letter to Levi Richards, 22 Mar. 1843, qtd. in Joseph Grant Stevenson, ed., *Richards Family History*, 3 vols. (Provo, Utah: Stevenson's Ge-nealogical Center, 1991), 3:93.

19. William W. Phelps, History Draft, ca. Mar. 1842–Aug. 1843, Joseph Smith History Documents (box 1, fd 5), CHL; Richards, Journal, 1 Aug. 1843, 9:44.

20. Dan Vogel, ed., *History of Joseph Smith and The Church of Jesus Christ of Lat-ter-day Saints: A Source- and Text-Critical Edition*, 8 vols. (Salt Lake City: Smith–Pettit Foundation, 2015), 1:lxxxvi, lxxxix. Phelps and Richards continued working closely to-gether into 1845, as indicated by notes they both kept titled "Material Facts Left Out of the History," which appear on unpaginated pages at the back of the Revelation Book 2 [Kirtland Revelations Book], Revelations Collection, CHL (*JSP*, MRB:659–63).

21. Smith, Journal, 8 Nov. 1843 (*JSP*, J3:127).

22. Richards, Journal, 7–8 Nov. 1843.

23. Brian Hauglid, *A Textual History of the Book of Abraham: Manuscripts and Edi-tions* (Provo, Utah: Neal A. Maxwell Institute for Religious Scholarship, Brigham Young University, 2010), 214n6; see also 2n3, 213n2.

probably assisted by W. W. Phelps, in 1843."[24] This is important because it contradicts the attempts of Nibley, Gee, and others to shift responsibility for the creation of the three Alphabets and bound Grammar to Phelps, not Smith, whereas Phelps, an eyewitness, and probably Smith, assigned authorship of the documents to Smith. It also means that the Alphabets and Grammar preceded the translation of Abraham and that the reverse-translation theory must be rejected.

Overview of the Three "Egyptian Alphabets"

The three "Egyptian Alphabets" documents are very similar in content. One is entirely in the handwriting of Phelps, another mostly in Smith's handwriting with a little of Cowdery's handwriting at the end, while the third is entirely in Cowdery's handwriting. Each document consists of five pages with hieratic characters, the names of the characters, and the definitions arranged in columns. The Alphabets are divided into five *parts* of what is called the "first degree." About a third of the way through the second part (of the five), the characters start to be copied sequentially from the columns on JSP I flanking Book of Abraham Facsimile No. 1. The major divisions of the Alphabets, sources, and characters may be summarized as follows:[25]

EGYPTIAN ALPHABETS		
Parts	*Sources*	*Character numbers*
[first part] first degree	Book of the Dead – Amenhotep	1–23
	Book of the Dead – Ta-sherit-Min	
second part first degree-A	Pure Language	1–13
second part first degree-B	col. 3 Breathing Permit – Hôr (mixed with invented characters)	14–42
second part first degree-C	col. 3 Breathing Permit – Hôr (sequential)	43–59

---

24. Kerry Muhlestein and Megan Hansen, "'The Work of Translating': The Book of Abraham's Translation Chronology," in J. Spencer Fluhman and Brent L. Top, eds., *Let Us Reason Together: Essays in Honor of the Life's Work of Robert L. Millet* (Provo, Utah: Brigham Young University, 2016), 158n5.

25. The numbering of the characters for parts 3, 4, and 5 comes from *JSP,* R4:369–77.

third part first degree	col. 2 Breathing Permit – Hôr	1–17c
fourth part first degree	col. 1 Breathing Permit – Hôr	1–14c
fifth part first degree	col. 5 Breathing Permit – Hôr	1–28

Note that there are twenty-three characters in part 1, which is the subject of the remainder of this chapter. The origin of the thirteen characters in part 2-A is discussed in chapter three. Characters 14–42 in part 2-B are from the Breathing Permit of Hôr (or JSP I, column 3), but are mixed with invented characters; they are discussed in chapter five. Beginning with character 43 in part 2-C, the characters are copied sequentially from JSP I, column 3. This sequential copying of characters is continued to the end of the Alphabets, with part 3 containing characters from column 2, part 4 from column 1, and part 5 from column 5. Discovering the origin of the characters and ideas in the first and second parts of the Alphabets is a key to understanding the initial phase of Smith's interaction with the Egyptian papyri beginning in July 1835 and renders the theory of a reverse translation insupportable.

"Egyptian Alphabet"—Part One

The first part of the Alphabets includes names and definitions for twenty-three hieratic characters. In 2000, Gee quoted the following definitions for the twenty-three characters:

1   the first being who exercises Supreme power
2   the first man or one who has Kingly power or K[ing]
3   universal reighn having g[r]eater dom[in]ion or power
4   rolyal family royal blood or pharaoah or supreme power <or> King
5   crown of a princess or queen or Stands for queen
6   Virgen unmaried or the pri[n]ciple of vi[r]tue
7   the name of a royal family in female line
8   An unmaried woman and a vi[r]gin pri[n]ces
9   young unmarried man a pri[n]cess
10 woman married or unmarried or daughter
11 Crown of a prince or King
12 the Earth
13 beneath or under water
14 the eye or to see or sight sometimes me myself
15 the land of Egypt first seen under water

16 what other person is that or who

17 government power or Kingdom

18 the begining first before pointing to

19 in the begining of the E[a]rth <or> Creation

20 Signifys to be in any as light in th[e] E[ar]th

21 the first Creation of any thing first insti[tu]tion

22 from the first to any Stated peried after

23 from any or some fix<ed> peried of time <back> to the beginning <of the creation>[26]

Gee then asked: "This is the Book of Abraham? How could anyone get the Book of Abraham from this?"[27] Since Nibley, Gee, and others have argued that the Alphabets and bound Grammar were created in an attempt to reverse engineer Smith's translation of the Book of Abraham, a better question would be: How could anyone get this from the Book of Abraham? Concerning the content of the Alphabets, Gee also asserted, "The English renderings in the last column are not connected with the Book of Abraham or astronomy [a topic the Book of Abraham broaches], although they should be were the critics correct."[28]

The unfolding of astronomy in Abraham does not occur until 1 October 1835, according to Smith's journal,[29] so no one should reasonably expect a discussion of astronomy in July 1835. Again, since defenders believe the Alphabets and bound Grammar were created by Phelps and others attempting a reverse translation of the Book of Abraham, it is they who need to explain the lack of Abraham material. Otherwise it is easy to explain that under the guise of creating an alphabet, Smith could hunt for a story line, brainstorm, and expand his ideas by degrees. In the translation phase, he might draw on some of what he created in the Alphabets and bound Grammar, leaving others unused.

---

26. Egyptian Alphabet-A, [1] (*JSP*, R4:57). Characters and names replaced with numbers.

27. John Gee, "Eyewitness, Hearsay, and Physical Evidence of the Joseph Smith Papyri," in *The Disciple as Witness: Essays on Latter-day Saint History and Doctrine in Honor of Richard Lloyd Anderson*, ed. Stephen D. Ricks, Donald W. Parry, and Andrew H. Hedges (Provo, Utah: Foundation for Ancient Research and Mormon Studies, 2000), 216–17n99.

28. Ibid., 201.

29. Smith, Journal 1 Oct. 1835 (*JSP,* J1:67).

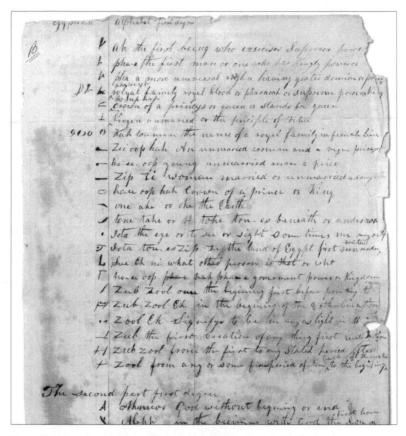

Figure 2.2. Egyptian Alphabet-A in the handwriting of Joseph Smith, showing twenty-three characters of the first part of the first degree.

Nevertheless, some material in the first part of the Alphabets, in fact, does appear later in the Book of Abraham, especially after it was expanded in the bound Grammar. The most obvious being character 15, which is translated in the Alphabets as follows:[30]

Smith's Alphabet	Cowdery's Alphabet	Phelps's Alphabet
Iota tou-es Zip-Zip the land of Egypt first seen under water	Iota-Tou-es-Zip-zi. The land of Egypt first discovered under water *by a woman*	Iota tou=es Zipzi= Egypt. The land first seen, *by a woman*, under water

30. Egyptian Alphabets-A–C, [1] (*JSP*, R4:57, 75, 87); emphasis added.

Note that Cowdery's and Phelps's Alphabets add that a woman had discovered Egypt while it was still under water. This appears to be an oversight by Smith rather than Phelps's and Cowdery's expansion of his definition. Iota tou-es Zip Zi is a compound character, consisting of three elements (characters 14, 13, and 10)—shown here from Smith's Alphabet:[31]

14   Iota the eye or to see or sight sometimes me myself

13   tone tahe or ~~th~~ tohe tou-es beneath or under water

10   Zip Zi woman married or unmarried or daughter

It may be seen that the element "woman" was included in one of the parts of the compound character, although not stated in Smith's definition. In the five degrees of the bound Grammar, the same compound character is translated as:

first degree   Iota toues-Zipzi: The land of Egypt

second degree   Iota tou-es Zip zi The land which was discovered under water by a woman

third degree   Iota toues Zip Zi. The women sought to settle her sons in that land. she being the daughter of Ham

fourth degree   Iota toues Zip Z[i] The land of Egypt discovered by a woman, who afterwards setled persons in it.

Fifth degree   Iota toues Zip Zi: The land of Egypt which was first discovered by a woman <wh[i]le underwater>, and afterwards settled by her Sons she being a daughter of Ham—any land over flown with water—a land seen when overflown by water:—land overflown by the seasons, land ~~by~~ enriched by being overflown low marshy ground.[32]

The progression from the first degree to the fifth degree is obvious and somewhat artificial. The third degree adds new information, revealing that the woman was a daughter of Noah's son Ham and

---

31. Egyptian Alphabet-A, [1] (*JSP*, R4:57).
32. GAEL, 5, 10, 14, 18, 21 (*JSP*, R4:125, 135, 143, 151, 157).

that she settled her sons in Egypt. The fifth degree generalizes the character as referring to any land that gets flooded or is marshy.

When dictating his translation of Abraham in November 1835, Smith drew on this material and his main scribe, Warren Parrish, wrote it down next to an invented grouping of characters partly made from the character in the Alphabets and bound Grammar:

> The land of Egypt. being first discovered, by a woman, who was the daughter of Ham, and the daughter of Zeptah, which in the Chaldea, signifies Egypt, which signifies that which is forbidden. When this woman discovered the land, it was under water, who after settled her sons in it; and thus from Ham sprang that race, which preserved, the curse in the land.[33]

Thus there is clearly a link between the first part of the Alphabets and the Book of Abraham, though, as I will demonstrate, the origin of the information had nothing to do with Abraham.

Princess Katumin and the Valuable Discovery Notebooks

While Abraham's name does not appear in the definitions in the first part of the Alphabets, another name does appear: a family named Kah tou man. The seventh character is given the following name and meaning in Smith's Alphabet:[34]

7   Kah tou man the name of a royal family in [the] female line

Because he left the names of the characters out of his list, Gee missed an important clue to understanding the content of the first part of the Alphabets. The name had previously appeared in two small notebooks. On the cover of one booklet, Frederick G. Williams wrote "Valuable Discovery of hid[d]en reccords that have been obtained from the ancient bur[y]ing place of the Egyptians," and which Joseph Smith then signed "Joseph Smith Jr."[35] This booklet contains three pages with hand-drawn copies of Egyptian fragments with some English text in the handwriting of Oliver Cowdery. The other notebook is untitled but also contains three

---

33. Book of Abraham Manuscript-B, 4 [Abr. 1:23–24] (*JSP*, R4:211).
34. Egyptian Alphabet-A, [1] (*JSP*, R4:57).
35. Historical Introduction, *JSP*, R4:27.

pages with hand-drawn copies of similar Egyptian fragments and English text in the handwriting of W. W. Phelps.

From these two notebooks, we learn that in addition to the two papyrus rolls—one known to Egyptologists as the Book of Breathings, once owned by a priest named Hôr, and the other roll known as the Book of the Dead, owned by a woman named Ta-sherit-Min—Joseph Smith also had in his possession fragments of another Book of the Dead owned by a man named Amenhotep. While Smith identified Hôr's scroll with Abraham and Ta-sher-it-Min's scroll with Joseph son of Jacob/Israel, he apparently associated one of the Amenhotep fragments with a record about a princess Katumin, who lived hundreds of years after Abraham. On the first page of Phelps's notebook appear the following two sentences under the heading: "A Translation of the next page" with "in part" added in pencil.

> Katumin, Princess, daughter of On-i-tas <King> of Egypt, who ~~reigned~~ began to reign in the year of the world, 2962.

> Katumin was born in the 30th year of the reign of her father, and died when she was 28 years old, which was <the year> 3020[36]

On the opposite page are four lines of hieratic characters, which according to Robert K. Ritner, an Egyptologist at the Oriental Institute, University of Chicago, were taken from Chapter 46 of the now-missing Amenhotep Book of the Dead.[37] Underneath the characters, Phelps wrote, "over this stood the figure of a woman," which Ritner explains was actually "the *male* owner, Amenhotep."[38] Cowdery was evidently referring to the Amenhotep fragments, which were copied into the Phelps and Cowdery notebooks, as well as the circular hypocephalus (now Facsimile 2 of the Book of Abraham), when he wrote in December 1835 that in addition to the two rolls, "two or three other small pieces of

---

36. Notebook of Copied Egyptian Characters, 1 (*JSP*, R4:35).

37. Ritner, *Joseph Smith Egyptian Papyri*, 211. Since Cowdery described only two rolls of papyrus, Smith only possessed a fragment of the Amenhotep papyrus, which Chandler probably sold to someone prior to his arrival at Kirtland ("Egyptian Mummies," 236).

38. Ritner, *Joseph Smith Egyptian Papyri*, 210.

Figure 2.3. Page 2 of Notebook of Copied Egyptian Characters in the handwriting of W. W. Phelps, showing a paragraph of hieratic characters from the now-lost Amenhotep Book of the Dead, a drawing of a falcon-headed canopic jar taken from Hôr's Book of Breathings (JSP I; Fac. 1), and walking snake taken from Ta-sherit-Min's Book of the Dead (JSP VIII).

papyrus, with astronomical calculations, epitaphs, &c. were found with others of the Mummies."[39]

When Nibley criticized the notion that a few Egyptian characters could yield a paragraph of English text, he commented that the English words on the first page and the hieratic characters on the second "preserve a very nice balance between the number of words in each."[40] In saying this, he seems to have overlooked Phelps's insertion of "in part" in pencil, which is not visible on the microfilm copy of the document. He also overlooked Cowdery's version of the same words in the "Valuable Discovery" notebook, which identified the specific characters that were "in part" translated in Phelps's notebook. On page 3 of his notebook, Cowdery included only the three groups of characters from Phelps's paragraph of the hieratic characters that were supposedly translated.

> Katumin, Princess, daughter of On-i-tas [Pharaoh King] of Egypt, who <began to> reigned in the year of the World 2962.

---

39. "Egyptian Mummies," 234.
40. Nibley, "Meaning of the Kirtland Egyptian Papers," 374.

Katumin was born in the 30th year of the reign of her father, and died when she was 28 years old, which was the year 3020.[41]

The first group of characters comes from the first line of Phelps's paragraph of hieratic characters, reading from right to left. The next group of three characters is transposed and copied into the middle of Cowdery's translation. Finally, the last group of characters is also transposed and appears at the beginning of the second sentence of the Katumin translation. Ritner translates the entire group of characters as "Recitation by the Osiris."[42]

A close examination of the two translation texts indicates that Cowdery and Phelps wrote simultaneously as Smith dictated. Both Cowdery and Phelps originally wrote "Onitas of Egypt." At some point, Cowdery added "Pharaoh" at the end of the first line, then canceled it and inserted "King," whereas Phelps inserted "King" above the line. For the second emendation, Phelps made an in-line correction: "who ~~reigned~~ began to reign," whereas Cowdery corrected his text differently: "who <began to> ~~reigned~~." This is clear evidence that Phelps and Cowdery were writing simultaneously from Smith's dictation.[43] As discussed in the previous chapter, Smith used the same method when dictating the text of Abraham 1:4–2:2 four months later with Frederick G. Williams and Warren Parrish as scribes.

If we use Bishop James Usher's 4004 BCE as the date of Creation, as Smith and his contemporaries did, then 2,962 years after Creation is 1042 BCE and 3,020 years is 984 BCE. According to Smith's/Rigdon's "Lectures on Faith" delivered in Kirtland during the winter of 1834–35, Abraham died in the 2,183rd year of the world, or 1821 BCE, which is 809 years before the birth of Katumin (b. 1012 BCE).[44] According to Adam Clarke's widely-circulated Bible commentary, Joseph son of Jacob/Israel died in 1635 BCE, or 623 years before the birth of Katumin.[45]

---

41. "Valuable Discovery" Notebook, 3 (*JSP*, R4:31).
42. Ritner, *Joseph Smith Egyptian Papyri*, 211n15.
43. Thanks to Brent Lee Metcalfe for this observation.
44. D&C, 1835 ed., 24.
45. Adam Clarke, *The Holy Bible ... With a Commentary and Critical Notes*, vol. 1 (New York: N. Bangs and J. Emory, for the Methodist Episcopal Church, 1825), 280; s.v. Exodus 1:6.

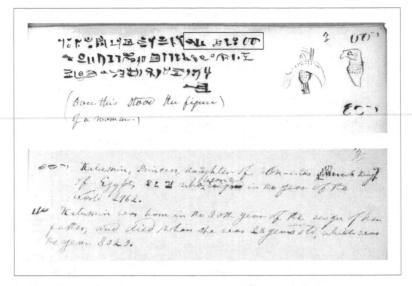

Figure 2.4. Comparison of page 2 of Notebook of Copied Egyptian Characters in the handwriting of W. W. Phelps (top) and page 3 of the "Valuable Discovery" Notebook in the handwriting of Oliver Cowdery (bottom) showing the portion of the hieratic characters that was supposedly translated.

Apparently, Smith's first translations pertained to the identities of the mummies. According to two independent reports, when Smith's mother, Lucy Mack Smith, exhibited the mummies in Nauvoo, Illinois, she identified them as King Onitas and his family. Shortly after viewing the mummies and papyri in Nauvoo in 1843, Charlotte Haven told her mother that Lucy Smith introduced her and her companions to "King Onitus and his royal household,— one [mummy] she did not know."[46] In December 1843, LaFayette Knight wrote that he visited Joseph Smith in Nauvoo and examined the four mummies "one of which his Mother told me was King Onitus, on whose breast was found the writing of Abr[a]ham."[47]

Kah-tou-man in the Alphabets

While the Katumin passage in the Valuable Discovery notebooks is about a specific princess and king, the Kah-tou-man of the Alphabets

---

46. Charlotte Haven, Letter to her mother, 19 Feb. 1843, in "A Girl's Letters from Nauvoo," *Overland Monthly* 16 (Dec. 1890): 623.

47. LaFayette Knight, Letter to James H. and Sharon Fellows, 21 Dec. 1843, CHL.

is a generic term applied to a royal female lineage extending back to the reputed founding of Egypt by the daughter of Ham. The first part of the Alphabets is about various aspects of the royal Kah-tou-man family line, and, as developed in the five degrees of the bound Grammar, the purpose of the passage was apparently to explain how two records of Hebrew patriarchs came into the possession of an Egyptian mummy.

In Smith's Alphabet, the character for Kah-tou-man is drawn differently from that in Phelps's and Cowdery's Alphabets:[48]

Smith's Alphabet		Kah tou man the name of a royal family in female line
Cowdery's Alphabet		Kah-tou=mun The name of the royal family– The female line
Phelps's Alphabet		Kah=tou<=>mun The name of the <a> royal family, in the female line

Smith's Alphabet appears to attempt three versions of the character. Apparently, there was some hesitation about how to draw the first character or characters, perhaps due to damage to or flaking of the ink. Ritner observes that the transcription of the first characters of the paragraph of hieratic text in Phelps's notebook are "garbled," as are those that appear "twice more at the right of the page, above and below a drawing of the falcon-headed canopic jar."[49] Note that Smith's Alphabet is closer to the top version, while Phelps's and Cowdery's are like the bottom. The characters have been restored by Ritner and others as "ḏd," which represent the hieratic cobra and hand for the word "recitation."[50]

In the bound Grammar, the development of the Katumin definition appears forced and artificial, but the fifth degree adds new information about one of the records:[51]

first degree	Kah-tou-mun The name of a Royal family in the female line

48. Egyptian Alphabets-A–C, [1] (*JSP*, R4:57, 75, 87).
49. Ritner, *Joseph Smith Egyptian Papyri*, 211n13.
50. To see how it is represented as "ḏd-w" on the Breathing Permit, see Nibley, *Message of the Joseph Smith Papyri*, 37, line 11.
51. GAEL, 4, 9, 13, 17, 21 (*JSP*, R4:123, 133, 141, 149, 157).

second degree	Kah tou mun, a distinction of royal female lineage
third degree	Kah tou mun descent from her by whom Egypt was discovered while it was under water.
fourth degree	Kah tou mun. a lineage, a daughter of Ham.
fifth degree	Kah tou mun: a lineage with whom a record of the fathers was intrusted by tradition of Ham, and according to the tradition of their elders, by whom also the tradition of the art of of embalming was kept.

The record found on the breast of one of the female mummies was the Book of the Dead belonging to Ta-sherit-Min, which Smith identified as the record of Joseph, son of Jacob/Israel. In the December 1835 issue of the *Latter Day Saints' Messenger and Advocate*, Cowdery gave a detailed description of the record of Joseph that leaves no doubt that he, Cowdery, was referring to Ta-sherit-Min's Book of the Dead. As described by Cowdery, the record of Joseph included:

The representation of the god head—three, yet in one …

The serpent … standing in front of, and near a female figure …

Enoch's Pillar, as mentioned by Josephus …

The inner end of the same roll, (Joseph's record,) presents a representation of the judgment: … the Savior seated upon his throne, crowned, and holding the sceptres of righteousness and power, before whom also, are assembled the twelve tribes of Israel … Michael the archangel, holding the key of the bottomless pit, and at the same time the devil as being chained and shut up in the bottomless pit.[52]

This last fragment, as noted by Ritner and others, is actually a vignette from a different papyrus once owned by an individual named Nefer-ir-nebu, specifically Chapter 125 of the Book of the Dead.[53] As may be seen, the first three items appear on JSP VI and JSP VIII. Smith therefore identified Ta-sherit-Min's scroll and the Nefer-ir-nebu vignette as the record of ancient Joseph just as

---

52. "Egyptian Mummies," 234.
53. Ritner, *Joseph Smith Egyptian Papyri*, 205–207; *JSP*, R4:20–21; Gee, *Guide to the Book of Abraham*, 10, 12.

Figure 2.5. Three vignettes from JSP VI and VIII consistent with Oliver Cowdery's description of a three-in-one godhead, walking snake, and Enoch's pillar.

he identified Hôr's scroll as the Book of Abraham. This raises an obvious question: Since Gee and Muhlestein have argued that the Book of Abraham was on the same scroll as Hôr's Book of Breathings, do they also want us to believe a real Book of Joseph was attached to the end of Ta-sherit-Min's Book of the Dead? One wonders if they have thought sufficiently through the implications of their "long-scroll" theory.

The fifth character in the Alphabets, which relates to the Kah-tou-man family, is named and defined in Cowdery's Alphabet as:[54]

| 5 | | Ho-oop-hah Crown of a pri[n]cess, or queen, or signifies queen. |

This character represents the crown for both a princess and a queen, and in the bound Grammar the character is developed in each of the five degrees—from a princess or unmarried queen, to a married queen, to a widowed queen, to a remarried queen, and finally to describe Queen Kah-tou-man, princess Katumin's mother, giving the same information about the record as was given for the seventh character previously discussed.[55]

first degree   Ho-oop=hah. Crown of a princes[s], or unmarried queen

second degree   Ho oop hah– Corwn [crown] of a married queen

third degree   Ho oop hah– Crown of a widowed queen

fourth degree   Ho oophah. Queen who has been married the second time

54. Egyptian Alphabets-A, [1] (*JSP*, R4:57).
55. GAEL, 3–4, 9, 13, 17, 21 (*JSP*, R4:121–23, 133, 141, 149, 157).

fifth degree   Ho oop hah Queen Kah tou mun, a distinction of Royal <female> lineage or descent, from her whom Egypt was discovered while it was under water, who was the daughter of Ham.– a lineage with whom a record of the fathers was intrusted by the tradition of Ham and accordding to the tradition of their elders; by who<m> also the tradition of the art of embalming in was kept.

Because Kah-tou-man is a lineage name, it is the name of both the queen mother and her princess daughter. As previously discussed, part of the compound character representing the discovery of Egypt by a woman while it was still under water, number 15 Iota tou-es Zip Zi, is number 13 tou-es, which the Alphabets define as "beneath or under water":

	Smith's Alphabet	*Cowdery's Alphabet*	*Phelps's Alphabet*
13			
15			

In the bound Grammar, this character is developed in the fifth degree as:

under the Sun: under heaven; downward; pointing downward going downward; stooping down going down in<to> another place,= any place: going down into the grave– going down into misery= even Hell; coming down in lineage by royal descent, in a line by onitas one of the royal families of the Kings the of Egypt.[56]

Here Katumin's father's name, Onitas, has also become a descent name. So even in the bound Grammar, the identities of the mummies is still very much on Smith's mind.

There is more to discuss about the first part of the Alphabets, such as the question of the legitimacy of the kings and queens of Egypt, which appears in my discussion of the bound Grammar in chapter four. I merely observe here that Smith later dropped this information about the origin of the Egyptians into his dictation of the Book of Abraham (Abr. 1:21–24, 25–27), but the source

---

56. GAEL, 5 (*JSP,* R4:125).

of the information came from papyri that were completely unrelated to Abraham.

Source

Comparing the three groups of characters in the Katumin passage in Cowdery's "Valuable Discovery" notebook with the characters and their explanations in the Alphabets is instructive, although piecing together what was intended is not always clear and necessitates some conjecture. However, such a comparison is further obstructed because the Katumin passage in the notebooks includes characters not found in the Alphabets and vice versa, and therefore any overlap is partial. Nevertheless, the relationship between the two groups of documents is clear.

COMPARISON OF CHARACTERS IN KATUMIN PASSAGE IN
"VALUABLE DISCOVERY" NOTEBOOK AND CHARACTERS IN PART I
OF EGYPTIAN ALPHABET-B WITH TRANSLATIONS

Cowdery "Valuable Discovery"	Cowdery Egyptian Alphabet	Translation
		Katumin, Princess, daughter of On-i-tas [Pharaoh King] of Egypt
	5	Ho-oop-hah Crown of a pri[n]cess, or queen, or signifies queen
	7	Kah-tou=mun The name of a royal family– The female lin
	11	Ho=e=oop-hah Crown of a prince, or King [Onitas]
	10	Zip-zi A women married or unmarried,.– daughter
		who <began to> reigned in the year of the World 2962
	6	Zi Virgin, unmarried, virtuous, or the principle of virtue
	4	Pha-ho-e-oop Royal family, royal blood, or pharaoh, or supreme power <power, or king>
	9	Ho=e-oop A young unmarried man, a prince

Cowdery "Valuable Discovery"	Cowdery Egyptian Alphabet	Translation
	22	Zub-zool From the first to any stated period after
	21	Zub First creation of any thing, first institution
	23	Zool From a fixed period of time back to the begin<ning or creation>
	10	Zip-zi A women married or unmarried,.– daughter
		Katumin was born in the 30th year of the reign of her father, and died when she was 28 years old, which was the year 3020
	2	Pha-e The first man, or one who has Kingly power, or king
	3	Pha a more universal reign, having greater dominion, or power
	7	Kah-tou=mun The name of a royal family— The female line

The twenty-three characters in part 1 of the Alphabets were not copied sequentially from any source but were gathered randomly, possibly from multiple sources, and arranged according to their shapes—which is what one would expect from an alphabet or dictionary. Hence, characters 1–4 are very similar in shape, as also are characters 8–10, 11–13, 16–17, and 18–23. Additionally, because part 1 of the Alphabets shows the dissection of two compound characters (number 15 and number 19), other characters in the list may have been taken from compound characters as well. Finding close approximations of the twenty-three characters of part 1 of the Alphabets among the Amenhotep fragments copied into the Valuable Discovery notebooks is not difficult, with the notable exception of one of the compound characters, number 19. However, the other compound character, number 15, is very similar to two characters in the Katumin paragraph of hieratic characters in Phelps's notebook as well as on the Ta-sherit-Min papyrus, most often in red ink and sometimes reversed. That the character representing the discovery of Egypt by a woman while it was under water appears in the Katumin passage in one of the Valuable Discovery notebooks and is a feature of the scroll associated with Katumin's mother is probably more than coincidence. Compare the following:

	Egyptian Alphabet	Valuable Discovery	Ta-sherit-Min papyrus
15			

The above shows the two compound characters—numbers 15 and 19—and the other characters in part 1 of the Alphabets that relate to them, which account for nearly one-half of the total number of characters. The three groups of characters in the last column were taken from the left margin of the Book of Abraham Manuscript-C, one of the English translations of Abraham. They are not hieratic Egyptian but were invented to fill in the missing portion of the Hôr papyrus. From this comparison, it may be seen that the invented characters incorporate elements from the characters found in part 1 of the Alphabets. By inserting these characters to fill in a gap in the Hôr papyrus, Smith could make it appear that later Egyptian understanding of the founding of Egypt as well as the legitimacy of the Hamite claim to authority derived from Abraham's record. In dictating the Book of Abraham in November 1835, Smith incorporated material he had translated in part 1 of the Alphabets and developed in the five degrees of the bound Grammar the previous July regarding Katumin and her mother.

COMPARISON OF TWO COMPOUND CHARACTERS FROM EGYPTIAN ALPHABET AND INVENTED CHARACTERS FROM BOOK OF ABRAHAM MANUSCRIPT[57]

Alphabet number	Alphabet character	Translation ms character
10		
13		

57. Alphabet characters are from Joseph Smith's Egyptian Alphabet-A, early July–Nov. 1835, p. 1 (*JSP*, R4:56). Translation characters are from Book of Abraham Manuscript-C, Nov. 1835, p. 5 (Ibid., 226).

Alphabet number	Alphabet character	Translation ms character
14		
15		
18		
19		
20		
21		
22		
23		

Conclusion

Katumin and her mother were in a line of royal females all with the same name extending back to a woman who discovered Egypt while it was under water. At this point, Abraham has not been mentioned, only Egypt, the Pharaohs, and the Kah-tou-mans.

Part 1 of the Alphabets and bound Grammar deal with Katumin and primarily Amenhotep's Book of the Dead and not with the Book of Abraham, although some of the Katumin–Amenhotep material was later used when Smith dictated his translation of the Breathing Permit of Hôr as the Book of Abraham. This is a problem for the theory that the Alphabets and bound Grammar derived from Smith's translation of Abraham. Rather, the first parts of the Alphabets and Grammar were independent translations of characters from a completely different papyrus. This discovery reveals how ideas that found their way into the Book of Abraham began to be developed prior to Smith's dictation of the English text of Abraham in November 1835.

3   The Pure Language

In chapter two, I discussed how the first parts of the Alphabets relate to fragments of the Book of the Dead once owned by Amenhotep, and which were copied into the Valuable Discovery notebooks and translated by Joseph Smith as the epitaph of Princess Katumin, who lived about a thousand years before Jesus. This discovery contradicts the theory that the Alphabets and bound Grammar were created after Smith translated the Book of Abraham and were an attempt by W. W. Phelps at reverse translation (that is, the Book of Abraham preceded the Alphabets and Grammar). In this chapter, I explore how part 2 of the Alphabets incorporates Smith's teachings about a pure Adamic language, dating to 1832, which also contradicts the reverse-translation theory. However, as I explain, Smith's previous thoughts on the pure language, like the Katumin material, also find their way into the Book of Abraham.

"Egyptian Alphabet"—Part Two

While John Gee sees nothing in the Alphabets that could produce the Book of Abraham, Brian Hauglid in 2011 referred to the similarities as evidence that the two groups of documents were connected, although he misstated the order of production. Concerning the Alphabets and bound Grammar, Hauglid asserted: "At this point the Egyptian manuscripts appear to be dependent on the text of the Book of Abraham. That is to say, the Book of Abraham was already in existence before the Egyptian papers were produced. … However, it is difficult to determine exactly what Phelps and some of the early brethren were trying to do with these papers. … But one thing is clear—the Book of Abraham is closely related to the Egyptian manuscripts."[1]

---

1. Brian M. Hauglid, "Thoughts on the Book of Abraham," in *No Weapon Shall Prosper: New Light on Sensitive Issues*, ed. Robert L. Millet (Provo, Utah: Religious Studies Center, Brigham Young University/Salt Lake City: Deseret Book Co., 2011), 257.

While Hauglid linked the Book of Abraham to the Alphabets and bound Grammar based on the similarity of some content, he did not explain the presence of material not in Smith's translation nor did he discuss the different contexts for the similar material. In the Alphabets and bound Grammar, the context for the founding of Egypt by the daughter of Ham is hundreds of years after Abraham. Part 2 of the Alphabets and bound Grammar begins with material unrelated to Abraham but eventually evolves into a discussion of Egyptian astronomy, which is also discussed in Abraham 3 but from a different source. Obviously, the reverse-translation theory cannot explain the presence of the unique material in the Alphabets and bound Grammar and is one reason why the theory must be rejected. My examination of part 2 of the Alphabets that follows shows that these documents are more complex than the theories of defenders can explain.

Part 2 of the Alphabets consists of fifty-nine characters that may be subdivided into three sections: (A) characters 1–13 are not Egyptian and some of them were taken from a document called the "pure language," which predated the arrival of the Egyptian papyri; (B) characters 14–42 were taken from the top portion of column 3 of the Breathing Permit of Hôr and mixed with invented or derivative characters, and that were eventually developed into an elaborate cosmology; and (C) characters 43–59 were copied sequentially from the bottom portion of column 3 of the same papyrus, and that were never named or given definitions.

OVERVIEW OF PART 2 OF EGYPTIAN ALPHABETS

Part	Source	Character numbers
second part first degree–A	Pure Language (invented characters)	1–13
second part first degree–B	col. 3 Breathing Permit – Hôr (mixed with invented characters)	14–42
second part first degree–C	col. 3 Breathing Permit – Hôr (sequential)	43–59

Part Two (A), Characters 1-13: The Pure Language

According to University of Chicago Egyptologist Klaus Baer, the first thirteen characters "differ in general appearance" from the

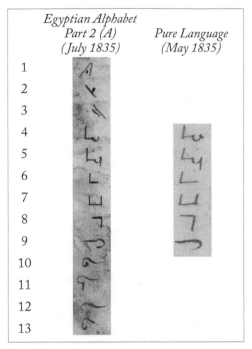

Figure 3.1. Comparison of the first thirteen characters in part 2 (A) of Egyptian Alphabet-C and W. W. Phelps's copy of the "pure language."

other characters and do not appear to be hieratic Egyptian.[2] At the time Baer examined Smith's Egyptian papyri and related documents in 1968, it was not known that characters 4–9 are identical to characters said to have come from the "pure language" spoken by Adam and his posterity until the confusion of tongues at the tower of Babel (Gen. 11:1–9).

On 26 May 1835, more than a month before Smith acquired the Egyptian papyri, Phelps, who was living with Smith and working as his scribe, wrote to his wife in Missouri and included "A specimen of some of the 'pure language'" (fig. 3.2).[3] Like the

2. Klaus Baer, "The Breathing Permit of Hôr: A Translation of the Apparent Source of the Book of Abraham," *Dialogue: A Journal of Mormon Thought* 3/3 (Autumn 1968): 128–29.

3. William W. Phelps, Letter, Kirtland, Ohio, to Sally Waterman Phelps, Liberty, Missouri, 26 and 27 May 1835, William W. Phelps Papers, BYU. Phelps arrived at Kirtland on 16 May 1835 and may have come across this material while working on the Doctrine and Covenants. Phelps recorded on 25 May that he "Worked in the office" until Saturday 30 May. On 16 June, he recorded: "Commenced cop[ying].

Egyptian Alphabets, this text is arranged in columns, although with different names and definitions:

ah	ahman–	God.
anz	sonahman=	Son of God
aintz	saunsahman	sons of God ordain[ed]
aine	anglo–	angels
oh	oleah	the Earth

The names and definitions of all but the last character were given by Smith as early as March 1832, while he and his family were living in Hiram, Ohio, with John Johnson and his family. This related document is headed "A Sample of pure Language given by Joseph the Seer as copied by Br Johnson," and conveys the same information in a question and answer format without characters:

Question What is the name of God in pure Language
Answer   Awman.

Q [what is] The meaning of the pure word A[w]man
A It is the being which made all things in all its parts.

Q What is the name of the Son of God.
A The Son Awman.

Q What is the Son Awman.
A It is the greatest of all the parts of Awman which is the Godhead the first born.

Q What is is man.
A This signifies Sons Awman. the human family the children of men the greatest parts of Awman Sons the Son Awman

Q What are Angels called in pure language.
A Awman Angls-man

Q What are the meaning of these words.
A Awman's Ser◊◊◊ts Ministerring servants Sanctified who are sent forth from heaven to minister for or to Sons Awman the greatest part of Awman Son. Sons Awman Son Awman Awman[4]

rev[elations]. at 3 [p.m.] [at] Josephs." This perhaps refers to the revelations Phelps copied into his journal. On 17 June, Phelps recorded: "Compared revelations" (William W. Phelps, 25–30 May, 16 and 17 June 1835, Diary and Notebook, CHL).

4. "A Sample of Pure Language," [Hiram Township, OH, between ca. 4 and ca. 20 Mar. 1832], Revelation Book 1, 144 (*JSP*, MRB:265; *JSP*, D2:213–15).

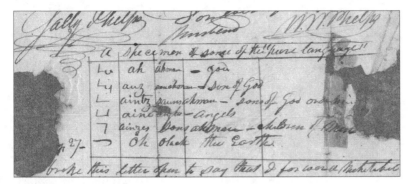

Figure 3.2. W. W. Phelps, Letter to Sally Phelps, 26 and 27 May 1835, showing characters and definitions from the "pure language."

Before Smith obtained the papyri, he was occupied with the idea of a pure Adamic language. The Book of Mormon contains the story of a people called the Jaredites whose language was not confounded at the Tower of Babel and so remained "pure." God allowed them to retain their pure language and sent them to the American continent.[5] As early as November 1830, Smith had emended Genesis to include mention of a "book of remembrance" that was kept among the ancient patriarchs, written "in the language of Adam … which was pure and undefiled" (Moses 6:4, 6).[6]

Smith and the early Mormons associated the gift of tongues with the pure language. Shortly after meeting Smith in Kirtland in November 1832, Brigham Young spontaneously broke into an ecstatic display of tongues, which, as Young later recalled, Smith declared was the "pure Adamic language."[7] After this, according to an early draft of Young's history, Smith stated that "the same spirit and gift is upon me, and I wish to speak in an unknown tongue, which he did and then interpreted, declaring it was the pure language which he spoke, and exhorted the brethren to seek after that gift."[8]

---

5. Book of Mormon, 1830 ed., 539–40 (Ether 1:33–37); Gen. 11:1–9.

6. Old Testament Revision 1, 11, CCLA. Also available in Scott H. Faulring, Kent P. Jackson, and Robert J. Matthews, eds., *Joseph Smith's New Translation of the Bible: Original Manuscripts* (Provo, Utah: Religious Studies Center, Brigham Young University, 2004), 97. On date, see p. 57.

7. "History of Brigham Young," *Millennial Star* 25 (11 July 1863): 439.

8. History of President Young, Historian's Office, Brigham Young History Drafts, 1856–1858, CHL. Joseph Smith's official history states, "I received the gift myself" (DHC 1:297). This appears in portion of the history that was added in JS History,

Elizabeth Ann Whitney received the gift of singing "inspirationally" in Kirtland in December 1835. "The first Song of Zion ever given in the pure language was sung by me then," she later wrote, "and interpreted by Parley P. Pratt, and written down; of which I have preserved the original copy. ... The Prophet Joseph promised me that I should never lose this gift if I would be wise in using it; and his words have been verified."[9] In nearby Painesville, skeptical newspaperman E. D. Howe reported in 1834 that the early Mormons sometimes "professed to believe that these 'tongues' were the same which were 'confounded' at the building of Babel."[10]

In addition to speaking occasionally in the pure language, Smith was also known to declare the Adamic names for contemporary geographic locations. As early as August 1831, while visiting Independence, Missouri, Smith declared it was the location of the prophesied city of Zion, which in the original language was "Zomar."[11] Another place was Adam-ondi-Ahman, which in 1838 Smith located 80 miles north of Zomar, explaining that "it is the place where Adam shall come to visit his people, or the Ancient of days shall sit as spoken of by Daniel the Prophet."[12] While making revisions in his revelations in early 1835 (before publishing them later that year), Smith expanded a revelation on priesthood originally dictated in November 1831. In this expansion, probably dictated some time in March or April 1835,[13] Smith declared:

Three years previous to the death of Adam, he called Seth, Enos, Cainan, Mahalaleel, Jared, Enoch and Methuselah, who were all high

vol. A-1, Addenda, 2, Note A, by Thomas Bullock possibly on 14 Jan. 1845 (see Dan Vogel, ed. *History of Joseph Smith and The Church of Jesus Christ of Latter-day Saints: A Source- and Text-Critical Edition*, 8 vols. [Salt Lake City: Smith–Pettit Foundation, 2015], 1:lxxxvi, 212n42).

9. Elizabeth Whitney, "A Leaf from an Autobiography," *Women's Exponent* 7 (1 Aug. 1878): 83.

10. E. D. Howe, *Mormonism Unvailed* (Painesville, Ohio: by the author, 1834), 133.

11. Ezra Booth, *Ohio Star*, 17 Nov. 1831. In Howe's reprint of Booth's letter, the name appeared as "Zomas" (Howe, *Mormonism Unvailed*, 199).

12. Joseph Smith, Journal, 19 May 1838 [D&C 116], Joseph Smith Collection, CHL (*JSP*, J1:271); Dan. 7:13–14.

13. The Joseph Smith Papers editors suggest that this revelation dates to after 1 March 1835, when the Quorum of Seventy was fully organized, and before the Twelve left Kirtland on 4 May 1835 on their mission to the east and Canada (*JSP*, D4:309–10).

priests, with the residue of his posterity, who were righteous, into the valley of Adam-ondi-ahman, and there bestowed upon them his last blessing. And the Lord appeared unto them, and they rose up and blessed Adam, and called him Michael, the Prince, the Arch angel. And the Lord administered comfort unto Adam, and said unto him, I have set thee to be at the head: a multitude of nations shall come of thee; and thou art a prince over them for ever.[14]

It is no accident that both Zomar and Adam-ondi-Ahman appear in one of Smith's definitions in the second part of the bound Grammar. In the Alphabets, character 15 (Beth) is defined as "mans first residence fruitful garden A val[le]y a place of happiness." As developed in the fifth degree in the bound Grammar, it is defined as:

> The place appointed of God for the residence of Adam; Adam ondi= Ahman a ~~fruit~~ garden made to be fruitful, by blessing or promise; great valley or plain given by promise, fitted with fruit trees and precious flowers, made for the healing of Man. Good to the taste pleasing to the eye; sweet and ~~precious~~ <deligh[t]ful> to the smell; place of happiness– purity, holiness, and rest: even Zomar– Zion.[15]

So even as Smith developed his ideas in the bound Grammar, the pure or Adamic language was on his mind, giving further evidence of the source of his ideas in the second part of the Alphabets. But why would Smith include his sample of the pure language in an Egyptian alphabet and grammar? The answer may be found in the prevailing widespread belief that ancient Egyptian hieroglyphics were visual representations of the language Adam spoke. Seventeenth-century German Jesuit Athanasius Kircher, as Umberto Eco noted, "firmly believed that ancient Egyptian was the perfect, Adamic language, and, according to the 'hermetic' tradition, he identified the Egyptian Hermes Trismegistus with Moses and said that hieroglyphs were Symbols, that is, expressions that

---

14. D&C, 1835 ed., 3:28 [D&C 107:53–55] (*JSP*, D4:317). According to John Corrill, Smith interpreted Adam-ondi-Ahman as: "The valley of God, in which Adam blessed his children" (John Corrill, *A Brief History of the Church of Christ of Latter Day Saints* [St. Louis: "Printed for the Author," 1839], 28; *JSP*, H2:163; see also Joseph Smith and Sidney Rigdon, Letter, Far West, Missouri, to Stephen Post, Bloomfield, Pennsylvania, 17 Sept. 1838, Stephen Post Papers, CHL, in *JSP*, D6:242).

15. GAEL, 23 (*JSP*, R4:161).

referred to an occult, unknown, and ambivalent content."[16] Eco also explains that Kircher believed "the symbols were initiatory because they were wrapped in an impenetrable and indecipherable enigma, to protect them from the idle curiosity of the vulgar multitudes."[17] Nevertheless, Kircher produced a three-volume dictionary of the Egyptian language titled *Oedipus Aegyptiacus*, which were filled with invented translations wherein a few characters could yield many words. If, as Smith believed, Egypt had been settled by the daughter of Ham, then the Egyptian language would not have been affected by the subsequent confusion of tongues at the Tower of Babel, and therefore the Egyptian hieroglyphics would be closer to the pure Adamic language than even Hebrew.

Concerning this pre-Champollion understanding of Egyptian, LDS scholar Samuel Brown has observed that "by the nineteenth century this belief had moved well beyond the esoteric literature from which it sprang."[18] Noah Webster's 1828 *American Dictionary of the English Language,* for example, defined "hieroglyphic" as "a mystical character or symbol, used in writings and inscriptions, particularly by the Egyptians, as signs of sacred, divine, or supernatural things ... which contained a meaning known only to kings and priests."[19] Eighteenth-century mystic Immanuel Swedenborg and his followers believed that Egyptian hieroglyphs preserved remnants of the "true original language of nature" that existed before the Flood, and that the Hermetic doctrine of "Correspondency" (that is, "the knowledge of nature in its correspondence to divine and heavenly things") was lost but "remained longest among the Egyptians, of which their Hieroglyphics or sculptures were a principal part."[20] Yale professor of English R. John Williams has noted that reports of "Champollion's discovery in North America in the late 1820s and early 1830s ... were framing these developments in

---

16. Umberto Eco, *Serendipities: Language and Lunacy,* trans. William Weaver (New York: Columbia University Press, 1998), 60.

17. Ibid.

18. Samuel Brown, "Joseph (Smith) in Egypt: Babel, Hieroglyphics, and the Pure Language of Eden," *Church History* 78/1 (Mar. 2009): 44.

19. Noah Webster, *American Dictionary of the English Language* (New York: S. Converse, 1828), s.v, "hieroglyphic."

20. Preface to the first American edition of Immanuel Swedenborg, *A Treatise Concerning Heaven and Hell* (Baltimore: Anthony Miltenberger, 1812), 31.

classic Swedenborgian fashion as only further *confirming* the important, priestly nature of Egyptian hieroglyphics. Even as these new findings revealed the characters to be primarily alphabetic, such revelations did not preclude the possibility—even the necessity—for these Anglo-American Swedenborgians that other, more spiritual, mystical, and theologically powerful messages were encoded in their pictographic etymologies."[21]

High and Patriarchal Priesthoods

Probably the most important feature of Smith's spring 1835 expansion of his 1831 revelation pertains to the recently introduced patriarchal priesthood, which was linked to the high priesthood.[22] On 6 December 1834, Smith had Sidney Rigdon ordain his father, sixty-two-year-old Joseph Smith Sr., to the new office of patriarch of the church. As the Hebrew Bible makes no mention of priesthood being handed down from Adam through the ancient patriarchs, Smith's expansion provided an ordination lineage, stating that the patriarchal priesthood was "instituted in the days of Adam, and came down by lineage" from father to son until Noah, as follows:[23]

1	Adam	6	Jared
2	Seth	7	Enoch
3	Enos	8	Methuselah
4	Cainan	9	Lamech
5	Mahalaleel	10	Noah

The expanded revelation then declares that in the valley of Adam-ondi-Ahman, "Adam stood up in the midst of the congregation, and notwithstanding he was bowed down with age, being full of the Holy Ghost, predicted whatsoever should befall his posterity unto the latest generation. These things were all written in the book of Enoch, and are to be testified of in due time."[24]

---

21. R. John Williams, "The Ghost and the Machine: Plates and Paratext in *The Book of Mormon*," in *Americanist Approaches to The Book of Mormon*, Elizabeth Fenton and Jared Hickman eds. (New York: Oxford University Press, 2019), 79n45.

22. D&C, 1835 ed., 3:17–29 [D&C 107:39–57] (*JSP*, D4:316–17).

23. D&C, 1835 ed., 3:19–27 [D&C 107:41–52] (*JSP*, D4:316).

24. D&C, 1835 ed., 3:29 [D&C 107:56–57] (*JSP*, D4:317).

Any "Book of Enoch" would have been written originally in the pure language. If Phelps's pure-language specimen of characters, names, and definitions were part of Smith's preliminary effort to produce a pseudepigraphic Book of Enoch, perhaps the characters and translation were intended to bolster confidence in Smith's followers that any eventual translation would have come from an actual record that—like the gold plates—would never be exhibited to the public. If so, Smith may have prepared his specimen of pure language characters for the same reasons he had produced a facsimile of Book of Mormon characters seven years earlier.

If Smith was, in fact, preparing to produce a pseudepigraphic Book of Enoch to support his introduction of patriarchal priesthood, it was interrupted by the arrival of the Egyptian papyri—which Smith used to accomplish the same thing: that is, to lend ancient support for his recent introduction of the patriarchal priesthood. This is evident in part 2 of the Alphabets and bound Grammar, as well as in the first lines of the Book of Abraham, where Abraham declares:

> I sought for the blessings of the fathers, and the right whereunto I should be ordained to administer the same: ... a rightful heir; a high priest, holding the right belonging to the fathers, from the begining of time; even from the begining, or before the foundation of the earth, down to the present time; even the right of the first born, or the first man, who is Adam, or first father, through <the> fathers, unto me.[25]

Less than two weeks before the arrival of Michael Chandler, Smith preached on the "Evangelical Order," meaning the patriarchal priesthood.[26] When Chandler arrived with his papyri, Smith was able to translate real ancient records that the learned had declared were undecipherable. Smith only had to persuade colleagues—especially Phelps—that he was actually translating. After identifying the mummies and authors of the two rolls of papyrus, Smith began recording his ideas in the Egyptian Alphabets. It would only be natural for him to transfer his thoughts about Adam, Enoch, and the patriarchal priesthood to the Egyptian

---

25. Book of Abraham Manuscript-C, ca. July/Nov. 1835, 1 [Abr. 1:2] (*JSP* R4:219).
26. "The twenty-first, being Sunday, I preached in Kirtland on the Evangelical Order" (DHC 2:234). The source for this 21 June 1835 entry in Smith's official history is unknown.

project. In doing so, the narrative necessarily shifted to patriarchs who had dealings with Egypt—most obviously Abraham and Joseph—who lived after the corruption of language at the Tower of Babel. Smith therefore explained that Abraham had access to the records of previous patriarchs—presumably Adam's Book of Remembrance and the Book of Enoch. Thus Abraham declares: "the records of the fathers, even the patraarch's, concerning the right of priesthood, the Lord my God preserved in mine own hands, therefore a Knowledge of the beginning of creation, and also of the planets and of the Stars, as it was made Known unto the fathers, have I Kept even unto this day."[27]

In discussing the record of ancient Joseph in December 1835, Oliver Cowdery made an explicit connection to the Book of Enoch and revealed the possible source of Smith's inspiration. Cowdery said that upon the papyrus scroll of Joseph son of Jacob/Israel was found a drawing of

Enoch's Pillar, as mentioned by Josephus, ... our present version of the bible does not mention this fact, ... but Josephus says that the descendants of Seth were virtuous, and possessed a great knowledge of the heavenly bodies, and, that, in consequence of the prophecy of Adam, that the world should be destroyed once by water and again by fire, Enoch wrote a history or an account of the same, and put [it] into two pillars one of brick and the other of stone; and that the same were in being [or existence] at his (Josephus') day.[28]

Is it coincidence that Josephus, a first-century CE Roman–Jewish historian who was well-known to Smith's contemporaries, mentions a prophecy of Adam and a record of Enoch as well as a knowledge of "heavenly bodies, and their order,"[29] being handed down by the descendants of Seth? Is it more than chance that Josephus refers to Egypt as "Mestre, and the Egyptians Mestreans,"[30]

27. Book of Abraham Manuscript-B, Nov. 1835, 5–6 [Abr. 1:31] (*JSP*, R4:213–15).

28. "Egyptian Mummies—Ancient Records," *Messenger and Advocate* 2 (Dec. 1835): 236.

29. Flavius Josephus, Antiquities of the Jews, Book 1, chap. 2, sect. 3, trans. William Whiston, *Josephus Complete Works* (Grand Rapids, Michigan: Kregel Publications, 1960), 27.

30. Antiquities of the Jews, Book 1, chap. 6, sect. 2 (Whiston, *Josephus Complete Works*, 31).

and that Smith in part 1 of the bound Grammar said that Abraham "was fore warned of God to go down into Ah=meh=strah, or Egypt, and preach the gospel <unto the> Ah meh strah ans"?[31]

Similar to the ten generations of patriarchs listed in Smith's expanded 1831 revelation, part 2 of the Alphabets traces the authority line from Adam to "Baeth-ku," or the "fifth high priest from Adam," who was Mahalaleel, Enoch's grandfather.

PATRIARCHAL PRIESTHOOD LINEAGE IN PART 2 OF EGYPTIAN ALPHABETS[32]

Character number	Definitions	Patriarchs
10	Baeth Ka Adam or the first man or first King	Adam
11	Baeth Ke the next from Adam one ordained under <him>	Seth
12	Baeth Ki the third patrearck	Enos
13	Baeth Ko the fourth from Adam	Cainan
14	Baethchu the fifth high preast from Adam	Mahalaleel

Josephus also described the right to govern being handed down through the patriarchs, that Enos "delivered the government to Cainan his son," and that several generations later Methuselah "delivered the government" to his son Lamech. When Lamech had "governed seven hundred and seventy-seven years, [he] appointed Noah his son to be ruler of the people ... and retained the government nine hundred and fifty years."[33] Thus both the Alphabets and Josephus mention a succession of patriarchal rulers, but which is completely absent in Genesis.

In late September 1835, while copying blessings into the new Patriarchal Blessing Book, Cowdery expanded blessings Joseph Smith had given to Smith family members in 1833, no doubt under Smith's supervision. To Joseph Sr.'s blessing was added a reference to his holding the "right of patriarchal priesthood," followed by a quote about Adam blessing his posterity in the valley

---

31. GAEL, 6 (*JSP*, R4:127).

32. Definitions are from Egyptian Alphabet-A, 1–2, in the handwriting of Joseph Smith (*JSP*, R4:57–58).

33. Antiquities of the Jews, Book 1, chap. 3, sect. 4 (Whiston, *Josephus Complete Works*, 28).

of Adam-ondi-Ahman from the 1831 revelation that Joseph Jr. had only recently expanded. The expanded blessing declares, "So shall it be with my father: he shall be called a prince over his posterity, holding the keys of the patriarchal priesthood over the kingdom of God on earth, even the Church of the Latter Day Saints."[34] Of course, Joseph Sr. had not been ordained to this office until December 1834; yet Cowdery claimed that the blessings he was about to record were "correct and according to the mind of the Lord."[35]

In his introduction to the patriarchal blessings, Cowdery stated that Joseph Sr. received authority to give blessings from Joseph Jr., "the first elder, and first patriarch of the church." Cowdery then explained that he and Joseph Jr. had received authority, first from the visitation of an angel in May 1829, and that later they "received the high and holy priesthood: but an account of this will be given elsewhere, or in another place."[36] Cowdery further explained that prior to the first—May 1829—reception of authority

> our souls were drawn out in mighty prayer—to know how we might obtain the blessings of baptism and of the Holy Spirit, according to the order of God, and we diligently saught for the right of the fathers and the authority of the holy priesthood, and the power to admin[ister] in the same: for we desired to be followers of righteousness and the possessors of greater knowledge, even the knowledge of the mysteries of the kingdom of God.[37]

Cowdery's words reflected the opening verses of the Book of Abraham, which by late September 1835 had been entered into the translation book by Phelps or were available to Cowdery in manuscript form.[38]

---

34. Joseph Smith, Expanded Blessing to Joseph Smith Sr. and Lucy Mack Smith, [Kirtland Township, Geauga County, Ohio], between ca. 15 and 28 Sept. 1835, Patriarchal Blessing Book 1, 9, CHL (*JSP*, D4:488; H. Michael Marquardt, ed., *Early Patriarchal Blessings of The Church of Jesus Christ of Latter-day Saints* [Salt Lake City: Smith–Pettit Foundation, 2007], 4).

35. Patriarchal Blessing Book 1, 9 (Marquardt, *Early Patriarchal Blessings*, 3).

36. Patriarchal Blessing Book 1, 8, 9 (Marquardt, *Early Patriarchal Blessings*, 3).

37. Patriarchal Blessing Book 1, 8–9 (Marquardt, *Early Patriarchal Blessings*, 3).

38. Phelps: Book of Abraham Manuscript-C, 1 [Abr. 1:2] (*JSP*, R4:219); Cowdery: Patriarchal Blessing Book 1, 9 (Marquardt, *Early Patriarchal Blessings*, 3).

BOOK OF ABRAHAM MANUSCRIPT	PATRIARCHAL BLESSING BOOK
W. W. Phelps	Oliver Cowdery
(ca. July 1835)	(late September 1835)

"I *sought* for the blessings of the *fathers*, and the *right* whereunto I should be ordained to *administer the same*: Having been a *follower of righteousness*, *desiring* to be one who *possessed great Knowledge*, a greater follower of righteousness; <*a possessor of greater knowledge*;> ..."	"we diligently *saught* for the *right* of the *fathers* and the authority of the holy priesthood, and the *power to admin[ister] in the same*: for we *desired* to be *followers of righteousness* and the *possessors of greater knowledge*, even the knowledge of the mysteries of the kingdom of God."

After this, Cowdery stated: "Therefore, we repaired to the woods, even as our father Joseph said we should, that is to the bush, and called upon the name of the Lord, and he answered us out of the heavens, and while we were in the heavenly vision the angel came down and bestowed upon us this priesthood; and then, as I have said, we repaired to the water and were baptized."[39]

Cowdery's narrative alludes to the supposed content of one of the scrolls of papyrus, identified by Smith as the record of ancient Joseph. The year previous, Cowdery had announced that he and Smith had been ordained by the unnamed angel prior to their baptizing one another in May 1829, which came as a surprise to leading members David Whitmer, William E. McLellin, and even Phelps.[40] A few months later (about spring 1835), Smith identified the angel as John the Baptist when he expanded an 1830 revelation about the use of wine in the sacrament to include God's declaring: "John [the Baptist] I have sent unto you ... to ordain you unto the first priesthood."[41] Cowdery's 1835 entry in the Patriarchal Blessing Book suggests what may have been a plan to use the newly acquired Egyptian papyri to support the recent announcement of angelic ordination to the priesthood.

---

39. Patriarchal Blessing Book 1, 8–9 (Marquardt, *Early Patriarchal Blessings*, 3).

40. Oliver Cowdery, Letter to W. W. Phelps, 7 Sept. 1834, *LDS Messenger and Advocate* 1 (Oct. 1834): 15 (*EMD* 2:419–20). See Dan Vogel, "Evolution of Early Mormon Priesthood Narratives," *John Whitmer Historical Association Journal* 34 (Spring/Summer 2014): 58–80.

41. D&C, 1835 ed., 50:2 [D&C 27:8] (*JSP*, D4:411).

On 2 October 1835, Cowdery copied a blessing into the Patriarchal Blessing Book that Smith had given him in 1833, which was now expanded to include a reference to a second angelic ordination. The expanded wording has Smith declare:

> He [Cowdery] shall sit in the council of the patriarchs, with his brother Joseph and with him have part in the keys of that ministry when the Ancient of Days shall come. ... For he shall have part with me in the keys of the kingdom of the last days, and we shall judge this generation by our testimony: and the keys shall never be taken from us. ...
>
> These blessings shall come upon him [Oliver] according to the blessings of the prophecy of Joseph, in ancient days, which he said should come upon the Seer of the last days and the Scribe that should sit with him, and that should be ordained with him, by the hand of the angel in the bush, unto the lesser priesthood, and after receive the holy priesthood under the hands of ~~they~~ <those> who had been held in reserve for a long season; even those who received it under the hand of the Messiah, while he should dwell in the flesh, upon the earth, and should receive the blessings with him, even the Seer of the God of Abraham, Isaac and Jacob, saith he, even Joseph of old.[42]

Cowdery did not name the ancient apostles, but Smith's 1835 expansion of the 1830 revelation not only mentions the appearance of John the Baptist but also "Peter, and James, and John, whom I have sent unto you, by whom I have ordained you and confirmed you to be apostles."[43] This expanded revelation retroactively provided Smith and Cowdery with authority to organize the Quorum of Twelve Apostles, which they had already done the previous February (1835), while the 1835 expansion of the 1831 revelation gave the new apostles authority to "ordain evangelical ministers," otherwise known as patriarchs.[44]

From Smith's spring 1835 expansions of his early revelations and Cowdery's September 1835 written introduction to Joseph Sr.'s blessings and the expanded portion of the blessing he, Cowdery, had received from Joseph Jr., it is apparent that Smith and perhaps

---

42. Patriarchal Blessing Book 1, 12 (*JSP*, D5:513–14; Marquardt, *Early Patriarchal Blessings*, 3).

43. D&C, 1835 ed., 50:3 [D&C 27:12] (*JSP*, D4:411).

44. D&C, 1835 ed., 3:17 [D&C 107:53–55] (*JSP*, D4:316).

Cowdery intended to use the Egyptian papyri to confirm the reality of the angelic ordinations and to provide pseudepigraphic evidence for the 1831 introduction of the high priesthood, the 1834 introduction of the patriarchal priesthood, and the 1835 organization of the Quorum of Twelve Apostles.

Source

As noted, characters 4–9 in part 2 of the Alphabets were taken from Smith's previous work on the pure language. Egyptologist Klaus Baer's comment that the first thirteen characters "differ in general appearance" from the other characters and do not appear to be hieratic Egyptian[45] indicates that the surrounding characters up to number 13 probably result from the pure language project that preceded the acquisition of the Egyptian papyri. How these Adamic characters could appear in the middle of an "Egyptian Alphabet" is not explained, but this creates a problem for those who want to argue that the Alphabets and bound Grammar represent a reverse translation of Abraham.

Similar to part 1 discussed in chapter two, the first thirteen characters of part 2 (A) are arranged by shapes: 1–3 are combinations of angled lines and a dot or short dash; 4–5 are very similar in shape; 6–8 are variations of right angles; and 9–13 are combinations of horizontal hooks.

The next group in part 2 (B)—characters 14–42—are copied from column 3 of JS-P I, and although sometimes difficult to match up with the characters on the papyrus, it is clear that some are copied out of sequence and sometimes separated by characters that are not from column 3. According to Baer, character 14, which looks like a caret symbol or upside down V, "probably represents the first traces of ink visible at the upper edges of line [or column] 3" of the Breathing Permit of Hôr, but which has since broken off.[46] This is followed by four variations of that shape (14–18). While Baer interpreted this as evidence that the characters were copied from the badly damaged top portion of column 3 and "shows that

---

45. Baer, "The Breathing Permit of Hôr," 128–29.
46. Ibid., 128.

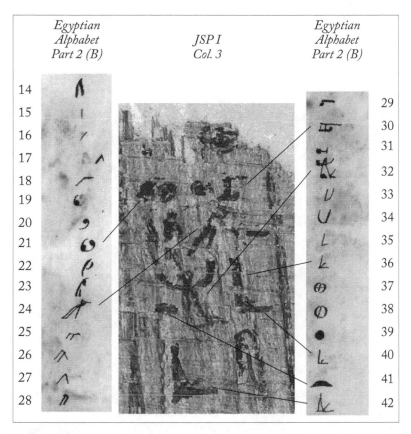

Figure 3.3. Comparison of characters in part 2 (B) of Egyptian Alphabet-C and column 3 of Joseph Smith Papyrus I.

the ink was flaked much as it is now,"[47] a more likely explanation is that Smith added characters derived from the shape of the character that he saw on the papyrus, which he does again in subsequent portions of column 3. Character 24, for example, is shaped like a bird and appears near the top of column 3, but characters 25–28, which are stylized versions of the bird character, are not found on the papyrus. It is as if Smith were inventing his own cursive writing from the hieratic characters in Hôr's Book of Breathings. It should

---

47. Baer also observed that characters 15–24 appear to have been copied from the badly damaged top portion of column 3 and that seven characters, 18–24, were originally four characters, which "shows that the ink was flaked much as it is now" (Baer, "The Breathing Permit of Hôr," 128). However, as I explain, the extra characters are actually the result of Smith's creation of variations of the characters he saw on the papyrus.

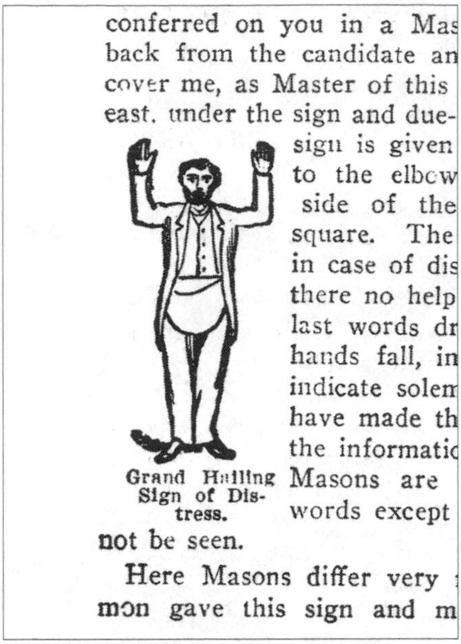

conferred on you in a Mas
back from the candidate an
cover me, as Master of this
east. under the sign and due-
sign is given
to the elbow
side of the
square. The
in case of dis
there no help
last words dr
hands fall, in
indicate solem
have made th
the informatic
Grand Hailing Masons are
Sign of Dis-
tress. words except
not be seen.

Here Masons differ very
mon gave this sign and m

Figure 3.4. Page 76 of William Morgan's *Illustrations of Masonry* (1827), showing sign of grief and distress.

be observed that in the Alphabets characters 24–42 are named but not defined, whereas in the bound Grammar they are named.

Character 32 looks like a man with his arms raised above his head, which reminded Smith of the Masonic sign for grief and distress (see fig. 3.4).[48] In the Alphabets, Smith named it "Ho-hah-oop" but did not define it. Later, in the bound Grammar, the character was defined as one who has been "appointed to intercede for another; [or] invocation."[49] Characters 33 and 34 are V and U shapes, apparently abstractions of the raised arms. They are not found on the papyrus but are similarly defined in the Grammar as "a sign among the Egyptians that is used for influence or power: [or] a sign made use of for one to escape his enemies."[50]

The appearance of Masonic-like signs/gestures at the time of the patriarchs is a theme Smith had discussed as early as April 1829,

---

48. William Morgan, *Illustrations of Masonry* (Batavia, New York: David C. Miller, 1827), 76.
49. GAEL, 31 (*JSP,* R4:177).
50. GAEL, 27 (*JSP,* R4:169).

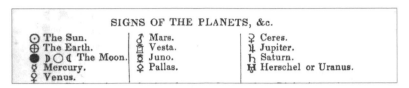

Figure 3.5. Page 3 of *The American Almanac and Repository of Useful Knowledge for the Year 1835.*

when he dictated the account in the Book of Mormon of Alma's commanding his son Helaman to suppress the records of the Jaredites so that people may not know "the mysteries and the works of darkness, and their secret works, ... retain all their oaths, and their covenants, and their agreements in the secret abominations; yea, and all their signs and their wonders ye shall keep from this people" (Alma 37:21, 27). The following month, Smith dictated the account in the Book of Ether of a conspiracy to murder the Jaredite king Omer, which states that "Akish did administer unto them the oaths which were given by them of old who also sought power, which had been handed down even from Cain, who was a murderer from the beginning" (Ether 8:15). In October 1830, as part of his revision of the King James Bible, Smith expanded Genesis to include an account of Cain making a secret oath with Satan and exclaiming: "Truly I am Mahan, the master of this great secret"—thereafter, "Cain was called Master Mahan" (Moses 5:30–31), an allusion to "Master Mason," the third degree of Freemasonry.

Character 35 is a right angle, which also is not on the papyrus but perhaps is related to the Masonic theme of the previous characters or simply a variation of the next character, which is on the papyrus and appears twice in the Alphabet list—once before the three circles and again after them. The three circles do not appear on the papyrus, but in Oliver Cowdery's Alphabet they are named and identified as follows:

Jah-oh-eh	(the earth &c)
Flo-ees	(Moon)
Flos-isis	(Sun)

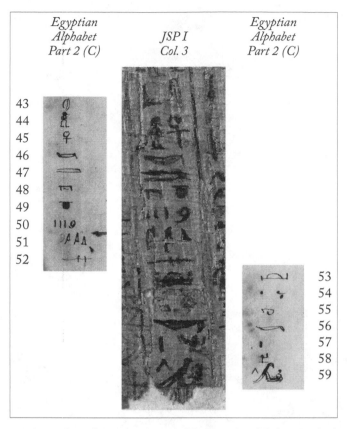

Figure 3.6. Comparison of characters in part 2 (C) of Egyptian Alphabet-C and column 3 of Joseph Smith Papyrus I.

It is unclear why, but the symbol for the earth appeared in almanacs of Smith's day, and the symbol for the sun appeared as the moon.[51]

Character 42 is the last to receive a name—Kolob—and is the first of an uninterrupted sequential copying of characters from column 3, making a total of fifty-nine characters for part 2 of the Alphabets (fig. 3.6). The sequential copying of characters from the columns of JSP I continues with part 3 containing characters from column 2, part 4 containing characters from column 1, and part 5 containing characters from column 5.

---

51. *The American Almanac and Repository of Useful Knowledge for the Year 1835* (Boston: Charles Bowen, 1834), 3.

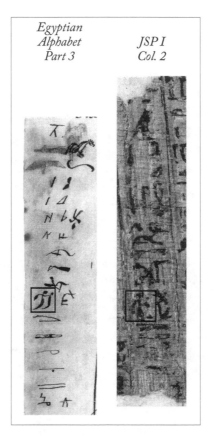

Figure 3.7. Comparison of characters in part 3 of Egyptian Alphabet-C and column 2 of Joseph Smith Papyrus I.

Analysis

We have seen how the Alphabets borrowed at least six characters from the pure language project that Smith was developing prior to the acquisition of the Egyptian papyri. The Adamic characters, names, and definitions in Phelps's letter to his wife were not simply a summary of Smith's 1832 answers to questions, but added new material about "the Earth" and division of humankind into "sons of God," or those ordained, and the "children of men." Part 2 of the Alphabets builds on the version of the pure language in Phelps's letter.

The two records—Phelps's letter and Smith's answers to questions—cover the same material, but the Alphabets multiply and refine the categories. The first nine characters discuss God, the firstborn son, two grades of angels (spirits and resurrected beings), four grades of ministers (high priests, lesser priests, priests ordained but not of God, and unordained ministers), and, finally, "all mankind."

Characters 10–14 list the five generations of patriarchal government previously discussed in Smith's spring 1835 expansion of his 1831 revelation. Character 15 represents humankind's first residence on the earth, followed by five degrees of improvement, which leads to the earth in its "purified" state, then to all the "heavenly bodies," and finally to the "Celestial kingdom, [or] God's residence." This is where part 2 of the Alphabets ended for a time. Later, Cowdery inserted the names to numbers 24–41 in Smith's Alphabet. Still later, Smith and Warren Parrish added the last name—Kolob, number 42—to two of the Alphabets.

As chapter five shows, when Smith added definitions to characters 24–42 in the bound Grammar, he picked up the theme of the celestial kingdom and expanded it to include a discussion of the different grades of "heavenly bodies," which evolved into an elaborate cosmology. Later, in Nauvoo, when resuming the Book of Abraham translation in March 1842, Smith drew on this cosmological material in the bound Grammar for his dictation of Chapter 3 of Abraham as well as his explanation of Facsimile 2. This means that the germ of Smith's ideas about a hierarchy of stars and planets began before his acquisition of the Egyptian papyri and grew out of his thoughts about a pure language, which were expanded in the Alphabets to include a hierarchy of heavenly and earthly beings and then projected onto the cosmos in the bound Grammar. This development of thought makes the reverse-translation theory untenable since it is clear that the evolution of thought actually went in the opposite direction.

COMPARISON OF CONCEPTS IN "PURE LANGUAGE"
AND PART 2 OF ALPHABETS[52]

Pure Language (Phelps)		Egyptian Alphabets Part 2		
ahman	God	1	Ahmeos	God
sonahman	Son of God	2	Aleph	Son of God

52. I switch the order of "angels" and "sons of God ordain[ed]" to facilitate comparison.

Pure Language (Phelps)		Egyptian Alphabets Part 2		
anglo	angels	3	Albeth	angels: spirits
		4	Alchabeth	angels: resurrected
saunsahman	sons of God ordain[ed]	5	Alchebeth	ministers: high priests, kings
		6	Alchibeth	ministers: lesser priests
		7	Alchobeth	ministers: not ordained of God
		8	Alchubeth	ministers: not ordained
Sons ahman	children of Men	9	Baeth	all mankind
		10	Baeth-ka	Adam, first king
		11	Baeth-ke	next from Adam, ordained
		12	Baeth-ki	third ordained patriarch, king
		13	Baeth-ko	fourth from Adam
		14	Baeth-ku	fifth high priest from Adam
oleah	the Earth	15	Beth	man's first residence, garden
		16	Beth-ka	another place, 5 times greater
		17	Beth-ke	a third place, 5 times greater
		18	Beth-ki	a fourth place, 5 times greater
		19	Beth-ko	a fifth place, 5 times greater
		20	Beth-ku	a sixth place, 5 times greater
		21	Beth-ku-ain-trieth	the whole earth, purified
[not represented]		22	E-Beth-ku-ain-trieth	the heavenly bodies
		23	E-Beth-ka	Celestial kingdom, God's residence

The Alphabets and Abraham

So far in our discussion of the Alphabets, Abraham's name has not been mentioned. This absence has caused Gee and Muhlestein to draw additional inaccurate conclusions about the Alphabets. Not knowing the origin of parts 1 and 2, Gee assumed in 2000 that all of the Alphabets' characters came from the Book of Breathings. Evidently not sensing the conflict of such an observation with the reverse-translation theory, Gee asserted: "The fact that the only one of these manuscripts to have Joseph Smith's handwriting on it matches JSP I but not the Book of Abraham would indicate that Joseph Smith did not think that the Book of Breathings was the Book of Abraham."[53] However, a problem with Gee's statement is that some of the Alphabets' definitions *are* related to the Book of Abraham, such as the discussion about a woman's discovery of Egypt while it was underwater. Another problem with Gee's comment is that the Alphabets do contain explicit references to Abraham when it translates three characters that were copied from the Breathing Permit of Hôr, not from a missing portion that Gee and Muhlestein speculate was attached to the end of the Breathing Permit. One of these characters was copied from column 2 of JSP I into part 3 of the Alphabets. Next to this character in each Alphabet is written:[54]

Smith's Alphabet		~~Ah broam=ah brahoam Ki Ahbraoam~~ <Ki-ah-bram, Ki-ah-bra-oam-Zub-zool-oan>
Cowdery's Alphabet		<Ki>-Ah-broan, <Ki>-Ah-bra-oam. Zub-zoal-oan.
Phelps's Alphabet		<Ki>Ah broam <ki>ah brah-oam zub zool oan

Here "Ah-broam"—a variant of Abraham—was written first and the prefix "Ki" was subsequently added by a different method in each of the Alphabets. We saw this character in the first chapter at the beginning of the Abraham text copied by Phelps into the translation

53. John Gee, "Eyewitness, Hearsay, and Physical Evidence of the Joseph Smith Papyri," in *The Disciple as Witness: Essays on Latter-day Saint History and Doctrine in Honor of Richard Lloyd Anderson,* eds. D. Ricks, Donald W. Parry, and Andrew H. Hedges (Provo, Utah: Foundation for Ancient Research and Mormon Studies, 2000), 201.

54. Egyptian Alphabets-A, -B, and -C, 3 (*JSP,* R4:64–65, 81, 91). In Smith's Alphabet, Phelps wrote, "Ah broam=ah brahoam," which was canceled when Smith added "Ki Ahbraoam," which was then canceled when Cowdery inserted "Ki-ah-bram, Ki-ah-bra-oam-Zub-zool-oan" (see *JSP,* R4:106n74 and 75).

book (fig. 1.2). On page 3 of the bound Grammar, Phelps broke this character down into its separate parts (see fig. 1.4):

Kiah broam = Kiah brah oam = zub zool oan

This character as shown dissected reads:

Kiah brah oam. Coming down from the beginning– right by birth– and also by blessing, and by promise– promises made; a father of many nations; a prince of peace; one who keeps the commandment of God; a patriarch; a rightful heir; a high priest.[55]

The middle part of the character—a dot and hook—is defined to reflect the promise Abraham received in Genesis 12:2–3 and closely follows the wording in Book of Abraham 1:2:[56]

EGYPTIAN GRAMMAR (ca. July 1835)	BOOK OF ABRAHAM MANUSCRIPT-C (ca. July–Nov. 1835)
Kiah brah oam. Coming down from the beginning– right by birth– and also by blessing, and by promise– promises made; *a father of many nations; a prince of peace; one who keeps the commandment of God*; a patriarch; *a rightful heir; a high priest.*	I sought for the blessings of the fathers, and the right whereunto I should be ordained to administer the same: Having been a follower of righteousness; desiring to be one who possessed great Knowledge; a greater follower of righteousness; <a possessor of greater Knowledge;> *a father of many nations; a prince of peace; one who keeps the commandments of God*; *a rightful heir; a high priest*, holding the right belonging to the fathers, from the begining of time …

The last two characters in the Alphabets (below) were not taken from the columns of JSP I, as Gee implied. Rather, they were the first two characters of JSP XI, which have since flaked off and are no longer visible.[57]

---

55. GAEL, 3 (*JSP*, R4:221).
56. Ibid.; Book of Abraham Manuscript-C, 1 (*JSP*, R4:219).
57. See Robert K. Ritner, *The Joseph Smith Egyptian Papyri: A Complete Edition* (Salt Lake City: Smith–Pettit Foundation, 2011), 84, 99; Baer, "The Breathing Permit of Hôr," 129; Brian Hauglid, *A Textual History of the Book of Abraham: Manuscripts and Editions*

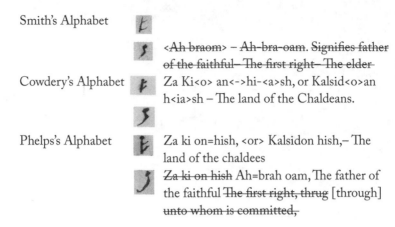

Smith's Alphabet

<Ah braom> – Ah-bra-oam. Signifies father of the faithful– The first right– The elder

Cowdery's Alphabet

Za Ki<o> an<->hi-<a>sh, or Kalsid<o>an h<ia>sh – The land of the Chaldeans.

Phelps's Alphabet

Za ki on=hish, <or> Kalsidon hish,– The land of the chaldees

Za ki on hish Ah=brah oam, The father of the faithful The first right, thrug [through] unto whom is committed,

Here we see the beginning of the translation of the Book of Abraham, with the top character representing "The land of the Chaldeans" and the bottom character representing "Ah=brah oam, The father of the faithful"—which, in Book of Abraham Manuscript-C (from the translation book), was connected to the first verse of the Book of Abraham (fig. 2.1). There, the first character is keyed to "the land of the Chaldeans," and the second character to "Abraham." In Smith's Alphabet, the translation of the characters was canceled by Cowdery, who turned to the next page, drew the bottom character, and then recorded its translation in all five degrees of its meaning:

> In the first degree Ah-broam– signifies The father of the faithful, the first right, the elders second degree– same sound– A follower of sig righteousness– Third degree– same sound– One who possesses great Knowledge– Fourth degree– same sound– A follower of righteousness, a possessor of greater knowledge. Fifth degree– Ah-bra-oam. The father of many nations, a prince of peace, one who keeps the commandments of God, a patriarch, a rightful heir, a high priest.[58]

To assert, as Gee does, that the Alphabets do not mention Abraham and that "Joseph Smith did not think that the Book of

---

(Provo, Utah: Neal A. Maxwell Institute for Religious Scholarship, Brigham Young University, 2010), 58. Phelps's Alphabet: Egyptian Alphabets-A–C, 4 (*JSP*, R4:68–69, 83, 93). In Smith's Alphabet (below), the characters were probably drawn by him but the transliteration and definition were inserted by Cowdery (*JSP*, R4:106n85).

58. Egyptian Alphabet-A, [5] (*JSP*, R4:70–71).

Breathings was the Book of Abraham" is erroneous and demonstrates unfamiliarity with the material.

At this point, needing more space for writing, the project shifted to the bound Grammar.

Was Phelps Responsible for the Alphabets and Bound Grammar?

While not directly connected to the Book of Abraham until the end of the Alphabets and beginning of the Grammar, these documents—the Alphabets and Grammar—give us a clear view of Smith's method of instilling confidence in his followers that his pseudepigraphic text was translated from Egyptian papyri, even though Smith's speculations were factually erroneous. Thus one should not be surprised that defenders of the Book of Abraham have tried to relieve Smith from responsibility for the creation of both the Alphabets and Grammar. Below, I review some of these arguments and reject the claim that Phelps was responsible for the Alphabets. I revisit the authorship issue in the next chapter as it specifically pertains to the bound Grammar.

According to Gee, Phelps is the true author of the bound Grammar. Moreover, the five degree system was entirely Phelps's, not Smith's, misunderstanding. Next to a photograph of the first page of the bound Grammar in his 2017 *Introduction to the Book of Abraham*, Gee asserted that it represented "W. W. Phelps's speculations on Egyptian grammar ... in his handwriting."[59] Obviously referring to the Alphabets, Gee further stated, "While some of the manuscripts use the terms 'degree' and 'part' as modern 'fragment' and 'column' to indicate where in the papyri the sign in question comes from, Phelps misunderstood them to be some sort of grammatical term."[60]

According to Gee, the "degree" and five-part system in the Alphabets had nothing to do with grammar but was merely a way of locating characters on the papyrus, that the word "part" was used for what is now called a "line" or "column" and "degree" means "fragment."[61] Thus part 1 of the first degree is fragment 1, or JSP I,

---

59. John Gee, *An Introduction to the Book of Abraham* (Provo, Utah: Religious Studies Center, Brigham Young Universities/Salt Lake City: Deseret Book Co., 2017), 39.
60. Ibid.
61. Ibid., 35.

column 1; part 2 is column 2 of the same fragment; and so forth. However, none of the Alphabet characters actually shows up where Gee's theory would predict.

As I have shown, part 1 of the first degree came from the missing Amenhotep papyrus copied into the Valuable Discovery notebooks, and the first third of part 2 of the first degree came from the pure language. The second third of part 2 was copied from column 3 but was mixed with invented and derivative characters and hence was not found on the papyrus. When the characters are copied sequentially from the columns of JSP I, only part 5 of the Alphabets matches Gee's theory.

The theory that the terms "degree" and "part" were part of a locating system was introduced in 1970 by John Tvedtnes, formerly a scholar at BYU's Institute for the Study and Preservation of Ancient Religious Texts, though in a different form than presented by Gee. Tvedtnes argued that the terms "degree" and "part" were intended as a directional system even in the bound Grammar and that modern readers have misunderstood them as grammar terms. In 1992, Tvedtnes told Gee:

> I showed that the terms *degree* and *part* in the Alphabet and Grammar were *not* intended as grammatical terms. Rather, they denote the location of the symbols on the papyri. The "first part," for example, is what we call Facsimile 1. The "first degree" of that "part" is the first column of script, while "the second degree" is the second column, and so forth. The "second part" is what Nibley termed the "Small Sensen Papyrus." It is pasted on paper marked with one-inch vertical rulings. The "first degree of the second part" denotes the first of these columns, counting from the right. Much of the Alphabet and Grammar is merely a means of giving "map coordinates" for locating the symbols on the papyri.[62]

It should be noted that Tvedtnes applied the terms in ways opposite from what Gee intends—*parts* refer to *fragments* not columns, and *degrees* to *lines* or *columns*. Hence, according to Tvedtnes, "part one" of the bound Grammar pertains to JSP I, and the five

62. John Gee, "A Tragedy of Errors," *FARMS Review of Books* 4/1 (1992): 114n59. John A. Tvedtnes, "The Critics of the Book of Abraham," in *Book of Abraham Symposium* (Salt Lake City: Salt Lake Institute of Religion, 1971), 73–74.

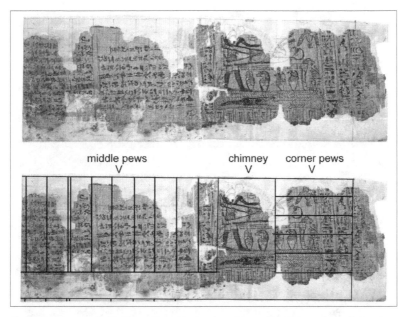

Figure 3.8. Joseph Smith Papyri XI and I, showing plans as bleed-throughs for in interior of the Kirtland temple on the backing paper.

"degrees" are the five "columns" of characters. The "second part," Tvedtnes maintained, is JSP XI, and the five parts pertain to the five columns created by the lines on the backing paper.

However, the grid of lines to which Tvedtnes refers is actually a sketch of the design of the interior of the Kirtland temple, the large pieces of drawing paper having been repurposed as backing to stabilize the delicate papyri.[63] On JSP XI the lines represent the middle pews, while on the JSP I the locations of a chimney and the corner pews are visible from behind the mounted papyrus (fig. 3.8). Comparing these fragments with a draft that Frederick G. Williams made in 1833 of a similar temple to be built in Independence, Missouri, the papyrus appears to have been mounted on the southwest corner of the discarded plan.

Moreover, JSP XI was still attached to the left side of Facsimile 1

---

63. See Kerry Muhlestein and Alexander Baugh, "Preserving the Joseph Smith Papyri Fragments: What Can We Learn from the Paper on Which the Papyri Were Mounted?" *Journal of Book of Mormon and Other Restoration Scripture* 22/2 (2013): 74. The editors of the Joseph Smith Papers have identified the plans as those of the Kirtland Temple (see *JSP*, D3:91–102).

when they were mounted together on the backing paper and only later cut into separate pieces.[64] It is doubtful that the papyri had been mounted before Smith, Cowdery, and Phelps began working on the Alphabets and bound Grammar. Indeed, Gee has suggested that the mounting of the papyri probably occurred in 1837.[65] This means that JSP I and JSP XI had not been separated and therefore would not have been considered different fragments. Tvedtnes's theory was based on a superficial understanding of the documents, and is wrong in most details. Nevertheless, in 1992, Gee used Tvedtnes's theory to criticize the works of some scholars.[66] In 2000, Gee adopted Tvedtnes's definitions and applied them to the Alphabets: "The columns on the left [in the Alphabets] are filled with characters from various columns of JSP I, identified by degree (column or line) and part (fragment)."[67] This is opposite from what he argued in 2017, quoted above. While scrapping Tvedtnes's grid theory, Gee nevertheless tries to salvage Tvedtnes's character-locating theory by limiting its application to the Alphabets and reversing the definitions. Gee seems to have decided that the five "degree" system in the bound Grammar, contrary to Tvedtnes, *is* a reference to grammar but was the result of Phelps's misunderstanding. Gee does not explain how Phelps could be confused about the meaning of the terms "degree" and "part" after supposedly taking the lead with Cowdery in the Alphabet phase of the project, as Gee also maintains.

The meaning of "degree" is not immediately apparent since the Alphabets deal only with five "parts" of the "first degree," whereas the bound Grammar deals with five "degrees" of only the "first part" and two-thirds of the "second part." Nevertheless, at the end

---

64. See Muhlestein and Baugh, "Preserving the Joseph Smith Papyri Fragments," 68, where it is observed: "The continuity of both the papyrus and the drawings on the paper indicates that the papyrus was originally glued to the paper in one piece and later cut." See also p. 70 for a photograph of the backs of JSP I and XI bearing the plans for the temple, showing that they were originally pasted together as one fragment.

65. "The current fragments of the Joseph Smith Papyri, however, were all mounted on heavy paper and placed in glass frames in 1837" (Gee, *Introduction to the Book of Abraham*, 84–85).

66. Gee, "A Tragedy of Errors," 114n59.

67. Gee, "Eyewitness, Hearsay, and Physical Evidence of the Joseph Smith Papyri," 201.

of Smith's Alphabet in Cowdery's handwriting, "Ah-broam" is given a definition in all five degrees, as noted. Thus the five-degree system can be traced to the end of the Alphabet project independent of any involvement from Phelps. Gee's assertion that Phelps misunderstood the term "degree" in the Alphabets as "some sort of grammatical term" and that the five-degree system in the bound Grammar was "Phelps's speculations on Egyptian grammar" is, I argue, completely without foundation.

To relieve Smith further from responsibility, Gee makes another mistaken suggestion about the Alphabets: "While Oliver Cowdery and W. W. Phelps worked on versions of this document, keeping different sections in different columns with labels, Joseph Smith copied their work, ignoring the column divisions and categories and dropping out text. This indicates that Joseph Smith cared less about the document than Cowdery or Phelps and that it probably was not his idea."[68]

Despite Gee's assertion, Cowdery also chose not to label his columns.[69] The fact that both Smith and Cowdery did not label their columns proves nothing about what they thought about the Alphabets.[70] Gee offered no evidence that Smith copied the work of Phelps and Cowdery. Rather, the evidence shows that the three men created their documents more or less independently and simultaneously. In 2000, Gee more accurately claimed just the opposite of what he claimed in 2017: "The three manuscripts are not copies of each other; free variants and synonyms abound indicating that the manuscripts are independent notes made on the same occasion."[71]

---

68. Gee, *Introduction to the Book of Abraham*, 39.

69. Despite Gee's assertion, it appears that Cowdery, like Smith, did not use column labels. Cowdery's document is missing the top left portion of the first page, so it is therefore not possible to determine if he used labels above the first two columns, although the portion where he would have written "explanation" is intact but blank; the remaining pages of Cowdery's document do not have column headings.

70. The lines for the four columns were drawn only on the first pages of Smith's and Cowdery's Alphabets and were evidently drawn before anyone knew what was needed. All three filled their first-page columns differently, and both Smith and Cowdery abandoned the use of columns altogether, although they continued with the character, name, and definition format.

71. Gee, "Eyewitness, Hearsay, and Physical Evidence of the Joseph Smith Papyri," 201–02.

Gee's recent claim that Smith copied from Phelps and Cowdery is difficult to maintain given the fact that Smith misspelled words which the other two men wrote correctly. If Smith had copied the work of Phelps and Cowdery and cared less, one wonders why he would change the spelling of the invented Egyptian names. And why he would change the wording or add to their explanations.

SPELLINGS IN EGYPTIAN ALPHABETS SHOWING SMITH'S INDEPENDENCE

Character number	Smith	Cowdery	Phelps
Part 1			
3	reighn	reign	reign
3	domion	dominion	dominion
4	pharaoah	pharaoh	pharaoh
6	Virgen	virgin	virgin
8	unmaried	unmarried	unmarried
17	goverment	government	government
19	begining	beginning	beginning
22	peried	period	period
Part 2			
5	preasts	priests	priests
5	minersters	Ministers	Ministers
15	valy	valley	valley
21	injoyment	enjoyment	
23	hapiness	happiness	

PROPER NAMES IN EGYPTIAN ALPHABETS SHOWING SMITH'S INDEPENDENCE

Character number	Smith	Cowdery	Phelps
Part 1			
4	phahoeup	Pha-ho-e-oop	Pha=ho=e=oop
5	ho up hah	Ho-oop-hah	Ho-oop-hah
7	Kah tou man	Kah-tou=mun	Kah=tou=mun
8	Zie oop hah	Zi-oop=hah	Zi=oop-hah
9	ho-ee-oop	Ho-e-oop	Ho=e=oop
11	ho-ee oop hah	Ho=e=oop-hah	Ho-e= oop=hah
13	tone tahe or tohe ton-es	Toan, Tah-e- Ta-e, or Tus	toan, tahe to,e or tou=es

Character number	Smith	Cowdery	Phelps
Part 2			
7	Alchobeth	Alkobeth	Alkobeth
8	Alchubeth	Alkubeth	Alkubeth
11	Baeth Kee	Baeth Ke	Baeth Ke
14	Baethchu	Baeth-Ku	Baeth ku
16	Bethcha	Beth-Ka	Beth ka
17	Bethche	Beth-Kee	Beth ke
18	Bethchi	Beth-Ki	Beth ki
19	Bethcho	Beth-Ko	Beth=ko
20	Bethchu	Beth-Ku	Beth ku
23	Ebethcha	E-Beth-Ka	Ebeth=ka

WORDINGS IN EGYPTIAN ALPHABETS SHOWING SMITH'S INDEPENDENCE

Character number	Smith	Cowdery	Phelps
Part 1			
5	<ho up hah> crown of a prin-cess or queen or *Stands for* queen	Ho-oop-hah Crown of a pri[n]cess, or queen, or *signifies* queen.	Ho-oop-hah Crown of a princes, or *signifies* Queen.
20	Zool Eh *Signifys* to be in *any* as light in th[*hole in page*]	Zub-z̶o̶o̶l̶ <eh> To be in, or be within— as light in the earth.	Zub=eh— To be in— as light in the earth
23	Zool from *any or some* fix\ed/ peried of time <back> to the begining <of the creation>	Zool From a fixed period of time back to the begin<ning or creation>	Zool From a <any> fixed period of time back to the begining
Part 2			
4	Alca{th|b}eth Angels in an unalte{a|r}able *immortal* <state>	Alkabeth Angels in an unalterable state— Sanctified, <or men after they are raised from the de[a]d>	Alkabeth Angels in an unalter-able state, men after they are raise <from the dead>

91

Character number	Smith	Cowdery	Phelps
16	Bethcha an other place of residence *or an <a> more fruitful Garden or larger place of hapiness greater hapiness 5 times*	Beth-Ka A garden, valley or plain, larger, more spacious, more pleasing, more beautiful— place of more complete happiness, peace & rest <for man.>	Beth ka Another place of Resi-dence, <5 times as great> more spacious, & larger <than the firsts>

Gee's assertion that Smith copied Phelps and Cowdery is not supported by the evidence. The situation was more fluid and dynamic, resulting from the fact that Smith was not simply dictating definitions but was giving "explanation[s]" of the characters, as the heading in Phelps's Alphabet states, and each man was keeping notes. Gee's claim that Smith dropped out text seriously oversimplifies what actually occurs in the documents.

Conclusion

While it is probable that parts 1 in the three Alphabets were created simultaneously, Smith's Alphabet shows the most hesitation and editing, which is not what one would expect if Smith simply copied Phelps's and Cowdery's Alphabets. In chapter two, I noted that Smith's Alphabet shows multiple attempts to draw the character for Katumin in the margin. Smith also canceled character 4 and drew another version of it in the margin. Moreover, three names were inserted above the line (two of them with unique spellings). There are also two instances of names being corrected as they were being created by Smith (numbers 13 and 17). These observations point to Smith being an active participant and likely the leader of the project.

In part 2 of the Alphabets, Smith again shows his independence in spelling names. While all three men alternated between "ch" and "k" for the k-sound in names—as in Alchabeth/Alkabeth—Smith favored "ch," whereas Phelps and Cowdery favored "k"; out of eighteen names with the k-sound, Cowdery and Phelps deviated from their preference only twice, Smith deviated four times. Such a situation cannot be explained by Gee's theory that Phelps and Cowdery worked together and then Smith merely copied their work.

Of the forty-six definitions in the Alphabets, there are twenty-eight instances where Smith could have copied from Phelps or Cowdery, as Gee argues, but there are also eighteen instances where Smith's text stands independent of Cowdery's and Phelps's, which is not what one would expect of someone passively copying the work of others. Gee's conclusion that "Joseph Smith cared less about the document than Cowdery or Phelps and that it probably was not his idea" because Smith did not use column headings, section breaks, and dropped out text is, in my opinion, based on a faulty, insufficient analysis of the sources.

It is unnecessary to speculate about Phelps's and Smith's roles in producing the Alphabets because Smith and/or Phelps has already told us what happened through, what I believe is, the best, most reliable source we have on this matter—Smith's official history—which states that during the latter part of July 1835 Smith "was continually engaged in translating an alphabet to the Book of Abraham, and arranging a grammar of the Egyptian language as practiced by the ancients."[72]

---

72. JS History, vol. B-1, 597 (DHC 2:238; Vogel, *History of Joseph Smith and The Church,* 2:244).

4 Race

In the fall of 1833 the Mormons were forcibly expelled from Jackson County, Missouri, largely because non-Mormon settlers found the Mormons' northern abolitionist leanings intolerable. The clash of cultures exploded into violence when W. W. Phelps, editor of the church's monthly paper *The Evening and the Morning Star*, published in Independence, Missouri, printed an article in July 1833 titled "Free People of Color," which invited free Blacks in other states to migrate to Missouri and join other Mormons gathering to Zion. Non-Mormons responded immediately, demanding that the Mormons leave the county and issuing a manifesto that listed their grievances, including Phelps's article "inviting free Negroes and mulattoes from other states to become Mormons and remove and settle among us." They feared that "the introduction of such a caste [of free blacks] amongst us, would corrupt our blacks and instigate them to bloodshed."[1]

Despite the publication of a retraction, a mob of 400–500 citizens descended on the Mormons, vandalized the press, and tarred and feathered Mormon bishop Edward Partridge and another Mormon in front of the courthouse. After several months of negotiations and stalling by the Mormons, about 1,200 of Joseph Smith's followers were driven from Jackson County the following November.

From this point on, Smith was preoccupied with attempts to regain the Mormon holy land, the land of Zion, in Jackson County, where his people were to build a temple complex and expanding community to await the presumed imminent return of Jesus. In the spring of 1834, Smith led about 200 armed Mormon men from Ohio to Missouri in an effort to reestablish Mormons on their Missouri lands, but the march ended in failure. Afterward,

---

1. Quoted in "To His Excellency, Daniel Dunklin," *The Evening and the Morning Star* 2 (Dec. 1833): 114.

Smith predicted the land of Zion would be redeemed by 11 September 1836. In a letter dated 16 August 1834, Smith wrote from Ohio to his brethren in Missouri and advised them to "use every effort to prevail on the churches to gather to those regions and situate themselves to be in readiness to move into Jackson Co. in two years from the Eleventh of September next which is the appointed time for the redemption of Zion."[2] When he identified the Egyptian mummies as descendants of Ham in July 1835, Smith knew he had to choose his words carefully if his prediction were to be fulfilled.

Like the Alphabets, part 1 of the Grammar deals with the Katumin royal lineage and becomes explicitly racial regarding the descendants of Ham, son of Noah. However, before I discuss the content of the bound Grammar, I must first address the notion that it was authored by W. W. Phelps instead of Smith.

Was Phelps Responsible for the Bound Grammar?

Smith's official history states that during the month of July 1835, "I was continually engaged in translating an alphabet to the Book of Abraham, and arrangeing a grammar of the Egyptian language as practiced by the ancients."[3] At some point during the creation of the Alphabets, it was decided that more space was needed and the project was moved to a bound volume titled "Grammar & A[l]phabet of the Egyptian Language" (hereafter GAEL). The bound Grammar not only incorporates and expands the Alphabets but contains imaginative lectures on Egyptian grammar.

---

2. Joseph Smith, Letter, Kirtland Township, Geauga County, Ohio, to Lyman Wight and Others, [Liberty, Clay County], Missouri, 16 Aug. 1834, Joseph Smith Letterbook 1, 86, CHL (*JSP*, D4:106). The date 11 September 1836 was derived from an 11 September 1831 revelation that said that God would "retain a stronghold in the Land of Kirtland for the space of five years," after which he would "not hold any guilty that shall go with open hearts up to the Land of Zion" (Revelation, Kirtland, Ohio, 11 Sept. 1831 [D&C 64:21–22], Revelation Book 1, 110; *JSP*, D2:65).

3. JS History, vol. B-1, 597 (DHC 2:238). Smith was not unfamiliar with the principles of grammar. On 4 November 1835, he attended school during the day, and, according to his journal, he lectured on grammar in the evening and again the next evening (Joseph Smith, Journal, 4 Nov. 1835, in *JSP*, J1:84). George A. Smith remembered that he attended "the School of the Prophets, which school was held in the room under the Printing office, taught by Joseph Smith Jr. & Sidney Rigdon. I studied English Grammar about six weeks: the school was removed to the attic story of the Temple" (G. A. Smith, Autobiography, 81, CHL).

Mormon defenders have expended considerable time and energy trying to distance Smith from authorship of the bound Grammar. According to John Gee, the bound Grammar represents "W. W. Phelps's speculations on Egyptian grammar … in his handwriting."[4] True, the bound Grammar is mostly in the handwriting of Phelps, who with Oliver Cowdery was Smith's scribe during the early phase of the Egyptian project. Phelps was also working on Smith's history with Willard Richards in 1843 when the entry about the Alphabets and Grammar was written assigning authorship to Smith, and presumably Phelps would have disagreed with Gee.

Gee attempts to assign authorship of the bound Grammar to Phelps because he believes it was kept in Phelps's personal "archive." Of course, this does not explain why Warren Parrish, who also worked as Smith's scribe, would write at the end of each of the degrees in a book owned by Phelps. Nevertheless, Gee presents no evidence that the bound Grammar as well as ten other documents among the Joseph Smith Egyptian papers, including all three Alphabets, was in Phelps's personal archive, as he claimed in 2017.[5] Rather, the bound Grammar was likely among the records listed in early LDS Church Historian's Office inventories as "Egyptian Grammar," as the editors of the Joseph Smith Papers state for Smith's Alphabet.[6] This includes the list of records packaged in boxes prior to the exodus West prepared in February 1846 by clerk Thomas Bullock.[7] As the Joseph Smith Papers editors note, these inventories show that these documents were in "continuous institutional custody," not in any theorized personal archive of Phelps.

Nevertheless, in an attempt to prove that Phelps owned the bound Grammar, Gee cites Smith's journal for 13 November 1843, which Gee believes, erroneously, documents that Smith went to Phelps's house to consult the Grammar. Although Phelps's

---

4. John Gee, *An Introduction to the Book of Abraham* (Provo, Utah: Religious Studies Center, Brigham Young University/Salt Lake City: Deseret Book Co., 2017), 39.

5. Ibid., 33–36.

6. Historical Introduction, *JSP*, D5:81.

7. "Schedule of Church Records, Nauvoo, 1846," [1], Historian's Office, CHL.

possession of the Grammar book would not necessarily prove his authorship, since Smith's scribes sometimes took church records home with them, a close examination of Gee's sources indicates that precisely the opposite of what Gee claims actually happened.[8]

On 9 November 1843, Smith assigned Phelps to answer a letter that James Arlington Bennett of New York City had written to him. As Phelps sometimes did, he sprinkled his text with phrases in various foreign languages, including Egyptian. The published letter, which appeared in the church's *Times and Seasons* periodical the same month, made reference to three astronomical Egyptian names from the bound Grammar: "Were I an Egyptian, I would exclaim, Jah-oh-eh, Enish-go-on-dosh, Flo-ees-Flos-is-is; [O the earth! the power of attraction, and the moon passing between her and the sun]."[9]

In the bound Grammar, Jah-oh-eh in the third degree is given the following explanation: "The earth under the government of an other <or the seconed> of the fixed stars, which is called Enish-go-an=dosh or in other words the power of attraction it has with the earth."[10] The explanation for Flo-ees in the third degree reads: "The moon– signifying its revolutions, also going between, thereby forming an eclipse."[11] And the explanation for Flos-isis in the third degree is: "The sun in its affinity with Earth and Moon– signifying their revolutions showing the power, the one has with the other."[12]

This passage in the letter to Bennett, however, underwent revision after Smith reviewed it. After working on the letter for a few

---

8. On 29 October 1835, for example, Smith went to Frederick G. Williams's house to retrieve his "large journal" (Smith, Journal, 29 Oct. 1835, in *JSP*, J1:76). On 25 January 1836, Smith received a letter from a sick Warren Parrish informing him that Parrish would be unable to perform his duties as scribe, stating "I therefore, with reluctance send your journal to you untill my health improves" (Warren Parrish, Letter, Kirtland Township, Geauga County, Ohio, to Joseph Smith, Kirtland Township, Geauga County, Ohio, 25 Jan. 1836, Smith, Journal, 25 Jan. 1836; *JSP*, J1:173; *JSP*, D5:161). On 8 February 1836, Smith's journal records: "Elder Parrish my scribe, received my journal again" (*JSP*, J1:183).

9. Joseph Smith, Letter, Nauvoo, Illinois, to James Arlington Bennett, 13 Nov. 1843, Arlington House, New York, *Times and Seasons* 4 (1 Nov. 1843): 373; Joseph Smith, *The Voice of Truth* (Nauvoo, Illinois: John Taylor, 1844), 11.

10. GAEL, 29–30 (*JSP*, R4:173–75).

11. GAEL, 30 (*JSP*, R4:175).

12. GAEL, 30 (*JSP*, R4:175).

days, Phelps went to Smith's office on the morning of 13 November 1843, and, according to Smith's journal, "Phelps read [the] letter to Jas A Bennet. & [Joseph Smith] made some correcti[o]ns."[13] An early draft of the letter does not include an English translation and exhibits signs of editing: "~~Was~~ <Were> I an Egyptian I would exclaim= ~~Floeese Floeese~~: <Jah oh=eh> Enish-go=on=dosh, ~~Jah=oh=eh~~ <Flo-ees-Floisis>."[14]

The draft copy also includes three characters from the bound Grammar in the left margin. Gee believes that during this process of editing Smith visited Phelps to consult the Grammar in Phelps's possession. According to Gee, "Apparently, the Egyptian quotation bothered Joseph Smith because that afternoon he 'called again & enqui[re]d for. the Egypti[a]n grammar,' apparently to check what Phelps had quoted."[15] A close reading of this entry makes it clear that the accurate meaning is not as Gee interprets. The entry for the morning is written twice with two locations for the meeting, although the entire entry was written by Willard Richards. In the first version, Smith "called at the office A M. ... and heard Judge Phelps read [the] letter to Jas A Bennet. & made some correcti[o]ns." The second version, probably written at the end of the day, reads: "In the morning Bro Phelps—called ~~on~~ at the mansion and read a letter which I [Joseph Smith] had dictated to Gen. Jam Ariligtn Bennet whi[c]h pleasd me much."

Smith's office was in the red brick store on Water Street in Nauvoo; his residence was one block east in the Mansion House. Phelps lived in a small house three blocks west of the red brick store on the northwest corner of Sidney Street and the "projected" Locust Street.[16] In the entry's first version, Smith "called at the office" and heard the letter read by Phelps, a clerk in Smith's office. In the second version, Phelps "called at the mansion" and read the letter. In neither instance was the letter read in Phelps's home, which is important to keep in mind when reading the remainder

---

13. Smith, Journal, 13 Nov. 1843 (*JSP*, J3:128).

14. Joseph Smith, Letter, Nauvoo, Illinois, to James Arlington Bennett, Flatbush, New York, 13 Nov. 1843, Joseph Smith Collection, CHL.

15. Gee, *Introduction to the Book of Abraham*, 36–37.

16. LaMar C. Berrett, ed., *Sacred Places: A Comprehensive Guide to Early LDS Historical Sites*, 6 vols. (Salt Lake City: Deseret Book Co., 1999–2007), 3:197.

of the entry for 13 November: "P.M. called again with Doct [John] Bernhisel & [William] Clayton. & read again. afte[r]wa[r]ds called again & enqui[re]d for. the Egypti[a]n grammar."

If it were Smith who "called again," it would have been in the office, where the grammar was likely located with other church records and where Phelps would have had access to it. On the other hand, if it were Phelps who "called again," it would have been in the Mansion House, which would still mean that the Grammar was not in Phelps's possession. In any case, Gee's interpretation is wrong. Gee never explains why Smith would consult a Grammar authored by Phelps and use it to correct and translate what Phelps had written.

Two days later, Smith "Suggested the Idea of preparing a grammar of the Egyptian Language," apparently for publication.[17] Gee misreads this passage as well, asserting that "it sounds like he may not have agreed with Phelps's treatment" and wanted to make his own. First, Smith did not disapprove of the Grammar. Why would Smith want to consult the Grammar if he did not approve of it? According to one account, the previous May 1843 Smith had compared the characters on the recently discovered Kinderhook plates (later shown to be a forgery) with characters in "his Egyptian alphabet."[18] There is no suggestion that Gee's theory of a replacement grammar existed. Rather, when Smith consulted the Grammar, he no doubt noted that it was incomplete and needed more work before it could be published.

Another way of distancing Smith from the bound Grammar is to assign a later date to its composition, sometime after Smith

17. Smith, Journal, 15 Nov. 1843 (*JSP*, J3:130).

18. *New York Herald*, 30 May 1843. The "Gentile" correspondent reporting from Nauvoo on 7 May 1843 mistakenly said the "Egyptian alphabet" had been taken from "the plates from which the Book of Mormon was translated." LDS apostle Parley P. Pratt writing on the same day to John Van Cott said that the Kinderhook plates had been brought to Smith "for examination & translation" and that "a large number of Citizens here have seen them and compared the characters with those on the Egyptian papyrus which is now in this city" (Parley P. Pratt and Orson Pratt, Letter to John Van Cott, 7 May 1843, CHL). The New York correspondent said that Smith "compared" the characters on the plates "in my presence with his Egyptian alphabet." The entry in Smith's journal for 7 May 1843 reads: "forenoon visited by several gentlemen concerning the plates which were dug out of a mound near quincy [Quincy, Illinois] sent by Wm Smith to the office for Hebrew Bible & Lexicon" (*JSP*, J3:13).

finished working on the Egyptian materials in the latter part of November 1835. In 2017, Gee dated the Grammar to "Between January and April 1836," explaining only that it contains a "Post-Seixas transliteration system."[19] Joshua Seixas was a non-Mormon scholar of ancient languages who began teaching Hebrew to Smith and other Mormons in Kirtland in January 1836 using his own textbook. Gee gave more details in 2015:

> the [Egyptian Grammar] book cannot date to 1835. How do we know that? The system of transliteration that Phelps used in the [Grammar] book follows the transliteration system taught by Josiah [Joshua] Seixas beginning in January of 1836. Words with long final vowels end in an "h." The transliteration system used before that does not have the "h" and this can be seen in the transcriptions of the same words made in October 1835 [referring to the Alphabets actually begun in July 1835]. Since the [Grammar] book has the later system, it must date after the later system was taught and thus must date after its introduction in January 1836.

Based on this evidence, Gee argued: "We have no record of Joseph Smith working on Egyptian materials from November 1835 until the beginning of 1842. ... This means that he was not working on the so-called Grammar and Alphabet, with its 1836 transliteration system. That work, instead, should be attributed to the man in whose handwriting it is ... W. W. Phelps."[20]

Here, again, Gee is sparse with details and makes it sound as if the Grammar is entirely reflective of Seixas's transliteration system, which is not the case. In fact, Gee's evidence consists entirely of Phelps's adding an "h" to the end of "Pha-e" thus" "Phah-eh," and three other times when "Pha" and "Pha-e" appear in connection with other words. Gee does not explain why Phelps would change one name in the Egyptian Grammar based on some newly learned rule of Hebrew when Egyptian names are not transliterations of an alphabetic language. Nor does Gee explain how he

---

19. Gee, *Introduction to the Book of Abraham*, 34–35.

20. John Gee, "Joseph Smith and Ancient Egypt," in *Approaching Antiquity: Joseph Smith and the Ancient World*, ed. Lincoln H. Blumell, Matthew J. Grey, and Andrew H. Hedges (Provo, Utah: Religious Studies Center/Salt Lake City: Deseret Book Co., 2015), 440–41.

knows "Pha" and "e" were pronounced as long vowels. If Phelps had been motivated by a rule of Hebrew, why are there no other changes? Despite many opportunities, no other "h" was added or deleted. "Ba-eth kee" is an interesting example since the long "e" is signaled by the double letter, but Phelps did not add an "h," as Gee's theory would suggest. The double *ee* is how Seixas transliterated the long *e*.[21] If Seixas had such a rule, it is not obvious from his published 1834 *Manual [of] Hebrew Grammar for the Use of Beginners.* Indeed, I can find nothing to suggest such a rule, as Gee represents.[22]

Gee's attempt to shift responsibility for the bound Grammar from Smith to Phelps does not stand up under scrutiny. Smith and/or Phelps have already told us through Smith's official history that it was Smith who began "arranging a grammar of the Egyptian language" during the latter part of July 1835.[23]

THE BOUND GRAMMAR

Part 1 (pp. 1–22)   Fifth degree (pp. 1–8)
                                Lecture on grammar (pp. 1–3)
                                [26 pages blank]
                           Fourth degree (pp. 9–12)
                                [6 pages blank]
                           Third degree (pp. 13–14)
                                [6 pages blank]
                           Second degree (pp. 15–19)
                                Lecture on grammar (pp. 15–16)
                                [11 pages blank]

---

21. Joshua Seixas, *A Manual Hebrew Grammar for the Use of Beginners* (2nd ed., enl. and impr.; Andover, Massachusetts: Gould and Newman, 1834), 6.

22. Ronald V. Huggins, formerly a professor at Salt Lake Theological Seminary and Midwestern Baptist Theological Seminary, assesses Gee's argument as follows: "Seixas's system of transliteration does not introduce the innovation Gee attributes to him, i.e., it does *not* reflect a practice where 'words with long final vowels end in an "h."' There never has been such a system of transliterating Hebrew where 'h' is added to *all* final long vowels. What he may have in mind are cases where a final *hê* ('h') marks lengthened vowels (i.e., certain kinds of 'a,' 'e' and 'o'). Yet, although some people today do add an h in their transliterations of those vowels, Seixas did not. Nor did he do so for any other final long vowels. Therefore, what Gee says about Seixas's introducing and employing such an innovation in his transliterations is simply incorrect." Ronald V. Huggins, Personal communication, 18 and 19 Aug. 2018, in my possession.

23. JS History, vol. B-1, 597 (DHC 2:238).

First degree (pp. 20–22)
>> Lecture on grammar (pp. 20–21)
>> [15 pages blank]

Part 2 (pp. 23–34)   Fifth degree (pp. 23–26)
>> [12 pages blank]
>> Fourth degree (pp. 27–28)
>> [22 pages blank]
>> Third degree (pp. 29–30)
>> [22 pages blank]
>> Second degree (pp. 31–32)
>> [22 pages blank]
>> First degree (pp. 33–34)
>> [42 pages blank]

Overview of the Bound Grammar

The bound Grammar is organized in two parts, each part subdivided into five degrees arranged in reverse order. Between each of the degrees many pages were left blank for expansion. The two parts of the Grammar coincide with parts 1 and 2 in the Alphabets, which contain only the first degree. In the first part of the Grammar, each of the twenty-three characters from the Alphabets receives a definition that is slightly different in each degree and enlarged in the fifth.

In the second part of the Grammar, the method was changed. Characters from part 2 of the Alphabets are not copied into all five degrees of the bound Grammar, but the first character of the Alphabets is copied only into the Grammar's first degree, the second into the second degree, and so on until the fifth degree. This process was repeated with the sixth character being copied into the first degree of the Grammar, the seventh into the second degree, and so on. This method was kept up until the 36th character. The last seven characters—36 through 42, which pertain to the so-called Egyptian astronomy—are copied and defined in all five degrees.

Included are three lectures on Egyptian grammar prefacing the first, second, and fifth degrees. The first lecture prefacing the fifth degree takes up the first two and a half pages of the Grammar and explains the five-degree system using the first three characters that appear in Phelps's transcription of the first three verses of the Book of Abraham in the translation book (fig. 1.2), but here they are given the names that appear in the Alphabets: Za Ki-oan Hiash (or Chalsidon hiash), Ah brah-oam, and Ki Ah-broam ki-ah-brah-oam Zub Zool oan (see below). As previously discussed, the first two characters are taken from the first line of JSP XI (fig. 2.1), while the last character would have appeared in the missing portion of the papyrus but is taken from JSP I, column 2, and appears in part 3 of the Alphabets (fig. 1.3).

In the first lecture on grammar, it is explained that a line above or below a character increases or decreases its significance and that as many as five lines may be added. Many instances in the text of the Breathing Permit and Book of the Dead may have suggested to Smith the use of such lines. Next, each of the three characters is "dissected" or broken down into "parts of speech" and each part given a meaning. Since the first character—Za Ki-oan Hiash—has five parts, when a line is added below, its meaning is increased five times (5 x 5) and therefore represents twenty-five parts of speech. With two lines this character would yield (5 x 25) 125 parts of speech; with three lines (125 x 5) 625 parts of speech, and so on. Such a language would be "very comprehensive,"[24] as Cowdery described, but it would also be impractical if not unworkable.

COMPARISON OF CHARACTERS AND NAMES FROM EGYPTIAN
ALPHABET-C AND BEGINNING OF GRAMMAR[25]

Alphabet (Phelps)		Grammar (Phelps)	
	Za ki on=hish <or> Kalsidon hish		Za Ki-oan Hiash (or Chalsidon hiash)
	Ah=brah oam		Ah brah-oam
	Ki Ah broam kiah brah-oam zub zool oan		Ki Ah-broam kiah-brah-oam Zub Zool oan

---

24. "Egyptian Mummies—Ancient Records," *Messenger and Advocate* 2 (Dec. 1835): 236.

25. Alphabet from Egyptian Alphabet-C, 4 (*JSP,* R4:93); Grammar from GAEL, 1, 2, 3 (*JSP,* R4:117, 119, 121).

Similar lectures on grammar preface the first and second degrees, using Beth from part 2 of the Alphabets.

The fact that the bound Grammar begins with the first three characters that Phelps recorded in the translation book (i.e., Book of Abraham Manuscript-C) and then deals with characters from the Alphabets is another reason to conclude that the translation was interrupted by the creation of the bound Grammar. Significantly, no other characters from JSP XI appear in the Grammar.

Bound Grammar: First Part

As mentioned in chapter three, Princess Katumin of the Valuable Discovery notebooks became a lineage name in the Alphabets, where we learned that she was descended from a woman who had discovered Egypt while it was covered by water, presumably from the Great Flood: "Iota-Tou-es-Zip-zi. The land of Egypt first discovered under water by a woman."[26] This subject was expanded in part 1 of the bound Grammar in the definitions of Kah tou mun and Iota-Tou-es-Zip-zi. In the fourth degree of the bound Grammar, for instance, we learn that females of the royal Kah tou mun lineage were descended from a daughter of Noah's son Ham.[27] According to the fifth degree:

 Kah tou mun: a lineage with whom a record of the fathers was intrusted by tradition of Ham, and according to the tradition of their elders, by whom also the tradition of the art of of embalming was kept.[28]

The record that was found on the breast of one of the female mummies was the Book of the Dead belonging to Ta-sherit-Min, which (see chapter two) Smith identified as the record of Joseph son of Jacob/Israel. Thus, according to the fifth degree, Katumin's mother was a descendant of Ham and therefore of the "lineage with whom a record of the fathers was intrusted." While Smith tried to explain how the records of two Hebrew prophets came into the possession of an Egyptian royal family, he left unexplained

---

26. Egyptian Alphabet-B, ca. July–Nov. 1835, 1 (*JSP*, R4:75).
27. GAEL, 9 (*JSP*, R4:133).
28. GAEL, 4 (*JSP*, R4:123).

why, after being handed down for several generations, they should be buried with mummies.

The bound Grammar's treatment of the compound character Iota-Tou-es-Zip-Zi contains additional information about the founding of Egypt. In the third and fifth degrees, we learn that this daughter of Ham, who discovered Egypt while it was still underwater, afterwards settled her sons in it.[29] The fifth degree, for example, states:

 Iota toues Zip Zi: The land of Egypt which was first discovered by a woman <wh[i]le underwater>, and afterwards settled by her Sons she being a daughter of Ham …[30]

Later, in November 1835, Smith drew on this information in the bound Grammar for his dictation of Abraham 1:23–24, which appeared next to a character that incorporated the Iota-Tou-es-Zip-Zi character.

 The land of Egypt being first discovered by a woman, who was the daughter of Ham; and the daughter of Zep-tah. which in the Chaldea signifies Egypt, which sign[i]fies that which is forbidden. When this woman discovered the land it was under water, who after settled her sons in it: And thus from Ham sprang that race which preserved the curse in the land.[31]

The character in the left margin is not hieratic but is one of the six groups of characters Smith created to fill the gaps in the damaged Hôr papyrus. Here, we see information from the Alphabets and bound Grammar originally associated with Katumin adapted to the Book of Abraham with the added information that the woman who discovered Egypt under water was the daughter of Ham and his wife Zeptah (and who is nowhere mentioned in Genesis). Later, prior to publication in 1842, Smith changed Zeptah to Egyptus, making it appear that both Ham's wife and daughter had the same name. It is unclear how Smith came up

---

29. GAEL, 5, 14 (*JSP*, R4:125, 143).
30. GAEL, 5 (*JSP*, R4:125).
31. Book of Abraham Manuscript-B, Nov. 1835, [3] [Abr. 1:23–24] (*JSP*, R4:199).

with the name Egyptus, but it appears in Josephus as a man's name from a later time.[32]

What Smith meant by preserving the curse in the land may be best explained in a letter Phelps wrote to Cowdery on 6 February 1835:

> Is or is it not apparent from reason and analogy as drawn from a careful reading of the Scriptures, that God causes the saints, or people that fall away from his church to be cursed in time, with a *black skin*? Was or was not Cain, being marked, obliged to inherit the curse, [upon] he and his children, forever? And if so, as Ham, like other sons of God, might break the rule of God, by marrying out of the church, did or did he not, have a Canaanite wife, whereby some of the *black seed* was preserved through the flood, and his son, Canaan, after he laughed at his grand father's nakedness, heired [inherited] three curses: one from Cain for killing Abel; one from Ham for marrying a black wife, and one from Noah for ridiculing what God had respect for?[33]

Significantly, Phelps's letter was written five months before Smith procured the Egyptian papyri, which indicates that the Book of Abraham only canonized what was already being discussed among Smith's followers about race and curses. In fact, both Phelps and Smith were expressing a version of what many of Smith's contemporaries believed was the origin of the Black race. Those who wanted to justify African slavery, however, did not refer to Ham's wife, but rather to Ham's son Canaan. According to the biblical account, Ham had seen the drunken and naked Noah passed out in his tent; and when Noah found out, he was displeased and cursed Canaan, saying: "Cursed be Canaan; a servant of servants shall he be unto his brethren" (Gen. 9:25). No doubt the pro-slavery persecutors of the Mormons in Missouri shared the views reported in John Blake's 1834 book *The Family Encyclopedia of Useful Knowledge and General Literature*: "In consequence of this irreverent act on the part of Ham, some have fancifully conjectured, that not only Ham

---

32. Flavius Josephus, *Against Apion*, Bk. 1, sec. 15, trans. William Whiston, *Josephus Complete Works* (Grand Rapids, Michigan: Kregel Publications, 1960), 612. On the change from Zeptah to Egyptus, see Brent Lee Metcalfe, "The Curious Textual History of 'Egyptus' the Wife of Ham," *John Whitmer Historical Association Journal* 34/2 (Fall/Winter 2014): 1–11.

33. William W. Phelps, Letter, Liberty, Missouri, to Oliver Cowdery, Kirtland, Ohio, 6 Feb. 1835, *LDS Messenger and Advocate* 1 (Mar. 1835): 82.

and Canaan, but all their posterity, became slaves, and the color of their skin was suddenly rendered black; and accordingly they maintain, that all the blacks have descended from Ham and Canaan."[34]

As early as 1831, Smith's revelations explained that the mark God had put upon Cain for murdering his brother, Abel, was black skin. In his revision of the King James Bible, Smith dictated to his scribe that Enoch beheld in vision that humankind "were a mixture of all the seed of Adam save it was the seed of Cain, for the seed of Cain were black, and had not place among them."[35] In August 1832, Phelps published Smith's "Prophecy of Enoch," which included the preceding statement, in *The Evening and the Morning Star*, perhaps to curry favor in the eyes of the suspicious, slave-holding Missourians.

While some of Smith's contemporaries associated Cain's curse with black skin, it remained to be explained how the curse was preserved through the Flood. One editor of a London newspaper noted that "doctors of divinity have differed as to what kind of mark was set upon Cain, some have asserted that his colour was changed to black, whence the negro race have sprung, but a difficulty is again started here, as Noah and his family according to the bible history must have pro-created the present race."[36]

Smith initially solved the problem by having Canaan's curse include black skin. As early as 1831, while revising the Bible, Smith reinforced the pro-slavery interpretation of the passage in Genesis: "And [Noah] said, Blessed be the Lord God of Shem; and Canaan shall be his servant, *and a veil of darkness shall cover him, that he shall be known among all men*" (emphasis added).[37]

---

34. J[ohn] L. Blake, *The Family Encyclopedia of Useful Knowledge and General Literature* (New York: Peter Hill, 1834), 434.

35. Old Testament Manuscript-1, 16 [Moses 7:22], CCLA (Scott H. Faulring, Kent P. Jackson, and Robert J. Matthews, eds., *Joseph Smith's New Translation of the Bible: Original Manuscripts* [Provo, Utah: Religious Studies Center, Brigham Young University, 2004], 105). This passage was dictated between December 1830 and 7 March 1831 (p. 57). Moses 7 was published in the August 1832 issue of *The Evening and the Morning Star* (1:18).

36. "Continuation of Reply to the Rev. Thomas Hartwell Horne's Pamphlet, Entitled Deism Refuted, &c. From Page 415," *The Republican* [London] 2 (14 Apr. 1820): 445.

37. Old Testament Manuscript-1, 25 [Gen. 9:26; I.V. Gen. 11:30] (Faulring et al., *Joseph Smith's New Translation of the Bible*, 118).

Earlier in his revision, Enoch, according to Smith, saw a vision of "the world for the space of many generations," and seemed to allude to Africa: "For behold, the Lord shall curse the land with much heat, and the barrenness thereof shall go forth forever; and there was a blackness came upon all the children of Canaan, that they were despised among all people."[38]

Smith therefore described a separate cursing of Canaan rather than a transmission of the curse through Ham's inter-racial marriage. In the intervening years between working on his Bible revision and dictating the text of the Book of Abraham, Smith modified his ideas about the origin of the Black race, possibly the result, in part, of Phelps's influence.

While Ham and Zeptah had other children, their daughter Egyptus would have had no claim to the patriarchal priesthood. Still the Book of Abraham makes a point of saying that although her son Pharaoh was a "righteous man" who imitated the patriarchal government of his fathers, he was nevertheless "cursed ... pertaining to the Priesthood" (Abr. 1:26). Pharaoh was therefore an illegitimate ruler not only because he was of the wrong race but because he had the wrong lineage. Nevertheless, the Book of Abraham states that "the Pharaohs would fain claim it from Noah, through Ham, therefore my father was led away by their idolatry" (Abr. 1:27), which may have been influenced by Isaiah 19:11, where the princes of the Egyptian city Zoan declare to Pharaoh, "I am the son of the wise, the son of ancient kings."[39]

While later Mormons interpreted this passage in Abraham as banning Blacks from all priesthood offices, the context of the statement pertained to the patriarchal priesthood. There is no indication that Smith envisioned an elaborate priesthood organization existing before Moses. To this point, his revelations spoke only of a

---

38. Old Testament Manuscript-1, 16 [Moses 7:20] (Faulring et al., *Joseph Smith's New Translation of the Bible*, 118).

39. A chronology accompanying the publication of some eighteenth- and nineteenth-century Bibles lists the founding of Egypt by one of Noah's grandsons and then states: "Egypt is called the land of Ham, and the Egyptian Pharaohs boasted themselves to be the sons of ancient Kings" (e.g., *The Holy Bible, Containing The Old Testament and the New* [London: Charles Bill, 1706]; *The Holy Bible, According to the Authorized Version* [Oxford, Engl.; Clarendon Press, 1818], unpaginated index at end of both volumes).

line of patriarchal ordinations, for which Shem was preferred over Ham. How this applied to Smith's church, and the priesthood Smith established, was never explicitly stated during Smith's lifetime, and historians have debated whether or not Brigham Young correctly interpreted Smith's teachings on the matter.[40] Regardless, under Young, it became LDS policy to restrict Black men from holding the priesthood, as well as Black men and women, from full participation in LDS temple ceremonies, until church president Spencer W. Kimball lifted the ban in 1978.

The subject of race continues in the Grammar. In part 1 of the Alphabets, character 9—named Ho-e-oop—is defined as relating to a young unmarried prince. In the bound Grammar, in the third degree, we are told that the character refers to "a prince of the line of the Pharaohs," and in the fourth "a true descendant from Ham— the son of Noah."[41] In the fifth degree, the definition of Ho-e-oop is expanded further to refer to an "inheritor of the Kingly blessings from under the hand of Noah, but *not according to the priestly blessing*, because of the trangrissions of Ham, which blessing fell upon Shem from under the hand of Noah" (emphasis added).[42] Later, as noted, when Smith dictated the text of the Book of Abraham in November 1835, he drew on the material in the bound Grammar dealing with Ham's priesthood restriction:

 Now the <first> government, of Egypt was established by Pharaoh, the Eldest son of Egyptes, the daughter of Ham, and it was after the manner of [the] government of Ham, which was patriarchal, Pharaoh being a righteous man established his Kingdom, and Judged his p[e]ople wise<ly> and justly all his days, seeking earnestly to imitate that order established by the fathers in the first generations, in the days of the first patriarchal reign, even in the reign of Adam; and also Noah his father, ~~for in his days~~ who blessed him, with the blessings of the earth, and with the blessings of wisdom, but cursed him as pertaining to the priesthood.[43]

40. See Armand L. Mauss, "The Fading of the Pharoahs' Curse: The Decline and Fall of the Priesthood Ban Against Blacks in the Mormon Church," *Dialogue: A Journal of Mormon Thought* 14 (Autumn 1981): 10–35.

41. GAEL, 9–10, 13 (*JSP*, R4:133–35, 141).

42. GAEL, 4 (*JSP*, R4:123).

43. Book of Abraham Manuscript-B, Nov. 1835, 4–5 [Abr. 1:26] (*JSP*, R4:211–13).

Again, it should be noted that the group of characters in the left margin is not hieratic Egyptian, but is another grouping of characters Smith created to fill in the gap in the damaged papyrus. The first character in the group appeared in the Alphabets and was named Zub-zool-eh and was said to mean "in the beginning of the earth, or crea<tion.>"[44] In the bound Grammar, this character was developed and defined in the fifth degree to mean:

Zub Zool eh: In the days of the first patrarchs In the reign of Adam; in the days of the first patriarchs; in the days of Noah; in the blessings of Noah; in the blessings of the children of Noah; in the first blessings of men; in the first blessings of the church:[45]

Thus a character representing the beginning of time in the Alphabets and associated with Katumin was developed in the Grammar to describe the patriarchal line of descent from Adam to Noah and Noah's blessing his children, which Smith subsequently incorporated into his dictation of Abraham. As discussed in chapter three, patriarchal government is not mentioned in Genesis but it is a key theme in the Book of Abraham and in Josephus.

Bound Grammar: Second Part

I move now to part 2 of the Grammar, which was begun in July 1835 but was still being created the following October. As discussed, the method of copying characters from the Alphabets changed. Instead of copying each character into all five degrees of the bound Grammar, the characters were copied sequentially, from the first to the fifth degree, repeatedly, until character 36, where the remaining seven characters (36–42) dealing with Egyptian astronomy were copied and defined in all five degrees. In chapter three, I discussed how part 2 of the Alphabets expanded and elaborated the definitions which had previously been given for characters belonging to Adam's "pure" language, a portion of which survives in Phelps's 26 May 1835 letter to his wife. Both sources—the Alphabets and Grammar—exhibit a progression of thought: from grades

---

44. See, e.g., Egyptian Alphabet-B, ca. July–Nov. 1835, [1] (*JSP*, R4:75).

45. GAEL, 6 (*JSP*, R4:127).

of beings, to grades of authority, to grades of geographic location, to grades of stars and planets. In the Alphabets the definitions end with character 23, which discusses the Celestial Kingdom, or residence of God. The bound Grammar continues this theme, defining the next two characters (24 and 25) as follows:

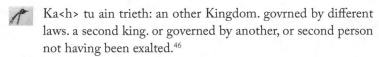 Ka<h> tu ain trieth: an other Kingdom. govrned by different laws. a second king. or governed by another, or second person not having been exalted.[46]

Kah tu=ain: Another Kingdom governed by different laws, composed of subjects who receive their place at a future period, and governed by those who are under the directions of another; a kingdom whose subject[s] differ one from another <in glory>; ... [they] behold not the face of of God.[47]

These definitions correspond to the Terrestrial and Telestial Kingdoms of Smith's and Sidney Rigdon's 1832 vision of three heavens.[48] The definitions are followed by three kingdoms of the devil, two names of which are derived from the Greek word Hades (the underworld). While Hades does not appear in the King James Version of the Bible, it appears in the Greek manuscripts of the Old and New Testaments and translated variously as "Hell," "grave," or "pit." Smith's contemporaries used the term as a synonym for "Hell." According to the bound Grammar, the three kingdoms of darkness are:

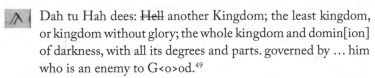 Dah tu Hah dees: ~~Hell~~ another Kingdom; the least kingdom, or kingdom without glory; the whole kingdom and domin[ion] of darkness, with all its degrees and parts. governed by ... him who is an enemy to G<o>od.[49]

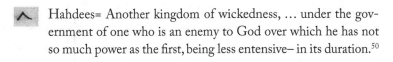 Hahdees= Another kingdom of wickedness, ... under the government of one who is an enemy to God over which he has not so much power as the first, being less entensive– in its duration.[50]

---

46. GAEL, 27 (*JSP*, R4:169).

47. GAEL, 23 (*JSP*, R4:161).

48. "The Vision," Hiram Township, Ohio, 16 Feb. 1832, Revelation Book 2, 1–10 [D&C 76] (*JSP*, D2:179–92).

49. GAEL, 33 (*JSP*, R4:181).

50. GAEL, 31 (*JSP*, R4:177).

De=eh, Another kingdom; ~~the least of all kig~~ over which Dah=Hah dees, or <the> king of Hell, ~~cannot~~ will not be permitted to exercise power at some fixed period.[51]

The Grammar then returns to the Celestial Kingdom:

Lish Zi hoe oop Iota: The glory of the celestial Kingdom: The connection of attributes; many parts perfected, and compounded into one Having been united; being united that which will be united, one glory above all other glories, as the the [sun] excels ~~in light~~ <the Moon> in light, this glory excels being filled: with the same glory equaility[52]

This is followed by characters 32–35—the four Masonic-like characters discussed in chapter three. Recall that character 32 was copied from column 3 of JSP I and that it appears as a man with his arms raised above his head:

Ho=hah=oop= – An intercessor; ... one who ~~is~~ <has been> appointed to intercede for another; invocation[53]

The character may have reminded Smith of the Masonic sign of grief and distress, as shown in William Morgan's 1827 exposé *Illustrations of Masonry*, published in Batavia, New York, about fifty-eight miles west of Palmyra (fig. 3.4). According to Morgan, Masons took an oath that "should I ever see that sign given or the word accompanying it, and the person who gave it appearing to be in distress I will fly to his relief at the risk of my life."[54]

The two characters that follow Ho=hah=oop are not from the papyrus but are abstractions of the shape of uplifted arms, similar to other derivative characters in part 2 of the Alphabets. These characters receive similar definitions that identify them with signs that may be used to escape one's enemies. The second Masonic-like character, which appears in the third degree, states:

---

51. GAEL, 29 (*JSP*, R4:173).
52. GAEL, 23 (*JSP*, R4:161).
53. GAEL, 31 (*JSP*, R4:177).
54. William Morgan, *Illustrations of Masonry* (Batavia, New York: David C. Miller, 1827), 74.

U Io=ho-hah oop: Tittle or dignity of one who is appointed to wait upon the king: one who is held in repute, trusty, honorable; who can be intrusted: The servant whom Abraham sent to get a wife for Isaac Most faithful: a tittle or dignity conferred upon women: a sign among the Egyptians that is used for influence or power: a sign made use of for one to escape his enemies: to excite commisseration, being had in honor, thereby affecting an escape.[55]

The sign associated with Abraham above alludes to Genesis 24:1–9, where Abraham instructs his servant to put his hand "under my thigh" and "swear by the Lord, the God of heaven, and the God of the earth, that thou shalt not take a wife unto my son of the daughters of the Canaanites" (v. 2). The third sign, which appears in the fourth degree, is defined as:

U Io=ho=hah oop zipzi: The title or dignity of one who is appointed to wait on the Queen; one who is held in repute; trusty honorable; who can be intrusted; a tittle or dignity conferred upon women: a sign among the Egyptians that is used for influence or power: a sign made use of for one to escape his enemies; to excite commisseration; being had in honor thereby effecting an escape[56]

The last of the four Masonic-like characters—character 35—is perhaps inspired by a Masonic square. It is also not on the papyrus but continues the theme of a messenger:

L Jah=ho=e=oop; An ambassador: one delgated with Kingly power; one authorized to ex[e]cute judgement for the King; a swift messenger one whose power cannot be escaped; one next to supreme;[57]

At this point in the bound Grammar, the method of copying the characters from the Alphabets changes with the last seven characters (36–42) being copied and defined in all five degrees. Since these last characters deal with so-called Egyptian astronomy, they date to 1 October 1835, which is discussed in the next

---

55. GAEL, 29 (*JSP*, R4:173).
56. GAEL, 27 (*JSP*, R4:169).
57. GAEL, 24 (*JSP*, R4:163).

chapter. It therefore seems probable that the change in copying characters coincides with a break or pause in the Egyptian project, which occurred in August 1835.

A Pause

In mid-August 1835 Smith left Kirtland with his scribe Frederick G. Williams on a trip to Michigan, and though he returned on 23 August, Smith would not resume the Abraham project until October. On 11 September, Phelps wrote to his wife in Missouri: "Nothing has been doing in the translation of the Egyptian Record for along time, and probably will not for some time to come."[58] In late September, while copying patriarchal blessings into a large book, Cowdery echoed some of the language in the Abraham 1:1–3 as recorded in the translation book by Phelps, and as discussed in chapter three.[59]

Conclusion

Smith's revelations reflected the theological prejudices of white Europeans concerning Blacks and the biblical justification for slavery. While Smith was sympathetic to slave owners, Mormons who migrated to Missouri from the North brought anti-slavery attitudes with them. Smith knew that if his campaign to retake Jackson County, Missouri, and establish his Zionic community there, had any chance of succeeding, he had to overcome the volatile subject of slavery. He had to change the image of his church as abolitionist. In April 1836, Smith published an article in his church's periodical the *Messenger and Advocate* in which he explicitly stated: "I do not believe that the people of the North have any more right to say that the South *shall not* hold slaves, than the South have to say the North shall."[60]

---

58. W. W. Phelps, Letter, Kirtland, Ohio, to Sally Phelps, Far West, Missouri, 11 Sept. 1835, CHL, quoted in Bruce Van Orden, "Writing to Zion: The William W. Phelps Kirtland Letters (1835–1836)," *Brigham Young University Studies* 33/3 (1993): 563.

59. Patriarchal Blessing Book 1, 8–9, Patriarchal Blessings, CHL.

60. Joseph Smith, Letter, Kirtland Township, Geauga County, Ohio, to Oliver Cowdery, Kirtland Township, Geauga County, Ohio, ca. 9 Apr. 1836, *LDS Messenger and Advocate* 2 (Apr. 1836): 289 (*JSP*, D5:238).

Smith also quoted the pro-slavery proof text in Genesis 9:25–26 concerning Canaan's curse and servitude, and declared: "I can say, the curse is not yet taken off from the sons of Canaan."[61] Smith then enunciated his church's policy regarding slavery: "We have no right to interfere with slaves, contrary to the mind and will of their masters. In fact, it would be much better, and more prudent, not to preach at all to slaves, until after their masters are converted, and then teach the master to use them with kindness."[62]

When citizens of Clay County, Missouri, demanded that the Mormons leave the county, in part, because they believed the Mormons were dangerous to societies "where slavery is tolerated and practiced,"[63] Smith and his counselors sent a letter, dated 25 July 1836, to alleviate tensions by denying the accusation and sending a copy of Smith's anti-abolitionist article.[64]

Although Smith's efforts failed and the deadline for the redemption of Zion came and went without fulfillment, I believe that the racial aspects of the Book of Abraham are best understood in this context. While not addressing slavery directly, Abraham supports the white supremacist ideology of slave owners. It speaks disapprovingly of Ham's interracial marriage as "forbidden" (Abr. 1:23). Because of Ham, the "curse" of a black skin was "preserved" through the Flood (Abr. 1:24). Delegitimizing Pharaoh's patriarchal government because he was "cursed … pertaining to the Priesthood" (Abr. 1:26) insured that Blacks could never be rulers in the patriarchal government that Smith was proposing for his Zion. But if Smith hoped to remove the barriers blocking the establishment of his Zionic community by promising to maintain the existing pro-slavery social order, he was mistaken. There were other things to dislike about the Mormons, and Missourians

---

61. Ibid., 290 (*JSP*, D5:240).

62. Ibid., 291 (*JSP*, D5:242). See D&C 134:12, included in the 1835 D&C as 102:12.

63. "Public Meeting," *Far West* (Liberty, Missouri), 30 June 1836; reprinted in "Public Meeting," *LDS Messenger and Advocate* 2 (Aug. 1836): 354.

64. Sidney Rigdon, Joseph Smith, Oliver Cowdery, Frederick G. Williams, and Hyrum Smith, Letter, Kirtland Township, Geauga County, Ohio, to John Thornton and Others, Clay County, Missouri, 25 July 1836, *LDS Messenger and Advocate* 2 (Aug. 1836): 355–59 (*JSP*, D5:258–68).

worried that the influx of Smith's followers would swing political power in the Mormons' favor. In two years Smith would be imprisoned and his people banished from the state.

5 The Cosmos

When Joseph Smith published the second installment of his translation of Abraham and interpretation of the circular hypocephalus (Facsimile 2) in the church's *Times and Seasons* periodical in March 1842, his translation contained a cosmology of planets and stars that was ascribed to the Old Testament patriarchs. However, Abraham's cosmology was not what one would expect from an ancient author. It did not describe the earth as flat. Nor did it mention the dome-like firmament in which stars were set as shining jewels.[1] Rather than luminous spots on the vaulted-canopy suspended above the earth, Abraham's scheme, according to Smith, was both unique and consistent with what was understood and believed by astronomers and natural theologians in the mid-nineteenth century. The mix of contemporary astronomy and theological concerns resulted in a cosmology that is as foreign to twenty-first-century readers of Smith's texts as ancient Hebrew cosmology was to Smith and his contemporaries.

With the invention of the telescope, scientists peered at the nearby planets and wondered if they too were inhabited. Some of Smith's contemporaries referred to the passage in Isaiah 45:18—"God ... created [the earth] not in vain, he formed it to be inhabited"—and, as the Revered Amos Pettengill (1780–1830) reasoned, "Jehovah intimates that it would have been inconsistent for him to create the Earth, had he not designed it to be inhabited. ... As he shows us a number of other worlds ... must we not infer from his perfections that he acted consistently in creating

---

1. See, e.g., Paul H. Seely, "The Firmament and the Water Above Part I: The Meaning of raqia' in Gen 1:6–8," *Westminster Theological Journal* 53/2 (Fall 1991): 227–40; Paul H. Seely, "The Firmament and the Water Above Part II: The Meaning of 'The Water above the Firmament' in Gen 1:6–8," *Westminster Theological Journal* 54/1 (Spring 1992): 31–46.

them, that he created them not in vain, but to be inhabited?"[2] In his book *A View of the Heavens, or Familiar Lessons on Astronomy*, published in 1826 in New Haven, Connecticut, and "adapted to the use of schools," Pettengill concluded that "the Planets are evidently calculated and designed to accommodate rational beings. They are like this Earth, and some of them vastly larger. ... Many circumstances constrain us to believe that they are filled with inhabitants; and that every fixed Star illuminates worlds peopled with creatures like ourselves, but not involved with us in rebellion against the Creator."[3]

It is against this backdrop that Smith developed his scriptural cosmology. When Smith and Sidney Rigdon declared in 1832 that through Jesus Christ "the worlds are and were created, and the inhabitants thereof are begotten sons and daughters unto God" (D&C 76:24), and that the inhabitants of this earth were destined to dwell in one of three eternal worlds, early Mormons understood it literally. In 1833, Oliver Cowdery commented: "It is a pleasing thing to let the mind stretch away and contemplate the vast creations of the Almighty; to see the planets perform their regular revolutions, and observe their exact motions; to view the thousand suns giving light to myriads of globes, moving in their respective orbits, and revolving upon their several axis, *all inhabited by intelligent beings.*"[4] While Smith's cosmology culminated in the 1842 publication of the Book of Abraham and explanation of Facsimile 2—which articulated a system of ruling planets headed by Kolob, the nearest planet to God's throne—Smith's text drew on the bound Grammar in which, in 1835, he had given more details of his unique cosmology.

Some Mormon scholars assert that Abraham is consistent with a geocentric or earth-centered cosmology. In this chapter, I show among other things that the "system of astronomy" in the bound Grammar and in Abraham 3 are best understood in the context of early nineteenth-century cosmology.

2. Amos Pettengill, *A View of the Heavens, or Familiar Lessons on Astronomy* (New Haven, Connecticut: Nathan Whiting, 1826), 64.

3. Ibid.

4. "Signs in the Heavens," *The Evening and the Morning Star* [Kirtland, Ohio] 2 (Dec. 1833): 116. Cowdery was editor.

Phase Two: Kirtland, October 1835

After a break of about two months, Smith resumed work on his "Grammar and Alphabet of the Egyptian Language." On 1 October 1835, Cowdery wrote in Smith's journal: "This after noon labored on the Egyptian alphabet, in company with brsr. O. Cowdery and W. W. Phelps: The system of astronomy was unfolded."[5] This refers to the bound "Grammar and Alphabet of the Egyptian Language," in which the last seven characters (numbers 36–42)—unlike the preceding characters in part 2—receive definitions in all five degrees, which describe a hierarchy of stars and planets organized much in the same manner as Smith had recently organized the priesthood authorities in his church, and which I discuss shortly.

Like Cowdery, Smith was aware of passages in Josephus that mention the descendants of Seth being "the inventors of that peculiar sort of wisdom which is concerned with the heavenly bodies, and their order."[6] Josephus also states that Abraham had "communicated" to the Egyptians "arithmetic, and delivered to them the science of astronomy, before Abram came into Egypt, they were unacquainted with those parts of learning; for that science came from the Chaldeans into Egypt, and from thence to the Greeks also."[7] It is no surprise that Smith would include a discussion of astronomy in his account of Abraham in Egypt. Of course, since Smith's Abraham received his knowledge from God through the medium of the Urim and Thummim, it comported not with ancient misunderstandings based on a belief in a flat earth, but with early nineteenth-century understandings of cosmology.

As mentioned, a cosmology unfolds in the definitions of the last seven characters (36–42) in the bound Grammar. Figure 5.1 shows these seven characters as well as their names and meanings. All but the three circular characters come from column 3 of the Breathing Permit of Hôr. The circular characters are similar to characters found elsewhere on the papyri and in the Valuable

---

5. Joseph Smith, Journal, 1 Oct. 1835, Joseph Smith Collection, CHL (*JSP*, J1:67).

6. Flavius Josephus, *Antiquities of the Jews*, Book 1, chap. 2, sec. 3, trans. William Whiston, *Josephus Complete Works* (Grand Rapids, Michigan: Kregel Publications, 1960), 27.

7. *Antiquities of the Jews*, Book 1, chap. 8, sec. 2 (Whiston, *Josephus Complete Works*, 33).

Discovery notebooks. While it is possible that Smith saw the three circular characters in some of the badly preserved portions of the papyri, he may have also been influenced by the almanacs of his day. No almanac has the circle with a single line and there is no clear example of the earth symbol among the Egyptian characters (fig. 3.5).[8] So the match of the earth sign in the Grammar and almanacs of Smith's day is significant.

ABRAHAM'S SYSTEM OF ASTRONOMY

Character number	Character	Name	Meaning
36	𝄆	Jah-ni-hah	messenger from the Celestial kingdom
37	⊕	Jah-oh-eh	earth
38	𝄢	Flo-ees	moon
39	●	Flos-isis	sun
40	𝄐	Kli-flos-ises	measurement of time
41	⌒	Veh-Kli-flos-isis	power of one of the fixed stars
42	𝄞	Kolob	a star nearest God's throne and slowest

The first character of the seven is "Jah-ni-hah," which is defined in the first degree as "one delegated with redeeming power; a swift messenger; one that goes before another; one having redeeming power, a second person in authority"—possibly referring to the Son, or Christ.[9] The fifth degree adds "one ... sent from the Celestial Kingdom."[10]

The next character's name is "Jah-oh-eh"—the earth—and its definition in each of the degrees leads to the unfolding of the Egyptian astronomy, with the fifth degree erupting into a long and elaborate explanation of the whole subject. Jah-oh-eh is developed in the four degrees as follows:[11]

8. *The American Almanac and Repository of Useful Knowledge for the Year 1835* (Boston, 1834), 3.
9. GAEL, 33 (*JSP*, R4:181).
10. GAEL, 24 (*JSP*, R4:163).
11. GAEL, 27, 29–30, 31, 33–34 (*JSP*, R4:169, 173–75, 177, 181–83).

first degree   Jah=oheh: The earth including its affinity with the other planets, with their govering powers: which are fifteen: the earth; the sun, and the moon, first in their affinity; including one power.

second degree   Jahoheh— The earth under the government of another, which is one of the fixed stars; which is called Oliblish.

third degree   Jah-oh-eh The earth under the government of another <or the seconed> of the fixed stars, which is called Enish-go-an=dosh or in other words the power of attraction it has with the earth.

fourth degree   Jah-oh-eh— The earth and power of attra[c]tion it has with the third fixed star, which is called Kai=e ven-rash.

So far, we learn that the earth is in a group of fifteen planets, which includes the earth, sun, and moon—the solar system as it was then understood, which, as one 1829 book on astronomy described it, consisted of "the Sun, eleven primary Planets, and eighteen Moons."[12] This same 1829 source then names the eleven primary planets: "Mercury, Venus, the Earth, Mars, Vesta, Juno, Pallas, Ceres, Jupiter, Saturn, and Uranus."[13]

German-born British astronomer William Herschel had discovered the planet Uranus in 1781, but Neptune and Pluto were not observed until 1846 and 1930. Vesta, Juno, Pallas, and Ceres were counted as planets from 1808 until 1845, but are now considered large asteroids in the main asteroid belt between the orbits of Mars and Jupiter. Thus Smith was referring to the eleven primary planets, the sun and moon, and two yet-to-be-discovered planets. He did not count the other moons. I discuss the significance of classifying the sun as a planet shortly.

These fifteen planets as understood by Abraham and the Egyptians were, according to Smith, governed by three fixed stars:

---

12. Richard Banks, *Astronomy; or, The solar system explained on mechanical principles* ... (London: Simpkin and Marshall, 1829), 19.

13. Ibid.

Oliblish, Enish-go-on-dosh, and Kae-e-van-rash. The elaboration of this system occurs in the fifth degree.

> ⊕ Jah-oh-eh The earth under the governing <powers> of oliblish, Enish go on dosh, and Kai-e van rash, which are the grand ~~governing~~ key or in other words, the governing power, which governs the fifteen fixed stars <(twelve besides themselves)> that ~~belong~~ governs the earth, sun, & moon, (which have their power <in> one,) with the other twelve moving planets of this system. Oliblish=Enish go on dosh, and Kaie ven rash, are the three grand central ~~stars which~~ powers that govern all the other creations, which have been sought out by the most aged of all the fathers, since the begining of the creation, by means of the urim and Thummim …[14]

The Grammar then gives the names of the twelve remaining fixed stars: "The names of the other twelve of the fixed stars are: Kolob, Limdi, Zip, Vurel, Venisti, Waine, Wagah=ox=oan, oansli, Sheble[,] Shineflis, flis, ots."[15] This is followed by the "Egyptian names" for the fifteen moving planets: "The Egyptian names, of the fifteen moving planets are: Oan isis, Flos-isis, flo'ese: Abbesele, Ele ash, Sabble, Slundlo, ear roam, Crash ma Kraw, obbles isim, Izinsbah, missel[,] Nah me,sile[,] ohee oop Zah, Zool."[16]

As we saw in our discussion of Smith's letter to James Arlington Bennett (in chapter four), the Grammar defines Flos-isis as the sun and Flo-ese as the moon. Oan-isis refers to the earth. Previously, Jah-oh-eh was defined in the Grammar as "the earth," but in the Alphabets the earth is named Oan.[17] Oan-isis appears first on the list of the fifteen moving planets, followed by Flos-isis and flo-ese—the sun and moon. As quoted, the earth, sun, and moon are described as a unit when it states that the three governing stars "governs the earth, sun, & moon, (which have their power <in> one,) with the other twelve moving planets of this system."

The pattern of fifteen "fixed stars," consisting of three "grand

---

14. GAEL, 24 (*JSP*, R4:163).
15. Ibid.
16. GAEL, 24–25 (*JSP*, R4:163–65).
17. It should be noted that in Abraham 3:13, the sun is called Shinehah and the moon Olea.

central stars" and twelve "fixed stars," as well as fifteen "moving planets," reflects Smith's recent organization of his church ecclesiastical hierarchy. In February 1834, Smith organized the "standing" high council in Kirtland, Ohio, which included three presidents and twelve high priests. In July 1834, Smith organized another high council to preside over the church in Missouri, again with three presidents and twelve high priests. In February 1835, the Quorum of Twelve Apostles was organized. Described as the "Traveling Presiding High Council" (D&C 102:3; 107:33), the apostles operated under the direction of the three presiding presidents: Joseph Smith, Sidney Rigdon, and Frederick G. Williams.

In October 1835, when Smith was dictating his Egyptian cosmology, the Kirtland temple was under construction and the plans for the first floor included an elaborate system of pulpits at the east and west ends of the building, one group of pulpits for the Melchizedek Priesthood leaders and the other group for the Aaronic Priesthood leaders. At the center of the west end of the interior meeting hall were three ascending levels of three pulpits each, where the presidencies of the various priesthood quorums sat during meetings. Smith and his two counselors were seated at the top. On the right sat the twelve apostles, on the left the twelve Kirtland high counselors. Thus Smith projected his priesthood organization into the organization of the cosmos.

Problematic Chronology

The cosmological scheme outlined in the bound Grammar fits the 1 October 1835 entry in Smith's journal, which states that Smith, Cowdery, and W. W. Phelps were working on the "Egyptian alphabet" when "the system of astronomy was unfolded."[18] For various reasons, John Gee and others have resisted making this obvious connection.

Because Gee wants the translation of Abraham to precede the Alphabets and bound Grammar, he cannot envisage the Grammar project coming to a close in October 1835. This would give validity to the statement in Smith's official history that he began

---

18. Smith, Journal, 1 Oct. 1835 (*JSP*, J1:67).

working on both the Alphabets and bound Grammar in July 1835. Although the statement in Smith's history was probably based on information from Smith and/or Phelps, Gee instead asserts that the 1 October 1835 entry in Smith's journal refers to the beginning of work on the Alphabets and dates the bound Grammar to sometime "between January and April 1836."[19] In proposing these dates in 2017, Gee never mentions the astronomical material in the bound Grammar.

In 2000, Gee argued that the unfolding of the "system of astronomy" mentioned in Smith's journal refers to the "explanation" of Facsimile 2 that was published in the *Times and Seasons* in 1842.[20] However, the only manuscript that contains such an explanation is in Willard Richards's handwriting and dates to 1842 in connection with the woodcut of Facsimile 2 published in the 15 March 1842 issue of the *Times and Seasons*.[21] Gee's argument proposes yet another missing text, whereas the more likely explanation is that Smith drew on the astronomical material in the bound Grammar when dictated his explanations of the woodcut.

In the same 2000 essay, Gee contends that the phrase in Smith's journal entry "labored on the Egyptian Alphabet" cannot refer to the bound Grammar because the bound Grammar bears a different title—"Grammar and Alphabet of the Egyptian Language." Thus, Gee writes, Smith's journal must refer to the three Alphabets.[22] Consequently, because the Alphabets do not deal with Egyptian astronomy, Gee argues that the part of the passage in the journal that mentions working on the Alphabet is unrelated to astronomy. Instead, Gee believes that either Smith's translation had reached Abraham 3 or Smith had interpreted Facsimile 2 in

19. Gee, *Introduction to the Book of Abraham*, 32.

20. John Gee, "Eyewitness, Hearsay, and Physical Evidence of the Joseph Smith Papyri," in *The Disciple as Witness: Essays on Latter-day Saint History and Doctrine in Honor of Richard Lloyd Anderson*, ed. Stephen D. Ricks, Donald W. Parry, and Andrew H. Hedges (Provo, Utah: Foundation for Ancient Research and Mormon Studies, 2000), 201.

21. Explanation of Facsimile 2, ca. 15 Mar. 1842 (*JSP*, R4:276–83); "A Fac-simile from the Book of Abraham, No. 2," *Times and Seasons* 3 (15 Mar. 1842): between pp. 719 and 721.

22. Gee, "Eyewitness, Hearsay, and Physical Evidence of the Joseph Smith Papyri." 201.

early October 1835, both of which are contradicted by the documentary evidence. The evidence clearly shows that in 1835 Smith's ideas about ancient astronomy were associated with his interpretation of characters taken from column 3 of Hôr's Breathing Permit (JSP I), not his translation of the characters from JSP XI or the hypocephalus.

Gee's argument that Cowdery's use of the term "Egyptian Alphabet" necessarily excludes the bound Grammar is faulty. There is no reason Cowdery could not have referred to the bound Grammar as an Alphabet. After all, the document was titled "Grammar and A[l]phabet of the Egyptian Language," because, unlike the three Alphabets, it included three brief lectures on grammar. However, the bulk of the Grammar was, in fact, an expansion of the Alphabets. At the top of page 9, at the beginning of the fourth degree in the first part, the page heading reads: "Egyptian Alphabet fourth degree." The same type of heading appears on pages 13, 15, 20, and 33. The top of page 33 reads: "Second part of the Alphabet 1s[t] Degree." In fact, none of the headings mention the title "Grammar." At some point, a label was added to the book's spine containing the words "Egyptian Alphabet." Because the system of astronomy occurs in the Alphabet part of the book, Cowdery would naturally and appropriately have referred to it as an "Egyptian Alphabet."

Gee also argues that the "Egyptian Alphabet" mentioned in the 1 October 1835 journal entry cannot refer to the bound Grammar because the latter contains the handwriting of Warren Parrish, who was not hired as Smith's scribe until the end of October. However, Parrish's handwriting does not appear until the end of the volume, occupying only the definitions for Kolob and three of the five degrees for the previous character, named Veh-Kli-flos-isis. The "system of astronomy was unfolded" several characters before Parrish's handwriting starts and is recorded in Phelps's handwriting.

The only reason anyone would have for not dating the astronomy portion of the bound Grammar to early October 1835 is to defend a dating of January–April 1836, which has no documentary evidence and contradicts Smith's official history.

Translation "Recommenced"

On 7 October 1835, Frederick G. Williams made an entry in Smith's journal stating that the Mormon prophet had "recommenced translating the ancient records."[23] Gee and Brian Hauglid suggest that this is when Williams made his "copy" of the translation manuscript covering Abraham 1:4–2:6.[24] But this is doubtful since, as discussed in chapter one, evidence shows that Warren Parrish and Williams wrote simultaneously from Smith's dictation and Parrish would not become Smith's scribe until end of October. By "recommenced," Williams means since 1 October, when the system of Egyptian astronomy began to be unfolded. Contrary to Gee and Hauglid, the Alphabets and Grammar were also considered translations. As Smith's history states, during the latter part of July 1835, Smith was "continually engaged in translating an alphabet to the Book of Abraham."[25] Thus the entry in Smith's journal refers, at a minimum, to character 37 as representing the earth, which contains most of the details of the ancient system of astronomy.

Continuing, there is nothing surprising in the Grammar's definitions of character 38—the moon—only that it is the "lesser light" and that it passes between the earth and sun "forming an eclipse." The definitions for character 39—Flos isis, or the sun—are not typical because the sun, while "the King of the day," is also a "central moving planet, from which, those other gove[rn]ing moving planets receive their light."[26]

In referring to the sun as both *central* and *moving* as well as a *planet*, Smith reflected the belief in his day, especially among theologians of nature, that the solar system is part of a larger system that moves around other systems, which in turn move around the throne of God. Commenting on the phrase "heaven of heavens" in Deuteronomy 10:14, Bible commentator Adam Clarke wrote that

---

23. Smith, Journal, 7 Oct. 1835 (*JSP*, J1:71). Frederick G. Williams's handwriting appears in Joseph Smith's journal for 3–7 Oct. 1835.

24. Gee, *Introduction to the Book of Abraham*, 17; Brian M. Hauglid, *A Textual History of the Book of Abraham: Manuscripts and Editions* (Provo, Utah: Neal A. Maxwell Institute for Religious Scholarship, Brigham Young University, 2010), 215.

25. JS History, vol. B-1, 597 (DHC 2:238).

26. GAEL, 34 (*JSP*, R4:183).

"the words were probably intended to point out the immensity of God's creation, in which we may readily conceive one system of heavenly bodies, and others beyond them, and others still in endless progression through the whole vortex of space, every *star* in the vast abyss of nature being *a sun*, with its peculiar and numerous attendant worlds! Thus there may be systems of systems in endless gradation up to the throne of God."[27] In *Philosophy of a Future State,* first published in Philadelphia in 1825, Thomas Dick commented on the phrase "throne of God":

> It is now considered by astronomers, as highly probable, if not certain, from late observations, from the nature of gravitation, and other circumstances, that all the systems of the universe revolve round one common centre,—and that this centre may bear as great a proportion, in point of magnitude, to the universal assemblage of systems, as the sun does to his surrounding planets. And, since our sun is five hundred times larger than the earth, and all the other planets and their satellites taken together; on the same scale, such a central body would be five hundred times larger than all the systems and worlds in the universe. Here, then, may be a vast universe of itself; an example of material creation, exceeding all the rest in magnitude and splendour, and in which are blended the glories of every other system. If this is in reality the case, it may, with the most emphatic propriety, be termed, *The Throne of God.* ... This grand central body may be considered as the *Capital* of the universe.[28]

Smith's definition of Flos-isis moves beyond the sun to include in the fourth degree "the high[es]t degree of light," which illuminates "the face of Millions of planets."[29] This is elaborated in the fifth degree to describe a grand center of light:

> Flos isis– The highest degree of light, because its component parts are light. The gover[n]ing principle of light Because God has said Let this be the centre for light, and let there be

---

27. Adam Clarke, *The Holy Bible ... With a Commentary and Critical Notes,* vol. 1 (New York: N. Bangs and J. Emory, for the Methodist Episcopal Church, 1825), 733–34; s.v. Deut. 10:14.

28. Thomas Dick, *Philosophy of a Future State* (New York: R. Schoyer, 1831), 224–25. Dick's book was discussed at length by Oliver Cowdery in the *Messenger and Advocate* in November 1836 (*LDS Messenger and Advocate* 3 [Nov. 1836]: 423).

29. GAEL, 28 (*JSP,* R4:171).

bounds that it may not pass. He hath set a cloud round about in the heavens, and the light of the grand govering or <15> fixed stars centre there; and from there its is drawn, by the heavenly bodies according to their portions; according to the decrees that God hath set, as the bounds of the ocean, that it should not pass over as a flood, so God has set the bounds of light lest it pass over and consume the planets.[30]

Smith believed that the sun was in an orbit around this grand light center, which explains why he described it, the sun, as both a central and moving planet. Indeed, as mentioned, he included the name of the sun—Flos-isis—among the fifteen moving planets. In referring to the sun as a planet, Smith reflected the belief among contemporaries that all the planets were inhabited worlds, including the sun. Astronomer William Herschel was one of the first scientists to receive popular notice for his ideas about the inhabitants of the sun and moon. As one scholar summarized, Herschel "thought it [was] possible that there was a region below the Sun's fiery surface where men might live, and he regarded the existence of life on the Moon as 'an absolute certainty.'"[31] The Reverend J. L. Blake's *First Book in Astronomy, Adapted to the Use of Common Schools*, which went through many editions, included a discussion about the sun in 1831:

[The sun] was formerly supposed to consist of liquid fire. ... By modern astronomers this theory has been found untrue. They have supposed, with more plausibility, that it is a solid body, surrounded by a luminous atmosphere. ... The similarity of the sun to the other globes of the system, in solidity, atmosphere, surface diversified with mountains and vallies, and rotation on its axis, lead us to conjecture that it is inhabited, like the rest of the planets, by beings whose organs are adapted to their peculiar circumstances. Dr. Elliot, an English astronomer, allows his imagination, in speaking of it, to depict the most

---

30. GAEL, 25 (*JSP*, R4:165).

31. Patrick Moore, *New Guide to the Moon* (New York: W. W. Norton & Co., 1976), 128. See also Steven Kawaler and J. Veverka, "The Habitable Sun: One of William Herschel's Stranger Ideas," *Journal of the Royal Astronomical Society of Canada* 75 (Jan. 1981): 46–55; and Simon Schaffer, "'The Great Laboratories of the Universe': William Herschel on Matter Theory and Planetary Life," *Journal for the History of Astronomy* 11 (June 1980): 81–111.

delightful rural scenery, with purling brooks, meandering streams, and rolling oceans, and with all the vicissitudes of foul and fair weather. And as the light of the sun is eternal, so he imagined, were its seasons. Hence, the Doctor infers, that this luminary offers one of the most blissful habitations which the mind of man is capable of conceiving.[32]

A revelation Smith dictated in 1832 declares poetically of God's creation: "The earth rolls upon her wings, and the sun giveth his light by day, and the moon giveth her light by night, and the stars also give their light, as they roll upon their wings in their glory, in the midst of the power of God" (D&C 88:45). The revelation then queries: "Unto what shall I [God] liken *these kingdoms*, that ye may understand?" (v. 46; emphasis added). The answer is given in the form of a parable in which a farmer visits his servants one at a time working in different areas of a field and concludes, "unto this parable I will liken all *these kingdoms* [i.e., earth, sun, moon, stars], and *the inhabitants thereof*" (vv. 51–57, 60–61; emphasis added). The parable implies that the earth, sun, moon, and stars are inhabited, which is precisely what early Mormons understood. Smith's older brother, Hyrum, alluded to this revelation when he declared in Nauvoo, Illinois, in 1843 that "*every* Star that we see is a world and is inhabited the same as this world is peopled. The Sun & Moon is inhabited & the Stars ... are inhabited the same as this Earth. ... They are under the same order as this Earth."[33]

Returning to the bound Grammar, characters 40 and 41—Kli-flos-isis and Veh-Kli-flos-isis—are measurements of time dealing with the twelve fixed stars. Three of the degrees for Veh-Kli-flos-isis as well as all five degrees of the last character, Kolob—numbers 41 and 42—are in the handwriting of Warren Parrish, whom, as mentioned, Smith hired as a scribe on 29 October 1835.[34] Smith saved what may be the best for last, for in the fifth degree:

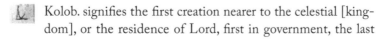 Kolob. signifies the first creation nearer to the celestial [king-dom], or the residence of Lord, first in government, the last

32. J[ohn]. L. Blake, *First Book in Astronomy, Adapted to the Use of Common Schools* (Boston: Lincoln and Edmands, 1831), 16, 17–18.

33. Eugene England, ed., "George Laub's Nauvoo Journal," *Brigham Young University Studies* 18 (Winter 1978): 177.

34. Smith, Journal, 29 Oct. 1835 (*JSP*, J1:76).

> pertaining to the measurement of time, the measurement ac-
> cording ~~according~~ to celestial time which signifies, one day to
> a cubit which day is equal to a thousand years according to the
> measurement of this Eearth or Jah=oh=eh[35]

The length of Kolob's revolution reminds one of Thomas Dick's speculations about the enormity of the throne of God and the vastness of the system in orbit around it. However, the slowness of Kolob's revolution conflicts with definitions Smith previously dictated in early October 1835 where Kolob is one of twelve fixed stars under the rule of the three grand ruling stars and is described as "swifter than the rest of the twelve <fixed stars;>; going before, being first in motion."[36]

In the first degree, we are told "Kolob ... signifies the first great grand governing fixed Star which is the fartherest that ever has been discovered by the fathers which was discovered by Methu-selar and also by Abraham."[37] In the second degree, "Kolob ... signfies the wonder of Abraham the eldest of all the stars, the greatest body of the heavenly bodies that ever was discovered by man."[38] This reminds one of what Josephus wrote about the de-scendants of Adam's son Seth being "the inventors of that peculiar sort of wisdom which is concerned with the heavenly bodies, and their order."[39] Recall, too, that Abraham "communicated" to the Egyptians "the science of astronomy."[40] Later, in Nauvoo in 1842, when Smith dictated Chapter 3 of the Book of Abraham (vv. 1–4), he drew on this language in the Grammar:

> And I, Abraham, had the Urim and Thummim, which the Lord
> my God had given unto me, in Ur of the Chaldees, and I saw the stars,
> that they were very great, and that one of them was nearest the throne
> of God; and there were many great ones which were near unto it; And
> the Lord said unto me: These are the governing ones; and the name

---

35. GAEL, 26 (*JSP*, R4:167).

36. GAEL, 25 (*JSP*, R4:165).

37. GAEL, 34 (*JSP*, R4:183).

38. GAEL, 32 (*JSP*, R4:179).

39. *Antiquities of the Jews,* Book 1, chap. 2, sec. 3 (Whiston, *Josephus Complete Works,* 27).

40. *Antiquities of the Jews,* Book 1, chap. 8, sec. 2 (Whiston, *Josephus Complete Works,* 33).

of the great one is Kolob, because it is near unto me ... I have set this one to govern all those which belong to the same order as that upon which thou standest.

And the Lord said unto me, by the Urim and Thummim, that Kolob was after the manner of the Lord, according to its times and seasons in the revolutions thereof; that one revolution was a day unto the Lord, after the manner of reckoning, it being one thousand years according to the time appointed unto that whereon thou standest.

When Smith published this account in March 1842, he included explanations of Facsimile 2, which also dealt with astronomy and were also inspired by the bound Grammar.

A Geocentric Cosmology?

Several Mormon scholars have argued that Abraham describes an earth-centered universe as would be expected of an ancient record, not a sun-centered solar system as assumed by Smith and his contemporaries. However, since Abraham relied on revelation through the Urim and Thummim, one might reasonably expect that his views would surpass those of his contemporaries and even those of Smith. In 2005, Gee, together with William Hamblin and Daniel Peterson, asserted: "If Joseph Smith is to be considered the author of the Book of Abraham under the influences of the astronomical speculations of his day, we would expect to see a heliocentric worldview espoused in the text. ... A careful reading of the Book of Abraham, however, shows that the text is describing a geocentric system."[41]

Of course, this assumes that Smith was unaware that heliocentrism (sun-centered) was a relatively new discovery. Nevertheless, the authors briefly describe four ancient versions of the geocentric (earth-centered) model. However, the model they use to interpret Abraham Chapter 3 requires the earth to be spherical with the sun, moon, and planets revolving in concentric circles around it, a model that, in fact, dates many centuries after Abraham. Indeed, all (but one) of the authors' examples range from the third

---

41. John Gee, William J. Hamblin, and Daniel C. Peterson, "'And I Saw the Stars': The Book of Abraham and Ancient Geocentric Astronomy," in *Astronomy, Papyrus, and Covenant*, eds. John Gee and Brian M. Hauglid (Provo, Utah: FARMS, 2005), 7.

century BCE (Greek philosophers) to fourteenth-century-CE Italy (Dante).[42]

The first version, they explain, has a single expanse of heaven, above the earth, which is occupied by the various luminaries; the second also has a single expanse of heaven but the stars and planets are arranged hierarchically; the third has multiple levels of heaven as well as a hierarchy of stars and planets; and the fourth has the planets arranged in concentric circles around the earth. Three versions describe the cosmos from the perspective of a flat earth, while the fourth organizes its cosmology around a spherical earth with planets revolving in concentric circles around it. They suggest that Abraham most likely reflects the third model—a layered heaven above a flat earth—but urge more research to "determine exactly which form of geocentrism best matches the Book of Abraham." This incompleteness allows them both to glide between versions and to conflate versions, as when they do not distinguish between a layered heaven and one with multiple planets in concentric orbits around the earth.

In discussing the *Apocalypse of Abraham*, a late first- or early-second-century CE pseudepigraphic work, Gee et al. claim that its description of "the earth at the center of the universe, with a series of concentric spheres culminating in the sphere of the stars … is … exactly as described in the Book of Abraham."[43] In fact, it is not. Layers of seven heavens, with the "hosts of stars" in the fifth firmament, spirit angels in the sixth, fiery angels in the seventh, and God

---

42. The exception is the Egyptian belief that the earth, personified by the god Geb, and sky, personified by the goddess Nut, are separated by Shu, god of air. While Gee et al. state that this concept of the cosmos "goes back at least as far as the Middle Kingdom (and thus to the approximate time of Abraham)," they do not explain that in the Egyptian cosmos the earth is flat and instead emphasize an Egyptian text which says the "Sun-disk encircles, that which Geb and Nut enclose" (Gee et al., "'And I Saw the Stars,'" 7). Thus they imply that Egyptians believed the sun revolved around the earth. In their description of the first of the four types of geocentricity, they state that the "sun, moon, stars, planets, etc.—surrounded and encompassed the earth in a single undifferentiated heaven" (ibid., 5). In the footnote they reference the "view of the heavens from the tomb of Seti I," which clearly shows the earth as flat with the heavens over it. The ancient Egyptians believed the sun (Ra) traveled on a barge through the underworld at night to emerge in the east the next morning, and not that the sun revolved around the earth.

43. Gee et al., "'And I Saw the Stars,'" 9.

in the eighth, is not what Abraham describes. Nothing is said in the *Apocalypse* about "concentric spheres," and stars are not arranged one above another in revolutions around the earth. Moreover, as one historian of ancient cosmology concludes, "There is no clear indication in the early Jewish and Christian apocalyptic writings that there is any connection between the seven heavens and the seven planets. ... The motif of seven heavens was probably borrowed from Babylonian tradition by Jewish apocalyptic writers."[44]

In 2017, Gee reproduced a depiction of a geocentric system by a sixteenth-century Portuguese cosmographer, not a depiction of what Bible scholars have generally depicted for the Old Testament. As mentioned, the concept of a spherical earth did not exist at the time of Abraham. Philosophers in sixth century BCE Greece are credited with the discovery of a spherical earth, although it would not become generally accepted until it was confirmed by Hellenistic astronomers 300 years later.

Again, in 2017, Gee quoted Abraham 3:4, which states that Kolob "was after the manner of the Lord, according to its times and seasons in the revolutions thereof," applied it to all the planets except the earth, and then stated, "These lights revolve around something," meaning the earth.[45] Gee has imposed a geocentric model onto the Abraham text, when the text itself says nothing about the revolutions of the planets or a central and motionless earth. The text only implies a measurement of time based on revolutions, but says nothing to exclude the earth from the same measurement or that its times and seasons, days or years, are measured differently.

In 2005, Gee, Hamblin, and Peterson also argued that the case for geocentricity is clear because there are "frequent references to a hierarchy of celestial bodies, each one higher than the preceding and all above the earth."[46] In other words, each succeeding planet is slower than the previous because its revolution around the earth is larger. As Gee stated in 2017, "The greater amount of time is

44. Adela Yarbro Collins, *Cosmology and Eschatology in Jewish and Christian Apocalypticism*, in *Supplements to the Journal for the Study of Judaism* (Leiden, Boston, Koln: Brill, 1 Nov. 1996), 53, 54.

45. Gee, *Introduction to the Book of Abraham*, 116.

46. Gee et al., "And I Saw the Stars," 7.

associated with a higher orbit. ... The higher orbits are larger and take more time to traverse; thus, the longer the time of revolution, the higher the light [or planet] is above the earth."[47] None of this scheme is stated explicitly in Abraham.

While this hierarchy is established by the slowness of movement and the text places "one planet above another" (Abr. 3:9), there is no reason to conclude that "above" means that each succeeding planet is slower than the preceding one because its orbit is longer. Rather, "above" refers to a planet's placement in the time hierarchy without reference to its position in a single system relative to a central earth. Indeed, the repeated hypothetical reasoning implies a random distribution. Abraham 3:8, for example, states: "And where these two facts exist, there shall be another fact above them, that is, there shall be another planet whose reckoning of time shall be longer still." Abraham 3:17 repeats this principle: "Now, if there be two things, one above the other, and the moon be above the earth, then it may be that a planet or a star may exist above it"—that is, somewhere in the universe, not the next planet in orbit around the earth. If a planet's position in the hierarchy is determined by the slowness of its revolutionary movement, then the text necessarily implies that the earth moves, contrary to a geocentric model, because it is positioned below the slower-moving moon in the time hierarchy (Abr. 3:5).

The randomness of the hypothetical is mirrored when Abraham parallels the hierarchy of planets with that of spirits: "Howbeit that he [God] made the greater star, as, also, if there be two spirits, and one shall be more intelligent than the other ... there shall be another more intelligent than they: I am the Lord thy God, I am more intelligent than they all" (Abr. 3:18, 19). In my opinion, Gee, Hamblin, and Peterson read too much into this hypothetical language.

While the authors restrict their analysis of Abrahamic cosmology to the text of Abraham, Smith provided more details in his Egyptian Grammar. Gee et al. note that the concept of Kae-e-vanrash governing fifteen "fixed planets or stars" mentioned in the English explanation of Facsimile 2 is "problematic from the

---

47. Gee, *Introduction to the Book of Abraham*, 116.

view of ancient and modern astronomy."[48] They conclude that "this seeming problem derives from Joseph Smith's modern interpretations, not from the ancient text of the Book of Abraham."[49] True, Smith and many of his contemporaries saw the stars as inhabited planets. However, Smith drew on the bound Grammar for his explanations of Facsimile 2, and the Grammar is said to be a translation of characters from column 3 of Hôr's Book of Breathings—the source of the Book of Abraham. The Grammar is the earliest text containing the unfolding of the "system of astronomy" mentioned in Smith's journal entry for 1 October 1835 and therefore provides a more complete interpretive context for understanding Abraham's cosmology. Unfortunately, because Gee et al. dismiss the bound Grammar as the work of Phelps, their analysis of Abrahamic cosmology is incomplete.

Gee et al. argue that Abraham 3:13, which defines Kokaubeam as "stars, or all the great lights, which are in the firmament of heaven," implies that the planets are stars and therefore it is "consistent with most ancient systems of astronomy, where the planets were seen as ... 'wandering stars.'"[50] However, it is not inconsistent with the general practice in Smith's day to describe the heavens as consisting of sun, moon, and stars, without specifically mentioning planets.[51] Thus, while a revelation Smith dictated in December 1832 mentions that "all things ... moove in there times, and there seasons," including "the earth, and all the planets," there is no mention of planets when it declares, "the Earth rolls upon her wings, and the sun giveth her light by day, and the moon giveth her light by night, and the stars also giveth there light as they roll upon, there wings, in there glory in the midst, of the power, of God."[52] One may therefore argue that planets are not mentioned in Abraham 3:13 because Smith did not consider them "great lights."

In a footnote, Gee et al. quote from figure 5 of Facsimile 2, which names "Enish-go-on-dosh ... one of the governing planets ... said

---

48. Gee et al., "'And I Saw the Stars,'" 11n41.
49. Ibid.
50. Ibid., 11.
51. See D&C 29:14; 34:9; 45:42; 88:45, 87; 121:87; 128:23; 133:49.
52. Revelation, [Kirtland Township, OH], 27–[28] Dec. 1833 [D&C 88:43, 45], Revelation Book 2, pp. 37–38 (*JSP*, D2:339).

by the Egyptians to be the Sun" and "Kae-e-vanrash … which governs fifteen other fixed planets or stars," as further "examples of the imprecise use of astronomical terminology."[53] However, a key difference between Smith and the ancients is that while the ancients saw everything, excluding the earth, sun, and moon, as stars, Smith and his contemporaries saw everything, including the sun, moon, and stars, as inhabited planets. Hence, Abraham 3:5 describes the moon as a planet, and figure 5 of Facsimile 2 refers to the sun and stars as planets.

In another footnote, Gee et al. observe that figure 5 of Facsimile 2 describes the sun as a moving planet, which they state "does not fit with nineteenth-century ideas but which perfectly matches geocentric thought."[54] However, these authors have both overlooked the ideas of nineteenth-century natural theologians like Thomas Dick and failed to consider the context of the sun's movement in Facsimile 2, which states that "the Moon, the Earth and the Sun" have "annual revolutions,"[55] which is inconsistent with their geocentric models. Joseph Smith took this statement from the bound Grammar, where in the fifth degree the word Flo-ees signifies "The moon, the earth and the sun in their annual revolutions."[56]

In the fourth degree, Flo-ees represents "The moon in its revolutions with earth, showing or signifying the earth going between, thereby forming an eclipse."[57] Here the earth moves into a position between the sun and moon causing a lunar eclipse, which eliminates any geocentric model requiring a flat earth like their example from the Middle Kingdom in ancient Egypt.

In the bound Grammar, Flos-isis—the sun—is said in the second degree to be "the central moving planet, from which the other governing moving planets receive their light—having a less motion—slow in its motion."[58] Obviously a central sun and a moving earth do not support a geocentric model. Yet the sun is also said to

---

53. Gee et al., "'And I Saw the Stars,'" 11n41.

54. Ibid., 11n43.

55. "Kae-e-vanrash … which governs fifteen other fixed planets or stars, as also Floeese or the Moon, the Earth and the Sun in their annual revolutions" (Fac. 2, fig. 5).

56. GAEL, 25 (*JSP*, R4:165).

57. GAEL, 27 (*JSP*, R4:171).

58. GAEL, 32 (*JSP*, R4:179).

be moving slowly around something, which is consistent with the model of the cosmos proposed by Dick and other natural theologians in Smith's day.

In the Grammar, Kolob is described as one of the fifteen fixed stars or planets, and in the Book of Abraham, figure 5 of Facsimile 2, it is also described as having a revolution. Abraham 3:4 states that "Kolob was after the manner of the Lord, according to its times and seasons in the revolutions thereof." The ancient model cannot account for Kolob being described both as a fixed star or planet and as moving in revolutions. The only explanation is that Kolob is at the center of a system which is at the same time revolving around the throne of God, much as natural theologians of Smith's day speculated. For example, Dick noted that it had recently been discovered that

> the principal fixed stars have a certain apparent motion, which is nearly uniform and regular. ... The stars in the northern quarter of the heavens seem to widen their relative positions, while those in the southern appear to contract their distances. These motions seem evidently to indicate, that the earth, and all the other bodies of the solar system, are moving in a direction from the stars, in the southern part of the sky, toward those in the northern. Dr. Herschel thinks, that a comparison of the changes now alluded to, indicates a motion of our sun with his attending planets towards the constellation *Hercules*. This progressive movement which our system makes in absolute space, is justly supposed to be a portion of that curve, which the sun describes [revolves] around the *centre* of that *nebula* to which he belongs; and, that all the other stars belonging to the same nebula, describe [mark out] similar curves. And since the universe appears to be composed of thousands of *nebulae*, or starry systems, detached from each other, it is reasonable to conclude, that all the starry systems of the universe revolve round one common centre, whose bulk and attractive influence are proportionable to the size and the number of the bodies which perform their revolutions around it.[59]

This model of the cosmos—which Adam Clarke called "systems of systems"—provides the best framework for interpreting Smith's explanation of Abrahamic cosmology circa October 1835.

---

59. Dick, *Philosophy of a Future State*, 225–26.

Later, when dictating chapter 3 of the Book of Abraham in 1842, Smith simplified the model for the purposes of making an analogy between the hierarchy of planets and the hierarchy of pre-mortal spirits. At the same time, he also drew on the bound Grammar for his explanations of Facsimile 2, suggesting that he may have viewed the Grammar's contents as inspired.

Dictating Abraham 1:4–2:18
(19–25 November 1835)

To this point in Smith's work on the Egyptian papyri, only a rough draft of the first three verses of the Book of Abraham existed, which Phelps had recorded in the translation book, from which the pages were subsequently removed. Two entries in Smith's journal for 19 and 20 November 1835 in the handwriting of Warren Parrish mark the probable time when Parrish and Frederick G. Williams served together as scribes for Smith's dictation of Abraham 1:4–2:2. The entry for 19 November states that Smith "went in company with Doct. [Frederick G.] Williams & my scribe [Warren Parrish] to see how the workmen prospered in finishing the house [of the Lord]," and that "I returned home and spent the day in translating the Egyptian records."[60] On the following day, Parrish records in the same journal that "[Smith] spent the day in translating, and made rapid progress"[61] As mentioned, this is likely one of the times that Parrish referred to when he later reported in 1838: "I have set by his [Smith's] side and penned down the translation of the Egyptian Hieroglyphicks as he claimed to receive it by direct inspiration of heaven."[62]

As discussed in chapter one, in Parrish's absence, Williams recorded an additional paragraph: Abraham 2:3–6. Very soon afterwards, Parrish copied his and Williams's transcriptions into the translation book, following Phelps's entry. After this, Parrish began writing from Smith's dictation directly into the translation book, which dictation brought the text to Abraham 2:18. This

---

60. Smith, Journal, 19 Nov. 1835 (*JSP*, J1:107).
61. Smith, Journal, 20 Nov. 1835 (*JSP*, J1:107).
62. Warren Parrish, Letter, Kirtland, Ohio, to the editor of the *Painesville Republican*, Painesville, Ohio, 5 Feb. 1838. *Painesville Republican*, 15 Feb. 1838.

likely took place on 24 and 25 November when Parrish recorded in Smith's journal (on the 24th): "in the after-noon, we translated some of the Egyptian, records"; and (on the 25th): "spent the day in Translating."[63]

TIMELINE FOR DICTATING BOOK OF ABRAHAM, KIRTLAND, OHIO, 1835

Date	Joseph Smith's journal	Scribe(s)	Text
ca. July		Phelps	Abr. 1:1–3
19 Nov.	"I returned home and spent the day in translating the Egyptian records"	Parrish Williams	Abr. 1:4–2:2
20 Nov.	"spent the day in translating, and made rapid progress"	Parrish Williams	Abr. 1:4–2:2
20 Nov.		Williams	Abr. 2:3–6
24 Nov.	"in the after-noon, we translated some of the Egyptian, records"	Parrish	Abr. 2:7–18
25 Nov.	"spent the day in Translating"	Parrish	Abr. 2:7–18

"Transcribing Egyptian Characters"

On 26 November, Parrish wrote the last entry in Smith's journal to mention work on the Egyptian materials until 1842: "we spent the day in transcribing Egyptian characters from the papyrus."[64] Brian Hauglid and others have suggested that the "transcribing" of Egyptian characters refers to the addition of characters in the margins of the three Kirtland translation manuscripts.[65] However, assigning a single day for adding the characters to all three documents is not feasible. The fact that two characters were misaligned in the translation book and had to be scrape-erased and repositioned up a few lines suggests that the characters in this instance were copied before the English text. This implies that the characters were already on the other two documents or, at least, on Parrish's shorter document, which ended with a character without any English text next to it, suggesting that the characters in that document were written as the dictation proceeded.

---

63. Smith, Journal, 24–25 Nov. 1835 (*JSP*, J1:109, 110).
64. Smith, Journal, 26 Nov. 1835 (*JSP*, J1:110–11).
65. Hauglid, *Textual History of the Book of Abraham*, 216n21.

On the other hand, Gee has speculated that this day could have been spent copying characters into one or both of the valuable discovery notebooks or on one of the single sheets bearing copies from the damaged Book of the Dead or hypocephalus.[66] However, the notebooks definitely pre-date the Alphabets, and the Alphabets were begun in July 1835, but it is possible that the last page of Phelps's notebook, which differs in style significantly from the preceding pages, was added at this time, and any of the loose sheets containing hieratic texts could, in fact, date to this time.[67]

Translation Interrupted

On the same day that Smith, Parrish, and possibly others spent "transcribing Egyptian characters from the papyrus," Smith complained that he was "severely afflicted with a cold."[68] On the next day, both Smith and Parrish were sick, and they blessed one another.[69] On the 28 November, Smith said that he was "considerably recovered from my cold, & I think I shall be able in a few days to translate again, with the blessing of God."[70] However, although Smith called the west room on the third story of the Kirtland temple his "translating room,"[71] there is no evidence documenting any translation during the remainder of Smith's residence in Kirtland (through January 1838).

Conclusion

On 1 October 1835, after a break of about two months, Smith resumed work on his "Egyptian alphabet." At this time, according to an entry in Smith's journal, "The system of astronomy was unfolded."[72] This refers to the last seven characters (numbers

---

66. Gee, *Introduction to the Book of Abraham*, 18, where Gee states that the "Valuable Discovery" notebooks and two sheets of copied of Egyptian characters "all fit this description, but which (if any of them) were written on this day is unknown."

67. See Notebook of Copied Egyptian Characters, ca. early July 1835, p. 3 (*JSP*, R4:336–37). For the loose sheets of hieratic texts, see Copies of Egyptian Characters, ca. summer 1835-A and -B; and Copy of Hypocephalus, between ca. July 1835 and ca. March 1842 (*JSP*, R4:44–47, 50–51).

68. Smith, Journal, 26 Nov. 1835 (*JSP*, J1:110–11).

69. Smith, Journal, 27 Nov. 1835 (*JSP*, J1:111).

70. Smith, Journal, 28 Nov. 1835 (*JSP*, J1:112).

71. Smith, Journal, 31 Dec. 1835 (*JSP*, J1:140).

72. Smith, Journal, 1 Oct. 1835, CHL (*JSP*, J1:67).

36–42) in the bound Grammar, which describe a hierarchy of stars and planets. There is no evidence to support the suggestion that Smith's journal refers to Abraham 3 or Facsimile 2, both of which date to 1842, according to our best evidence. In chapter six, I present evidence of Hebrew influence in both Abraham 3 and Facsimile 2, which necessarily dates them to after Smith's Hebrew lessons in early 1836.

There can be little doubt that Smith—like Oliver Cowdery—was aware that ancient Jewish historian Josephus credited Abraham with teaching the Egyptians astronomy. So it is no surprise that Smith would include a discussion of astronomy in his account of Abraham in Egypt. Unlike Josephus, Smith's Abraham learned astronomy, not from the Babylonian astronomers, but from God through an instrument that operated much like Smith's seer stone (with which he had formerly scryed for buried treasure and lost objects). The cosmology Smith ascribed to Abraham—with sets of twelve moving planets and twelve fixed stars, each governed by three ruling stars or planets—reflects Smith's recent organization of his church's ecclesiastical hierarchy into a high council, with three presidents and twelve high priests, as well as the Quorum of Twelve Apostles, which operated under the direction of Smith and his two counselors in the presidency.

In addition, Smith's cosmology also comported, not with ancient Earth-centered models, but with early nineteenth-century understandings of the universe. While several LDS scholars have argued that Abraham 3 describes a geocentric universe, their arguments are incomplete and not supported by the evidence. Because the bound Grammar is the earliest text containing the unfolding of the "system of astronomy" mentioned in Smith's journal, it provides a more complete interpretive context for understanding Abraham 3. Flo-ees, in the fourth degree, describes a lunar eclipse, eliminating any geocentric model requiring a flat earth; and Flos-isis, the sun, is defined as a "central moving planet," which gives light to the other planets. Smith's 1842 explanation of Facsimile 2, which drew on the bound Grammar, also states that the earth, along with the sun and moon, has "annual revolutions." Finally, Abraham 3:5, also dictated in 1842, implies the earth moves when it places the earth in the planetary hierarchy below the slower-moving moon. While a central sun and a moving earth do not support a geocentric model, the description of the sun as a central and moving planet is consistent with the model of a multi-system cosmos proposed by Thomas Dick and other natural theologians in Smith's day.

6   A Student of Hebrew

On 26 January 1836, Joshua Seixas, a Sephardic-Jewish scholar from nearby Western Reserve College, began teaching Hebrew to Joseph Smith and other Mormons in Kirtland, Ohio, using his own textbook, for what was intended as a six-week curriculum (fig. 6.1).[1] Interest in Kirtland was high, and Seixas stayed on to teach additional classes. For eight of the next nine weeks, Smith and about 80–120 students received lessons from Seixas. Classes met every day, except Sunday, on the third floor of the unfinished House of the Lord or temple.

Following lessons in grammar, Seixas had his classes begin translating portions of the Hebrew Bible during the third week, which included passages from Genesis 1 on the Creation. On 15 February 1836, Smith's journal records "on this day we commenced translating the Hebrew-language, under the instruction of professor Seixas, and he acknowledg's that we are the most forward of any class he ever taught, the same length of time."[2]

Smith proved to be a good student of Hebrew, for he and nine others were selected by Seixas to receive additional instruction.[3] After attending Hebrew school on 17 February 1836, Smith recorded in his journal, "My soul delights in reading the word of the Lord in the original, and I am determined to persue the study of

---

1. See Joshua Seixas, *A Manual Hebrew Grammar for the Use of Beginners* (2nd ed.; Andover, Massachusetts: Gould and Newman, 1834), iv. On Smith as a student of Hebrew, see Matthew J. Grey, "'The Word of the Lord in the Original': Joseph Smith's Study of Hebrew in Kirtland," in *Approaching Antiquity: Joseph Smith and the Ancient World*, ed. Lincoln H. Blumell, Matthew J. Grey, and Andrew H. Hedges (Provo, Utah: Religious Studies Center/Salt Lake City: Deseret Book Co., 2015), 249–302.

2. Joseph Smith, Journal, 15 Feb. 1836, Joseph Smith Collection, CHL (*JSP*, J1:186).

3. Smith, Journal, 19 Feb. 1836 (*JSP*, J1:187). The nine others were Oliver Cowdery, W. W. Phelps, Sidney Rigdon, Edward Partridge, William E. McLellin, Orson Hyde, Orson Pratt, Sylvester Smith, and Warren Parrish.

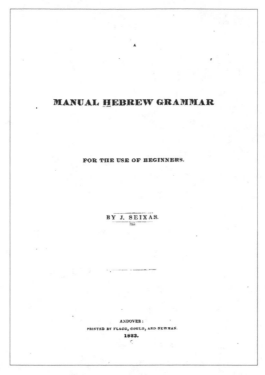

Figure 6.1. Title page of Joshua Seixas's *A Manual Hebrew Grammar for the Use of Beginners* (1833).

the languages until I shall become master of them, if I am permitted to live long enough."[4]

In addition to attending classes taught by Seixas, Smith also devoted considerable time to studying Hebrew on his own. As the editors of the Joseph Smith Papers have observed, "Between 23 November 1835 and 29 March 1836, J[oseph] S[mith]'s journal mentions his studying Hebrew—whether in class, with colleagues, or by himself—no fewer than seventy times."[5] On 30 March 1836, Seixas gave Smith a certificate verifying his completion of his course in Hebrew: "Mr Joseph Smith Junr has attended a full course of Hebrew lessons under my tuition; & has been indefatigable in acquiring the principles of the Sacred Language of the

---

4. Smith, Journal, 17 Feb. 1836 (*JSP*, J1:186).
5. Historical Introduction, *JSP*, D5:216.

Old Testament Scriptures in their original tongue. He has so far accomplished a knowledge of it, that he is able to translate to my entire Satisfaction."[6]

This event had a profound effect on Smith's continued translation of the Book of Abraham in Nauvoo in March 1842. The last three chapters of Abraham bear the marks of Smith's Hebrew lessons with Seixas in early 1836, which creates a problem for defenders who require that the entirety of the Book of Abraham translation must precede the creation of the bound "Grammar and A[l]phabet of the Egyptian Language." Reversing the chronology is necessary because such writers want to assign authorship of the Grammar to W. W. Phelps, not Smith. If the Grammar preceded the English translation of Abraham, as the evidence shows, it becomes impossible to assign authorship of the Grammar to Phelps, since doing so makes it appear that Smith drew on Phelps's Grammar to translate Abraham and explain Facsimile 2. As becomes apparent in this chapter, defenders of the Book of Abraham go to great lengths to defend their reverse-translation theory.

Editing and Publishing the Book of Abraham, 1841–1842

The first installment of the Book of Abraham and Facsimile 1 appeared in the 1 March 1842 issue of the *Times and Seasons*.[7] However, typesetting began in mid-February, and before that Smith's scribe Willard Richards had prepared a printer's copy of the text by copying and revising the translation text from the translation book which had been prepared in Kirtland by Phelps, probably in July 1835, and Warren Parrish the following November.

In 2010 Brian Hauglid asserted that the translation document Richards prepared for the printer in 1842 (which Hauglid labeled as Ab5) was "copied from an unknown earlier manuscript," implying that there is a now lost manuscript.[8] Later, Hauglid explained:

---

6. Joshua Seixas, Certificate to Joseph Smith, Kirtland Township, Geauga County, Ohio, 30 Mar. 1836, Joseph Smith Collection, CHL (*JSP*, D5:214–16).

7. "A Translation," *Times and Seasons 3* (1 Mar. 1842): 703–06.

8. Brian Hauglid, *A Textual History of the Book of Abraham: Manuscripts and Editions* (Provo, Utah: Neal A. Maxwell Institute for Religious Scholarship, Brigham Young University, 2010), 22.

"Some cancellations strongly suggest Ab5 [Willard Richards's copy] is derived from an earlier exemplar. ... However, it is difficult to determine which manuscript Ab5 was copied from." He suggested that Ab5 could have been copied from one of the extant Kirtland manuscripts in the handwritings of Frederick G. Williams and Parrish or from the manuscript cut from the translation book in the handwritings of Phelps and Parrish or from "another nonextant manuscript, or a combination of earlier exemplars."[9]

Despite Hauglid's speculations, there is no reason to think that Richards did not simply copy the longest and most complete Kirtland translation text from the translation book, making some revisions at Smith's direction. This explains why Richards's copy ends at exactly the same point as the translation book ends, that is, at Abraham 2:18. If there had been a longer, more complete text to which Richards had access, as some defenders maintain, there would have been no reason for Richards to have stopped at verse 18. Indeed, a more natural breaking-off point would have been seven verses later at the conclusions of the chapter, allowing the next installment in the *Times and Seasons* to begin with Abraham's vision of the cosmos (what is now chapter 3).

An indication that Richards was copying from Book of Abraham Manuscript-C (or translation book) is his misreading of Parrish's capital "K" for "R" in the word "Kahleenos." The letter is clearly "K" in Parrish's shorter document as well as in Frederick G. Williams's document, but when Parrish copied the text into the translation book, his "K" was formed in a way that could be mistaken for "R," which is how Richards read it (fig. 6.2). Additionally, in a passage naming four heathen gods on page 3, Richards copied "and the god of Koash," which is only in Parrish's text in the translation book. More recently, Hauglid, with Robin Scott Jensen, acknowledged that Richards's 1842 copy "is textually dependent upon the Kirtland-era manuscript in the handwriting of William W. Phelps and Warren Parrish (Book of Abraham Manuscript-C), suggesting that Richards copied directly from that document."[10]

---

9. Ibid., 150.
10. *JSP*, R4:245.

Figure 6.2. Showing Willard Richards mistaking Warren Parrish's "K" for an "R" in "Kahlee-nos": (a) Parrish writing "Kahleenos" in Book of Abraham Manuscript-B, p. 3; (b) Frederick G. Williams writing "Kahleenos" in Book of Abraham Manuscript-A, p. 2; (c) Parrish writing "Kahleenos" in Book of Abraham Manuscript-C, p. 3; (d-e) Parrish writing "King" in Book of Abraham Manuscript-C, pp. 2 and 3; and (f) Richards writing "Rahleenos" in Book of Abraham Manuscript, 1842, p. 5.

On the back of the second sheet of the printer's copy, Richards wrote out Smith's explanation of Facsimile 1. The type was then set for the publication of the first installment of the Book of Abraham using Richards's manuscript, which exhausted all the translation text that Smith had dictated in Kirtland. However, publication of the 1 March 1842 issue of the *Times and Seasons* was delayed while Reuben Hedlock, the printmaker, made some adjustments to the printing block of Facsimile 1. On 1 March, Richards recorded in Smith's journal: "During the fore-noon at his office. & printing office correcting the first plate or cut. of the Records of father Abra-ham, prepared by Reuben Hadlock for the Times & Seasons."[11] On

---

11. Smith, Journal, 1 Mar. 1842 (*JSP*, J2:39).

the following day, Richards added: "[Smith] Read the Proof of the 'Times and Seasons' as Editor for the First time, No. 9-Vol 3d in which is the commencement of the Book of Abraham."[12]

Phase Three: Nauvoo, 1841–1842

While type continued to be set for the 1 March 1842 issue,[13] Smith and Richards were busy preparing the second installment of the translation of Abraham to appear in the 15 March issue. On 4 March, Richards recorded in Smith's journal: "Exhibiting the Book of Abraham, in the original, To Bro Reuben Hadlock. so that he might take the size of the several plates or cuts. & prepare the blocks for the Times & Seasons. & also gave instructions concerning the arrangement of the writing on the Large cut. illustrating the principles of Astronomy."[14]

Preparations were being made for the second installment, which was to include a fold-out sheet containing an illustration of what Egyptologists today call a hypocephalus. However, there was no text of the Book of Abraham to go with it. On 8 March, Richards recorded in Smith's journal: "Commenced Translating from the Book of Abraham, for the 10 No of the Times and Seasons— and was engaged at his office day & evening."[15] On the next day (9 March), Richards recorded: "In the afternoon continued the Translation of the Book of Abraham ... & continued translating & revising, & Reading letters in the evening."[16] While dictating a letter that evening, Smith mentioned, "I am now very busily engaged in Translating, and therefore cannot give as much time to Public matters as I could wish."[17]

The new translation material and Facsimile 2 (the hypocephalus) were published in the 15 March 1842 issue, the tenth number of the *Times and Seasons*, and contained the remainder of the Book of Abraham as we have it, that is, Abraham 2:19–5:21.

---

12. Smith, Journal, 2 Mar. 1842 (*JSP*, J2:39).

13. The editorial section is dated 15 March (*Times and Seasons* 3:710).

14. Smith, Journal, 4 Mar. 1842 (*JSP*, J2:40). See fig. 6.3.

15. Smith, Journal, 8 Mar. 1842 (*JSP*, J2:42).

16. Smith, Journal, 9 Mar. 1842 (*JSP*, J2:42).

17. Joseph Smith, Letter, Nauvoo, Illinois, to Edward Hunter, West Nantmeal, Chester County, Pennsylvania, 9 and 11 Mar. 1842, Joseph Smith Collection, CHL (Dean C. Jessee, *Personal Writings of Joseph Smith* [Salt Lake City: Deseret Book Co., 2002], 550).

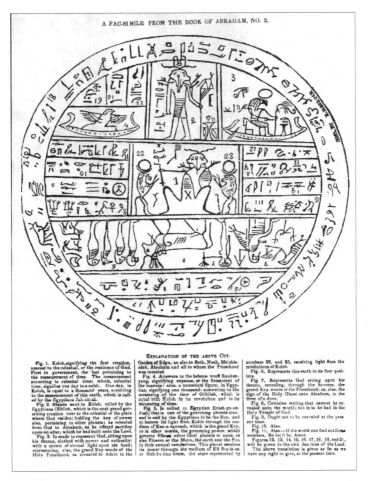

Figure 6.3. Facsimile 2 as it appeared in the 15 March 1842 issue of the *Times and Seasons*.

Contents and Dating of the New Material

The Kirtland translation material had stopped with a reworking of Genesis chapter 12 up to verse 6, where Abraham pauses in his journey toward Canaan to offer sacrifice to God. This reworking of the biblical text is similar to what Smith had done in revising the King James Bible between 1830 and 1833—although for his Abraham project, Smith transformed the text into a first-person account.

Now, in Nauvoo in 1842, Smith continued morphing Genesis 12, beginning at verse 7, where Abraham receives a vision of God, who promises him, "Unto thy seed will I give this land" (Gen. 12:7;

Abr. 2:19). As Abraham continues his journey to Egypt, he begins to worry that the Egyptians might murder him to gain sexual access to his beautiful wife, Sarah. However, instead of Abraham's telling Sarah to inform the Egyptians that she is his sister, as the Genesis story states, Smith's version has God tell Abraham to tell Sarah to lie about their marital status (Abr. 2:24).[18]

In Genesis, Abraham's conversation with Sarah is immediately followed by the account of his entering Egypt, Pharaoh taking Sarah into his house, and the discovery of Sarah and Abraham's true relationship (Gen. 12:14–20). This story does not appear in Abraham but rather is interrupted by a revelation Abraham receives through the Urim and Thummim, an instrument which had been given him while he was still in "Ur of the Chaldees" (Abr. 3:1). Smith then dictated twenty-eight verses on astronomy, comparing the hierarchal order of the stars and planets to the varying degrees of "intelligences" (like spirits but not exactly) in a pre-mortal existence. From the records in his possession, Abraham already has "a knowledge of the beginning of the creation, and also of the planets, and of the stars, as they were made known unto the fathers" (1:31), but just before he enters Egypt, he is given his own revelation on astronomy. Within the revelation, the Lord says, "Abraham, I show these things unto thee before ye go into Egypt, that ye may declare all these words" (3:15). This was inspired by passages in Josephus, which declare:

> Berosus mentions our father Abram without naming him, when he says thus:— "In the tenth generation after the Flood, there was among the Chaldeans a man righteous and great, and skillful in the celestial science." ...
>
> Abram communicated to them [the Egyptians] arithmetic, and delivered to them the science of astronomy, before Abram came into Egypt, they were unacquainted with those parts of learning; for that

---

18. Susan Staker suggests that this change provides a rationalization for Smith's own deceptions regarding the beginnings of his plural marriage doctrine. See Staker, "'The Lord Said, Thy Wife Is a Very Fair Woman to Look Upon': The Book of Abraham, Secrets, and Lying for the Lord," *Sunstone*, Jan. 1996, at www.sunstonemagazine.com.

science came from the Chaldeans into Egypt, and from thence to the Greeks also.[19]

As discussed in chapter five, Smith's dictation of Abraham 3 as well as his explanations of Facsimile 2 drew on the cosmology in the bound Grammar, which Smith dictated in early October 1835. While Smith's cosmology was unique, it still resembled the cosmology espoused by Thomas Dick and other natural theologians. Dick and others may have also impacted Abraham's discussion of pre-mortal "intelligences" in the second half of Abraham 3, which parallels Abraham's previous discussion of the hierarchy of stars and planets. It was probably on 8 March 1842 when Smith dictated the following verses:

> And the Lord said unto me: Abraham ... if there be two things, one above the other, and the moon be above the earth, then it may be that a planet or a star may exist above it; ... also, if there be two spirits, and one shall be more intelligent than the other ... there shall be another more intelligent than they; I am the Lord thy God, I am more intelligent than they all. ... Now the Lord had shown unto me, Abraham, the intelligences that were organized before the world was; and among all these there were many of the noble and great ones; And God saw these souls that they were good, and he stood in the midst of them, and he said: These I will make my rulers; for he stood among those that were spirits, and he saw that they were good; and he said unto me: Abraham, thou art one of them; thou wast chosen before thou wast born. (Abr. 3:15, 17, 18, 19, 22–23)

As Smith biographer Fawn M. Brodie pointed out, Thomas Dick believed that "the stars were peopled by 'various orders of intelligences,' and that these intelligences were '*progressive* beings' in various stages of evolution towards perfection."[20] Specifically, Dick discussed "the gradations of intellect, or the various orders of intelligences which may people the universal system" of stars and

---

19. Flavius Josephus, Antiquities of the Jews, Book 1, chap. 7, sec. 2; chap. 8, sec. 2, trans. William Whiston, *Josephus Complete Works* (Grand Rapids, Michigan: Kregel Publications, 1960), 32, 33.

20. Fawn M. Brodie, *No Man Knows My History: The Life of Joseph Smith* (2d ed. rev.; New York: Alfred A. Knopf, 1971), 172.

planets.[21] Smith would have been familiar with Dick's well-known speculations. Oliver Cowdery even quoted a large portion Dick's book *A Philosophy of a Future State* in the Mormon periodical *Messenger and Advocate* in December 1836, in which Dick argues:

> It is highly unreasonable; if not absurd, to suppose that the thinking principle in man will ever be annihilated. ... For, if amid the perpetual transformations, changes, and revolutions that are going forward throughout universal nature in all its departments, no particle of matter is ever lost, or reduced to nothing, it is in the highest degree improbable, that the thinking principle in man will be destroyed, by the change which takes place at the moment of his dissolution. ... And the Creator is under no necessity to annihilate the soul for want of power to support its faculties, for want of objects on which to exercise them, or for want of space to contain the innumerable intelligences that are incessantly emerging into existence: for the range of immensity is the theatre of his Omnipotence, and that powerful Energy, which has already brought millions of systems into existence, can as easily replenish the universe with ten thousand millions more.[22]

Dick's speculation recalls a May 1833 revelation in which Smith declares: "Man was also in the beginning with God. Intelligence, or the light of truth, was not created or made, neither indeed can be" (D&C 93:29). Abraham 3:18 similarly states: "yet these two spirits, notwithstanding one is more intelligent than the other, have no beginning; they existed before, they shall have no end, they shall exist after, for they are gnolaum, or eternal."

Gnolaum is one of the Hebrew words with which Smith sprinkled the text of Abraham 3–5, which he dictated in March 1842. In 1968, Louis C. Zucker, a professor of Hebrew at the University of Utah, commenting on Smith's use of Hebrew in Abraham 3, wrote that "gnolaum ... is an exact Seixas transliteration; however, the Hebrew word is not an adjective but a noun, which in the plural may act as an adverb. ... Gnolaum, in the English idiom 'everlasting,' is, in the Hebrew idiom, a noun, 'eternity.'"[23]

---

21. Thomas Dick, *Philosophy of a Future State* (New York: R. Schoyer, 1831), 196.

22. "Egyptian Mummies—Ancient Records," *LDS Messenger and Advocate* 3 (Dec. 1836): 423, 424, 425. Dick, *Philosophy of a Future State*, 88, 90, 92.

23. Louis C. Zucker, "Joseph Smith as a Student of Hebrew," *Dialogue: A Journal of Mormon Thought* 3 (Summer 1968): 51.

Zucker also verified that Kokob and Kokaubeam in Abraham 3:13 were correctly translated "star" and "stars."[24] The presence of these Hebrew words is one reason to date Abraham 3 to after Smith's lessons from Seixas in early 1836, rather than to July 1835 as John Gee and others believe.

Abraham's discussion of astronomy and intelligences is followed by fifty-two verses patterned after the Creation account in Genesis 1 and 2 (Abr. 4:1–5:21), only they too display Smith's familiarity with Hebrew, changing "God" to "Gods" throughout as well as replacing "without form and void" with "empty and desolate," "created" with "organized and formed," and "firmament" with "expanse." In an 1844 sermon, Smith recounted a conversation he had with "a learned Jew" about the Hebrew word *Elohim* translated in the Bible as "God": "I once asked a learned Jew, 'If the Hebrew language compels us to render all words ending in *heim* in the plural, why not render the first *Eloheim* plural?' He replied, 'That is the rule with few exceptions; but in this case it would ruin the Bible.' He acknowledged I was right."[25]

This story most likely refers to Seixas, who evidently failed to persuade his student. If so, the exchange may have occurred during the third week of class, when students translated Genesis 1.[26] Indeed, Seixas's *Hebrew Grammar* defined Elohim as "a sing[ular]. noun with a *plur[al]. form*."[27] The student is instructed to "see Lexicon" under Elohim. Seixas's grammar referred students to the second edition of Josiah W. Gibbs's *A Manual Hebrew and English Lexicon*.[28] On page 12, Gibbs explains that Elohim is defined as

---

24. Ibid.

25. Joseph Smith, Jr., *History of the Church of Jesus Christ of Latter-day Saints*, ed. B. H. Roberts, 7 vols. (2nd ed. rev.; Salt Lake City: Deseret Book Co., 1948–51), 6:475. This is based on notes kept by Thomas Bullock (see Andrew F. Ehat and Lyndon W. Cook, *Words of Joseph Smith: The Contemporary Accounts of the Nauvoo Discourses of the Prophet Joseph* [Provo, Utah: Religious Studies Center, Brigham Young University, 1980], 379).

26. The grammar supplement published by the church also contained the Hebrew text of Genesis 1 for translation (Seixas, *Manuel Hebrew Grammar*, 28–32). See also Grey, "'The Word of the Lord in the Original,'" n113.

27. Seixas, *Manuel Hebrew Grammar*, 85.

28. Josiah W. Gibbs, *A Manual Hebrew and English Lexicon* (2nd ed.; New Haven, Connecticut: Hezekiah Howe, 1832). There are three copies of this edition in the Community of Christ Library-Archive, Independence, Missouri.

"*a god*; by way of eminence, *the true God, Jehovah*" and "as the ordinary plural, *gods*." Gibbs also notes, "This pluralis excellantiae is generally construed with singular adjectives and verbs, but there are many exceptions."[29] Smith questioned this explanation.[30]

Other passages in Abraham 4–5 reflect Smith's 1836 Hebrew lessons from Seixas. As mentioned, instead of following the King James Version of Genesis 1:2—"And the earth was without form and void"—Abraham 4:2 reads: "And the earth, after it was formed, was empty and desolate, because they [the Gods] had not formed anything but the earth." In addition to correcting the problem of how the earth could be created yet without form, Smith's use of "empty and desolate" is exactly how Seixas translated the Hebrew words (*tohu* and *vohu*) on page 78 of his Hebrew grammar.[31]

More than a year before dictating his translation of Abraham 4 to Willard Richards, Smith delivered a sermon in Nauvoo in which he expressed another of his translation preferences for the Creation account in Genesis. On 5 January 1841, Smith declared: "In the translation, 'without form and void' it should read 'empty and desolate.'" At the same time, he also said: "The word 'created' should be formed or organized."[32] This is reflected in Abraham 4:1: "and they, the Gods, organized and formed the heavens and the earth"—although Seixas used "created."[33] On page 36, Gibbs's *Lexicon* translates the Hebrew word as "to form, make, create." While speaking at the funeral of King Follet on 7 April 1844, Smith declared: "You ask the learned doctors why they say the world was made out of nothing, and they will answer, 'Doesn't the Bible say He created the world?' And they infer, from the word create, that it must have been made out of nothing. Now, the word create came from the word *baurau*, which does not mean to create out of nothing; it means to organize; the same as a man would or-

---

29. Ibid., 12.

30. If Smith had such a conversation in 1836 about "Gods," it likely pertained to members of the Godhead, as his views on the subject were evolving to distinguish more clearly God the Father from God the Son.

31. Seixas, *Manual Hebrew Grammar*, 78. See also Michael T. Walton, "Professor Seixas, the Hebrew Bible, and the Book of Abraham," *Sunstone* 6 (Mar. 1981): 42.

32. "Extract from William Clayton's Private Book," as cited in Ehat and Cook, *The Words of Joseph Smith*, 60.

33. Seixas, *Manual Hebrew Grammar*, 85.

ganize materials and build a ship."[34] Thus Smith's use of "organize" in Abraham came from his understanding of the Hebrew word usually translated "create."

Smith's Hebrew lessons are also apparent when he changed "moved" in Genesis 1:2—"And the Spirit of God moved upon the face of the waters"—to "brooding" in Abraham 4:2, and "firmament" in Genesis 1:6—"And God said, Let there be a firmament in the midst of the waters, and let it divide the waters from the waters"—to "expanse" in Abraham 4:6, both of which are consistent with Seixas's translations of the same Hebrew words.[35]

Did Richards Copy Abraham 3–5 or Record It from Dictation?

Only a fragment survives of what Smith dictated to Richards on 8–9 March 1842: a single sheet containing Abraham 3:18–26 written on both sides with the page numbers 7 and 8. Because Gee and others posit that all of Abraham was dictated in July 1835 before the Egyptian Alphabets and bound Grammar were produced, they believe that the Smith–Richards fragment represents a longer text comprising Abraham 2:19–5:21 that Richards copied from a now-missing original manuscript dating to 1835.

Hauglid, for example, had originally argued that this fragment of Abraham 3 is a copy of a lost manuscript because some corrections are "possible copy errors."[36] However, none of the errors are definitive copy errors but rather what might be expected of corrections being made during editing for publication, which Smith's journal for 9 March mentions: "continued the Translation of the Book of Abraham ... & continued translating & revising."[37] One emendation was apparently made while Smith dictated the text to Richards, not from Richards copying an existing text:

they shall exist after, for they are ~~immortal~~ ~~ol~~ Gnolaum, or Eternal.[38]

---

34. DHC 6:308 (Ehat and Cook, *The Words of Joseph Smith*, 359).

35. For Seixas translating *mirahephet* as "brooding," see Seixas, *A Manual Hebrew Grammar*, p. 31; and for *raukiah* as "expanse," see pp. 21 and 78. See also Walton, "Professor Seixas," 42–43.

36. Hauglid, *Textual History of the Book of Abraham*, 151.

37. Smith, Journal, 9 Mar. 1842 (*JSP*, J2:42).

38. Book of Abraham Manuscript, ca. 15 Mar. 1842, 7 (*JSP*, R4:287).

In this emendation, Richards first wrote "they [spirits] shall exist after, for they are immortal." He then crossed out "~~immortal~~" and started to write *ol-m*, which Ashkenazi Jewish peoples often employ to mean "eternity" or "everlasting," but changed his mind and instead wrote *gnolaum*, which is the Sephardic term that Smith learned from Seixas to mean "or Eternal."[39] The text continues on the same line, demonstrating that the correction was done at the time of dictation and not the result of copy error or an emendation added later. In their 2018 publication of Book of Abraham documents, Jensen and Hauglid date this fragment to 8–9 March 1842 citing the entry in Smith's journal and observe: "The Handwriting on the manuscript appears rushed, suggesting that this document is part of the original manuscript dictated by JS to Richards."[40]

Even if it could be demonstrated that the Richards fragment were a copy, it would not necessarily be of an original text dating to 1835. If there had been more text in 1835, Parrish would, no doubt, have copied it into the translation book. The only reason to insist that that particular fragment of Abraham 3 is a copy of an 1835 original is to insist on a theory that the Abraham translation predates the Alphabets and bound Grammar. As Gee stated in 2017, "The grammar seems to have been produced from the Book of Abraham and not the other way round."[41] Maintaining this theory has led to several erroneous interpretations and assertions.

Origin of Shinehah

Some Mormon scholars believe there is evidence that the original translation had, in fact, surpassed Abraham 2:18, which is where the translation book—the longest extant text produced in

---

39. Concerning the correction of "~~ol~~" before Gnolaum, Gee speculates: "Joseph Smith used a Sephardic transliteration system for Hebrew instead of the now more common Ashkenazi system, which often disguises the word to us today, yielding, for instance, 'gnolaum' instead of the more familiar 'ôl-m. Given the transliteration system, one can then see that Joseph Smith's sentence … is good Aramaic (known in Joseph's day as Chaldean)" (John Gee, "Tragedy of Errors," *FARMS Review of Books* 4/1 [1992]:119). Actually, the correction of "~~ol~~" was done by wipe erasure and is smudged. Hauglid initially read this as "ol" (Hauglid, *Textual History of the Book of Abraham*, 197) but since, in his publication with Robin Scott Jensen, renders it "~~of~~" (*JSP*, R4:287).

40. *JSP*, R4:285.

41. John Gee, *An Introduction to the Book of Abraham* (Provo, Utah: Religious Studies Center, BYU/Salt Lake City: Deseret Book Co., 2017), 37.

Kirtland in 1835—ends. They argue that the name Shinehah—in Abraham 3:13—was used four times as a code name in two revelations published in the 1835 Doctrine and Covenants, which was released for sale in September.[42] These code names do not appear in the original manuscripts of the revelations[43] but were added before type was set for the 1835 edition, sometime between May and September, probably from a list of code names prepared by Smith before he left for Michigan in mid-August. In 2017, Gee used this evidence to argue that "the Book of Abraham had at least reached Abraham 3:13 before Joseph Smith left for Michigan."[44] In 2010, Hauglid had similarly argued: "In August 1835, the name 'Shinehah' appeared in the 1835 Doctrine and Covenants four times as a code name for Kirtland ... suggesting that the translation was at least up to Abraham 3:13 by this time, and perhaps further."[45]

Hauglid has since changed his mind.[46] However, the argument was more recently repeated by Muhlestein and Hansen:

> The word "Shinehah" is attested in Abraham 3:13, where it is part of the astronomical explanation given there. However, in section 86 of the 1835 edition of the Doctrine and Covenants, the word "Shinehah" is used as a code for "Kirtland." This happens again in the heading of section 96, as well as three times in section 98. While it is possible that this was a code word that Joseph [Smith] randomly created and then later inserted into Abraham 3 [in 1842], it seems more likely that he translated through Abraham 3 and then borrowed a word from the text [for the Doctrine and Covenants]. If this assumption is correct, then, again, Joseph had translated Abraham 3 before the end of 1835.[47]

---

42. See D&C, 1835 ed., 86:4 (82:12) and 98:3, 7, and 9 (104:21, 40, 48).

43. Compare 1835 Doctrine and Covenants with manuscript copies in *JSP*, MRB:228–29, 364–67.

44. Gee, *Introduction to the Book of Abraham*, 16. On page 28, Gee also argues: "References to the context from later sections of the Book of Abraham (e.g., Shinehah from Abraham 3:13) show up after the translation commenced but come from sections later in the translation than the manuscripts surviving from Kirtland."

45. Hauglid, *Textual History of the Book of Abraham*, 2.

46. *JSP*, R4:285.

47. Kerry Muhlestein and Megan Hansen. "'The Work of Translating': The Book of Abraham's Translation Chronology," in J. Spencer Fluhman and Brent L. Top, eds., *Let Us Reason Together: Essays in Honor of the Life's Work of Robert L. Millet* (Provo, Utah: Brigham Young University, 2016), 144.

Despite what Muhlestein and Hansen suggest, it is more likely that the order of events was exactly as the original relevant documents show: the code name Shinehah came first in mid-1835 and then Smith used it in dictating Abraham 3 in March 1842. As noted, the only manuscript evidence we have for Abraham 3 is a single sheet of two pages covering verses 18–26 in the handwriting of Richards, which dates to shortly before its publication in the *Times and Seasons* on 15 March 1842, according to Smith's journal.[48]

The bound Grammar and Alphabet of the Egyptian Language (GAEL)—the earliest document—contains many more names than contained in the explanation for Facsimile 2 and Abraham 3. In fact, Facsimile 2 introduces two new names (Raukeeyang and Hah-ko-kau-beam),[49] and Abraham 3 adds five (Shinehah, Kokob, Kokaubeam, Olea, and gnolaum). In other words, these seven names are nowhere found in the English documents associated with the Egyptian papyri dating to 1835. There is a reason for this: five of the seven names are Hebrew and date to after early 1836 when Smith and other Mormons studied Hebrew under Seixas. The two non-Hebrew names are Shinehah and Olea from Abraham 3:13, where they are said to mean sun and moon. This departs from the bound Grammar, which names the moon Flo-ees and the sun Flos-isis. Even Facsimile 2 gives a different name for the sun: Enish-go-on-dosh. The differences in the names may be explained as a difference in languages. The passage in Abraham 3:13 gives the Hebrew names for *star* and *stars*, Kokob and Kokaubeam. This was before Abraham went into Egypt. The bound Grammar specifies that the names of the fifteen moving planets, which includes Flos-isis and Flo-ese, were "Egyptian names." In Facsimile 2, Enish-go-on-dosh is one of the three ruling planets, which is "said by the Egyptians to be the Sun"—thus the word "sun" used in two systems receives different names. Although Shinehah and Olea appear in the same verse with the Hebrew words for star and stars, they are not Hebrew words themselves. So where did they come from?

---

48. "The Book of Abraham," *Times and Seasons* 3 (15 Mar. 1842): 719–22; Smith, Journal, 9 Mar. 1842 (*JSP*, J2:42).

49. Book of Abraham, Fac. 2, figs. 4 and 5.

Shinehah, used as a code name in the 1835 Doctrine and Covenants, pre-dates the arrival of the Egyptian papyri in July 1835. In fact, there is no indication that any of the code names was influenced by the Egyptian project. Rather, the code names date to the time when Smith was revising the revelations for publication, particularly Section 107, which mentions the Book of Enoch—Enoch also being one of Smith's code names. The editors of the Joseph Smith Papers date this revision and expansion to between about 1 March and 4 May 1835.[50] By 26 May 1835, when W. W. Phelps wrote to his wife about a pure language, typesetting of the Doctrine and Covenants had reached page 98, at least.[51] Most likely, the code names were determined before typesetting began, and, after the arrival of the Egyptian papyri in early July, Smith's primary focus would have been the papyri, not editing the revelations for publication.

Among the twenty or so code names, there are also three variants of Shinehah, which was code for Kirtland, Ohio—shinelah (print), Laneshine (printing office) and shinelane (printing). This links Shinehah with printing, not the sun. The only link to sun would be a play on the English word "shine," as if to say the truth would shine forth from Kirtland through its printing press. The word Shinehah is more at home among these invented names than with the Egyptian materials.

CODE NAMES IN 1835 DOCTRINE AND COVENANTS 86:4
(82:12), 98:3, 7, AND 9 (104:21, 40, 48)

1	Enoch, Gazelam, Baurak Ale	Joseph Smith
2	Pelagoram	Sidney Rigdon
3	Olihah	Oliver Cowdery
4	Ahashdah	Newel K. Whitney
5	Alam	Edward Partridge
6	Mahalaleel	A. Sidney Gilbert
7	Horah	John Whitmer

---

50. Instruction on Priesthood, between ca. 1 Mar. and ca. 4 May 1835, *JSP* 4:308–21.

51. Phelps wrote a letter to his wife in Liberty (Missouri) in which he included prints of "the Six first forms of the Doctrines and Covenants" (Letter, Kirtland, Ohio, to Sally Phelps, Liberty, Missouri, 26 and 27 May 1835, William W. Phelps Papers, BYU).

8	Shalemanasseh	W. W. Phelps
9	Shederlaomach	Frederick G. Williams
10	Zombre	John Johnson
11	Mahemson	Martin Harris
12	Shinehah	Kirtland, Ohio
13	City of Enoch	Zion or Independence, Missouri
14	Laneshine	printing office
15	Ozondah	mercantile establishment
16	Tahhanes	tannery
17	shinelah	Print
18	shinelane	Printing
19	Cainhannoch	New York
20	Baneemy	mine elders

The probable source of Shinehah and Olea in Abraham 3:13 is an 8 July 1838 revelation that speaks of both the "mountains of Adam-ondi-Ahman" and the "plains of Olaha Shinehah, or the land where Adam dwelt" (D&C 117:8). An early copy of this revelation in the handwriting of Edward Partridge as well as two other sources close to Smith read "Olea Shinihah."[52] Because the use of "Olea Shinihah" in the 8 July revelation is intended as a place name comparable to Adam-ondi-Ahman, it seems likely that Abraham 3:13 actually blends Hebrew and Adamic terminology, thus pointing to an 1842 date for the composition of Abraham 3. This being the most likely chronology, the appearance of Shinehah in Abraham 3:13 does not prove that Smith's dictation of Abraham had reached that verse in 1835.

Defenders themselves undermine their appeal to Shinehah when they argue that Smith could have added Hebrew words to the Book of Abraham prior to publication in 1842. Muhlestein and Hansen, for example, argue:

> transliterations such as "Kokob" and "Kokaubeam" are clearly influenced by the Hebrew grammars Smith was studying [in 1836]. On

---

52. Revelation, Far West, Caldwell County, Missouri, 8 July 1838, Revelations Collection, CHL (*JSP*, D6:193). Also, Smith, Journal, 17 Jan. 1842 (*JSP*, J2:27), which has "Olah Shinehah"; and Joseph Smith, Sidney Rigdon, and Hyrum Smith, Revelation and Letter, Far West, Missouri, to William Marks and Newel K. Whitney, Kirtland, Ohio, 8 July 1838, 1, Joseph Smith Collection, CHL, which has "Oleashinihah."

the surface, this suggests Joseph translated these phrases after he began his study of Hebrew and his transliterations were influenced by his [Hebrew] grammar book. Yet it seems equally as likely that these are glosses, the "translation" efforts of 1842 were actually Joseph editing translated text [from 1835] and that this editing included inserting newly acquired Hebrew phrases.[53]

Contrary to the impression Muhlestein and Hansen give, emending the passage in Abraham 3:13 would not be a simple matter of inserting Hebrew words. Note how the passage combines the pure Adamic words with the Hebrew words:

And he [the Lord] said unto me: This is Shinehah, which is the sun. And he said unto me: Kokob, which is star. And he said unto me: Olea, which is the moon. And he said unto me: Kokaubeam, which signifies stars, or all the great lights, which were in the firmament of heaven. (Abr. 3:13)

If Kokob and Kokaubeam are influenced by Smith's Hebrew lessons, why are not Shinehah and Olea influenced by his 1838 revelation? Obviously, it is inconsistent to argue that Smith added the Hebrew words in 1842 in Nauvoo, while at the same time asserting that Shinehah in the same passage was not added but is evidence that Abraham 3 was dictated in 1835. Contrary to the above speculation, it is not "equally as likely" that the Hebrew words are glosses added to an 1835 text. In fact, the presence of the Hebrew words is clear indication that Abraham 3–5 were dictated by Smith in 1842, as his journal states.

More Problematic Evidence

Muhlestein and Hansen also refer to LDS Apostle Wilford Woodruff's journal, which mentioned Kolob in two entries for 1837 and 1838 and which, they argue, "likely serve as evidence of familiarity with Facsimile 2 or Abraham 3" prior to March 1842.[54] It is as if Muhlestein and Hansen are unaware of the contents of the bound

---

53. Muhlestein and Hansen, "'The Work of Translating,'" 150.

54. Ibid., 145. In 1837, Woodruff was blessed that "I should visit COLUB & Preach to the spirits in Prision" (Wilford Woodruff, Journal, 3 Jan. 1837, CHL). On 12 December 1838, Woodruff mentioned "COLOB" (Wilford Woodruff, Journal, 12 Dec. 1838).

Grammar, which recorded the unfolding of the "system of astronomy" mentioned in Smith's journal under 1 October 1835 and in which Warren Parrish recorded the definition for Kolob shortly after being hired as Smith's scribe in late October and before his departure from the church in December 1837. This seeming lack of awareness continues when they quote a 6 May 1838 entry in Smith's journal: "This day, President Smith, delivered a discourse, to the people. ... He also instructed the Church, in the mistories of the Kingdom of God; giving them a history of the Plannets &c and of Abrahams writings upon the Plannettary system &c."[55] After quoting this entry, they assert: "The most straightforward reading of this journal entry is that Joseph Smith had read Abraham's writings about astronomy. Only Abraham 3 fits this description. Because this is the most straightforward reading, it should be assumed that Joseph translated Abraham 3 during 1835."[56]

In fact, as I explained in chapter five, the fullest description of the planetary system is given in the bound Grammar, which is based on the translation of characters taken from column 3 of the Breathing Permit of Hôr on JSP I (the characters in the margins of the Abraham manuscripts indicate that the text supposedly came from JSP XI). Moreover, the Grammar describes a system of three ruling stars, twelve fixed stars, and fifteen moving planets, including the earth. Abraham 3 does not describe such a system, although it implies a hierarchy of planets and stars, of which Kolob is the greatest. Muhlestein and Hansen date the bound Grammar to "the latter half of 1835"[57]—well before Woodruff mentioned Kolob in his journal. However, like Gee, their dating of the Grammar ignores Smith's official history, which dates the beginning of the Grammar to July 1835.[58]

Next, Muhlestein and Hansen attempt to demonstrate that Abraham 3 was translated before the bound Grammar was created, arguing that the phrase on page 3 of the Grammar—"The first Being—supreme intelligence"—was inspired by the passage

---

55. Smith, Journal, 6 May 1838 (*JSP*, J1:266).
56. Muhlestein and Hansen, "'The Work of Translating,'" 145.
57. Ibid., 144.
58. JS History, vol. B-1, 597 (DHC 2:238).

in Abraham 3:19, which states that some spirits are "more intelligent" than others but that God is "more intelligent than they all." From this, they argue, "This does not necessitate that Abraham 3:19 had been translated by the time GAEL [Grammar and Alphabet of the Egyptian Language] [page] 3 was created, but it strongly suggests it."[59]

Even if we assume that the parallel is close enough to conclude one source inspired the other, which is not the case, nothing in the texts indicates which came first. However, the contexts of the two passages are completely different; therefore one source does not "strongly suggest" the other, in either direction. Moreover, the Grammar's definitions of Ahlish evolved from the Alphabets' definition of Ah, not Abraham 3. To quote the Grammar's fifth degree as proof is to miss the directionality of development. Indeed, there is a clear development that takes place within the Alphabets as well as within the Grammar, a development independent of Abraham 3. Ah is the first of four similar-looking characters in the Alphabets that deal with power. In the Alphabets, the definition of Ah only mentions "Supreme power," nothing about intelligence; the next three characters also deal with power.[60]

In the Grammar, Ahlish—the name given to the same character as Ah in the Alphabets—is defined in the first degree as "The name of the first being," which is then developed in each succeeding degree with a different attribute: "supreme intelligence," "supreme power," and "supreme glory." In the fifth degree are added "supreme Justice" and "supreme mercy."[61] Clearly, Ahlish has a development of its own independent of Abraham 3 and provides no support for Muhlestein and Hansen's assertion. Continuing, Muhlestein and Hansen argue: "Likewise, a few pages later in the grammar a discussion of Abraham being foreordained and chosen to go to Egypt to preach the gospel appears. These are concepts found only in Abraham 3, again strongly suggesting the translation had proceeded at least that far before the end of 1835."[62]

---

59. Muhlestein and Hansen, "'The Work of Translating,'" 144.
60. See, e.g., Egyptian Alphabet-A, ca. July–Nov. 1835, [1], 7 (*JSP*, R4:57).
61. GAEL, 3, 9, 13, 17, 157 (*JSP*, R4:121, 133, 141, 149, 157).
62. Muhlestein and Hansen, "'The Work of Translating,'" 144.

Again, there is nothing—except speculation—to indicate which came first. However, Muhlestein and Hansen do not accurately describe the content of the Grammar, which only uses Abraham (the person)—not the Book of Abraham—as an example of what Zub-zool means. After defining Abraham (the person) as "having foreordained, or decreed or having before seen," the Grammar explains:

> For instance: Abraham haveing been chosen before [he] was sent by commandment into the Land of Canaan: Having preached the gospel unto the heathen, was fore warned of God to go down into Ah=meh= strah, or Egypt, and preach the gospel <unto the> Ah meh strah ans;[63]

The Grammar associates Zub-zool with foreordination, meaning God's will and foreknowledge, and gives Abraham as an example. There is no mention of Abraham being chosen before birth, which would have been an obvious example to use if Abraham 3 were dictated before the Grammar. Instead, the Grammar refers to Abraham's being "chosen" by God to become a "great nation" before going into the land of Canaan (not Egypt), and which is stated in Genesis 12:2. Neither the Grammar nor the Book of Abraham says Abraham (the person) was "foreordained and chosen to go to Egypt to preach the gospel."

The Grammar is unique in stating that Abraham was "fore warned of God to go down into Ah=meh= strah, or Egypt," presumably to avoid the famine. Neither Genesis nor the Book of Abraham mentions Abraham's being "fore warned of God" to go to Egypt. Instead, the Book of Abraham states, "I, Abraham, concluded to go down into Egypt, to sojourn there, for the famine became very grievous" (2:21). Muhlestein and Hansen do not quote the Grammar, which allows them to blur the distinction between the Book of Abraham and Grammar, and avoid quoting the terms "Ah=meh= strah" and "Ah meh strah ans"—terms inspired by Josephus's report that the Jews called "Egypt Mestre, and the Egyptians Mestreans."[64] Moreover, since the Book of Abraham does not use these terms, it is difficult to explain their presence

---

63. GAEL, 6 (*JSP,* R4:127).

64. GAEL, 6 (*JSP,* R4:127); Antiquities of the Jews, Book 1, chap. 6, sect. 2 (Whiston, *Josephus Complete Works,* 31).

in the Grammar if the Grammar was created from the text of the Book of Abraham, as defenders of the Book of Abraham maintain.

Plurality of Gods

Problems multiply when defenders attempt to escape the anachronisms their creative chronologies produce. The account in Abraham 4–5 of "Gods" creating the heavens and the earth is difficult to date to 1835 because there is otherwise no indication that Smith was a polytheist at that time, although he held an unorthodox interpretation of the Trinity. As mentioned, these two chapters exhibit information Smith obtained while studying Hebrew under Seixas in early 1836, reworking Genesis and changing "God" to "Gods" throughout, as well as replacing "without form and void" with "empty and desolate," "created" with "organized and formed," and "firmament" with "expanse." None of this is surprising since prior to the 1842 publication of the second installment of the Book of Abraham, as noted, Willard Richards recorded in Smith's journal that Smith was busy translating on 8–9 March 1842.[65]

Recognizing that the Hebrew "elements are so thoroughly interwoven in the text of Abraham 4 and 5 that it is difficult to imagine them as glosses," Muhlestein and Hansen argue that Smith re-translated and updated his 1835 translation with knowledge he had gained in his subsequent Hebrew lessons. They note that Smith's journal entry for 9 March mentions "translating & revising," then state:

> [Smith's] Hebrew study must have … heavily influenced the way he reworded his translation of the Book of Abraham as he prepared it for publication. This would also explain why he spent time "translating" before the second installment of the Book of Abraham and not the first. It is in that second installment he would need to so thoroughly rework the text in order to incorporate the Hebrew-influenced phrases that said so well what he already learned when he first translated the text.[66]

Smith's journal did not mention "translating" before the first installment because that issue printed all that had been translated

---

65. Smith, Journal, 8–9 Aug. 1842 (*JSP*, J2:42).
66. Muhlestein and Hansen, "'The Work of Translating,'" 150, 152.

in Kirtland, and the reference to "translating & revising" before the second installment pertained to the tenth number of the *Times and Seasons,* as stated in the journal. As discussed, the fragment of Abraham 3 shows that "Gnolaum" was added at the time of dictation, after which the text was lightly edited for publication. If there had been an 1835 manuscript, editing would have been added to that and then a fair copy produced from it. Nevertheless, Muhlestein and Hansen agree that Abraham 4–5, as we have them, was created in 1842, while their speculation that the two chapters were a re-translation of an 1835 manuscript is without foundation and reflects a need that the entire Book of Abraham precede the Egyptian Grammar, which is unnecessary since the latter does not depend on the former in content.

Muhlestein and Hansen attempt to establish that Smith's later teachings on the plurality of Gods originated with the Book of Abraham prior to his 1836 Hebrew lessons, which is both unnecessary and inconsistent given their assertion that Abraham 4–5 was re-translated in 1842 to add the Hebrew elements. They refer to the 1844 sermon previously cited in which Smith recounted the conversation he had with "a learned Jew" about the Hebrew word *Elohim* as "Gods."[67] They observe that the learned Jew was likely Seixas and argue that Smith would not have questioned his teacher unless he had previously encountered the plural "Gods" in the Genesis-like chapters 4 and 5 in the Book of Abraham. In 2016, they contended:

> It is almost certainly during his study of Hebrew at the end of 1835 and the beginning of 1836 that Joseph first saw any linguistic evidence in Hebrew that supported the notion of a plurality of gods. Yet the way he would have encountered this does not seem like it would have propelled him towards that interpretation. ... The Prophet would probably not have disagreed with his respected teacher, his teacher's grammar book, and the other Hebrew books he was using, if he had not already come to believe that there was more than one god at work in the creation story.[68]

---

67. Ehat and Cook, *Words of Joseph Smith,* 379.
68. Muhlestein and Hansen, "'The Work of Translating,'" 151, 152.

To assume Smith would not have disagreed with established Hebrew authorities is to commit the idealist fallacy, a "presumption of rationality in human behavior."[69] Yet as Smith related in 1844, his Hebrew instructor "acknowledged I was right." Although it is doubtful that Seixas would have made such an acknowledgment, the story is not about a disagreement but rather about raising a question that many students have probably asked concerning the word *Elohim*. At this point in his life, Smith may have only seen the plural *Elohim* as representing the Father and the Son, who were becoming distinct and separate beings in his theology. Regardless, the idea that Smith would not dare question his teacher is flawed since Smith built a career on interpreting the scriptures differently from learned priests and rabbis.

Disproportion

In a final attempt to establish the theory that Abraham 3–5 were originally translated in Kirtland in 1835, Muhlestein and Hansen argue that dating these chapters to March 1842 creates a disproportion between the amount of translation text produced in Kirtland versus what was produced in Nauvoo. They contend:

> Joseph spent at least eight and a half days translating in the latter half of 1835. If we were to suppose that he translated from Abraham 1:1 through Abraham 2:18 during that time, that would mean that he translated 49 verses, or 2,149 words, averaging almost 6 verses or 253 words per day.
>
> In contrast ... there are only one and a half days [in 1842] where Joseph Smith noted he was translating. ... If we suppose that on these days he translated Abraham 2:19–5:21, then during that day and a half he translated 88 verses, or 3,340 words, averaging just over 58 verses or 2,226 words a day. This would suggest he translated about 9 times faster in 1842 than 1835. This seems unlikely.[70]

To arrive at their estimated 8.5 days that Smith translated in 1835, Muhlestein and Hansen guess that he translated "at least three days" but "likely more" in July. Counting the unfolding of

---

69. David Hackett Fischer, *Historians' Fallacies: Toward a Logic of Historical Thought* (New York: Harper & Row, 1970), 199.

70. Muhlestein and Hansen, "'The Work of Translating,'" 143.

astronomy on 1 October as well as "other days we know he spent on translating … in the latter half of 1835," as mentioned in Smith's journal, they arrive at their estimated 8.5 days.

However, their estimation for 1835 is based on the false assumption that the Alphabets and bound Grammar are not translations and that therefore every time Smith's journal mentions "translating," it must refer to the text of the Book of Abraham. As reconstructed in the previous chapters, after Smith's initial identification of the two rolls of papyri as the records of Abraham and Joseph, the project switched to the Valuable Discovery notebooks, then to the Alphabets and bound Grammar. The unfolding of astronomy on 1 October referred to the last part of the bound Grammar, not to Abraham 3 or a missing portion of the Book of Abraham. Smith did not return to his dictation of the English text of the Book of Abraham until 19 November 1835, when his journal mentions that Warren Parrish and Frederick G. Williams were with him while inspecting the temple and afterwards, as Parrish recorded, that "[Smith] spent the day in translating the Egyptian records."[71] Smith's journal mentions translating on 19–20 and 24–25 November, during which Parrish and Williams were scribes for Abraham 1:4–2:18.[72] This reconstruction cuts Muhlestein and Hansen's calculations of time Smith spent translating in 1835 at least in half and doubles the textual output—in other words, Smith translated approximately twelve verses or 506 words per day.

The higher output numbers for 1842 are boosted by the fact that Abraham 2:19–25 closely follows Genesis 12:7–13 and that Abraham 4–5 are a reworking of Genesis 1–2, which leaves only twenty-eight verses of Abraham 3 as unique. Nevertheless, Muhlestein and Hansen's claim that Smith "spent two days frantically translating in order to publish Abraham 2:19–5:21 in the next edition of the newspaper" in 1842 is probably inaccurate since Smith, as Gee observed, is known to have dictated long revelations fairly quickly.[73]

---

71. Smith, Journal, 19 Nov. 1835 (*JSP,* J1:107).

72. Smith, Journal, 19–20 and 24–25 Nov. 1835 (*JSP,* J1:107–10).

73. Gee, *Introduction to the Book of Abraham,* 22.

Did Smith Translate More Text than We Have?

Muhlestein and Hansen's argument from disproportion and Gee's assertion that the entire Book of Abraham was dictated in July 1835 has led defenders to conclude that Smith translated additional text beyond the present text of the Book of Abraham. Obviously, to maintain that the translation of the Book of Abraham came first and that the Alphabets and bound Grammar were created from it, one must explain material in the latter that does not appear in the former. One must also explain subsequent references in Smith's journal to translating in October and November 1835 and March 1842. Defenders have little choice but to postulate that Smith translated more of the Book of Abraham than what he published in Nauvoo in 1842. For example, Gee argues:

> The manuscripts of the Book of Abraham dating to that time [in 1835] vary in length, between one and ten pages of text, all of which fit within the range of what Joseph Smith was known to dictate in a single day at that time. ... We can account for only three hypothetical translation sessions ... and we have six recorded in his journal. This is another indication that the manuscripts are incomplete.[74]

Gee's three hypothetical translation sessions based on natural divisions in the manuscripts are: (1) Abraham 1:1–3, with Phelps as scribe; (2) Abraham 1:4–2:6, with Parrish and Williams as scribes; and (3) Abraham 2:7–18, with Parrish only as scribe. From this, Gee reasons that the other references to Smith translating took the translation well beyond the Kirtland-era manuscripts. Again, Gee's calculation—like Muhlestein and Hansen's—is based on the incorrect assumption that the Alphabets and bound Grammar are not translations and that all references to Smith's "translating" must pertain to the Book of Abraham. This assumption is not supported in Smith's official history, which states that during the latter part of July 1835 he "was continually engaged in translating an alphabet to the Book of Abraham."[75] Postulating that Smith translated more text than we presently possess does not arise from any compelling evidence but from the need to resolve problems

---

74. Ibid.
75. JS History, vol. B-1, 597 (DHC 2:238).

arising from the reverse-translation theory, which requires that the Book of Abraham precede the Alphabets and bound Grammar.

Anson Call's Reminiscence

To support the assertion that Smith only published a small portion of the Book of Abraham in 1842, Gee and other scholars have drawn on the reminiscence of Utah Mormon Anson Call, who, in recalling an incident in 1879 that supposedly occurred forty years earlier in Missouri in "late July 1838," said:

> While at Far West [Missouri] I happened in John Cor[ril]l's or the church store and my attention was called by Vincent Knights who was opening some boxes of goods.
>
> Say he, "Joseph will be much pleased with these. He had been very uneasy about the translation of the Bible and Egyptian Records. Here they are," placing them on the table. Said he to me, "If you will take one of these, I will the other and we will carry them over to Joseph's office."
>
> There we found Joseph and six or seven other brethren. Joseph was much pleased with the arrival of the books, and said to us "Sit down and we will read to you from the translations of the Book of Abraham." Oliver Cowdery then read until he was tired when Thomas Marsh read making altogether about two hours.[76]

Gee argues that because "it takes about half an hour" to read the Book of Abraham aloud, "this indicates that by 1838, Joseph Smith had translated approximately four times as much as we currently have in the Book of Abraham."[77] This speculation has been repeated by other researchers.[78] However, the accuracy of Call's reminiscence has been challenged since by "late July 1838" Cowdery was no longer a member of the church and had left Far West. Mormon writer H. Donl Peterson noted: "This entry

---

76. Anson Call, "Copied from the Journal of Anson Call," Feb. 1879, CHL.

77. John Gee, "Eyewitness, Hearsay, and Physical Evidence of the Joseph Smith Papyri." In *The Disciple as Witness: Essays on Latter-day Saint History and Doctrine in Honor of Richard Lloyd Anderson*, ed. Stephen D. Ricks, Donald W. Parry, and Andrew H. Hedges (Provo, Utah: Foundation for Ancient Research and Mormon Studies, 2000), 201.

78. Muhlestein and Hansen. "'The Work of Translating,'" 147; Hauglid, *Textual History of the Book of Abraham*, 4.

contains several valuable insights except for one problem: Oliver Cowdery was not in good standing in the Church in 1838 and would not have been in such a gathering by September 1838. Apparently Anson Call confused Oliver Cowdery's name with that of another person when he recorded this episode."[79]

In 2016, Muhlestein and Hansen also conceded that "Cowdery had been excommunicated some months earlier and was not in Far West at this date." Yet these authors want to argue: "This source strongly suggests that the Book of Abraham had been translated beyond Abraham 5 before the end of 1835. It would take fairly strong evidence to discard this historical source, as problematic as it is."[80] They believe: "His [Call's] writing seems to have taken place sometime afterwards, yet his ability to give a precise date suggests he was consulting a diary."[81] How is "late July 1838" a precise date? If Call had a "diary" with specific dates, as Muhlestein and Hansen speculate, it was not evidently used to write his autobiography when it covers the same period of time. Call gives no day or month for his arrival at Far West, but implies that it was during the "summer."[82] The next date he gives is "the month of September [1838]," when he says he "received a visit from Joseph, Hyrum and Sidney Rigdon" at the Three Forks settlement located about thirty miles northwest of Adam-ondi-Ahman in Clinton (now Gentry) County, Missouri. From Smith's own contemporary journal, this visit actually took place on 12 August 1838.[83] In my opinion, Muhlestein and Hansen's attempt to bolster Call's 1879 reminiscence despite the demonstrably inaccurate reference to Cowdery by suggesting the use of a "diary" is wishful thinking.

The only source available for Call's statement is located in the LDS Church History Library in Salt Lake City and claims to

---

79. H. Donl Peterson, *The Story of the Book of Abraham: Mummies, Manuscripts, and Mormonism* (Salt Lake City: Deseret Book Co., 1995), 140–41.

80. Muhlestein and Hansen. "'The Work of Translating,'" 147.

81. Ibid.

82. Anson Call, "Autobiography of Anson Call," 3–4, typescript, BYU.

83. Smith, Journal, 12 Aug. 1838 (*JSP,* J1:303n232). The Kirtland Revelation Book includes "material facts left out the history of the church," compiled by W. W. Phelps and Willard Richards, which mentions: "1838. Aug 16 to 20. Joseph was att the 3 forks of grand river, with Rigdon Hyrum & Babbit, to see the country, with Anson Call—mob tried to intercept him on his retrn" (*JSP,* MRB:661).

have been "Copied from the Journal of Anson Call" in February 1879. Early Mormons sometimes used the term "journal" to refer to retrospective accounts. Smith, for example, published in the July 1839 issue of the *Times and Seasons*, "Extract, from the Private Journal of Joseph Smith Jr.," which detailed his experiences in Missouri the previous year but, as the editors of the Joseph Smith Papers acknowledge, "was not in fact based on a journal source."[84] Extracts from what were purported to be "Elder [Heber C.] Kimball's Journal" were published serially in the *Times and Seasons* in 1845. They gave an account of his journey from Ohio to Missouri in the spring and summer of 1834 as a member of Zion's Camp, but biographer Stanley B. Kimball warned that the 1845 publication was "not a journal in any sense of the word, but is rather a memoir of events."[85] Smith's official history includes a lengthy account of an interview between Smith and the Pottawattamie Indian chiefs in Nauvoo in July 1843, which is said to have been copied from "W[ilford]. Woodruff's journal."[86] Despite the claim, the excerpt is nowhere in Woodruff's journal but was evidently composed ex post facto on 29 April 1855.[87]

The sequence of events may not have been as Call recalled them in his 1879 statement. In one autobiographical narrative, Call said he left Kirtland on 20 March 1838 with a company of other Mormons, which included his father and brother. Travelling southward about 100 miles, they stopped at Wellsville on the Ohio River. He says he left his family in Wellsville and went on the river to Missouri with Asael Smith Jr. and George Gee and their wives. His father, Cyril, also accompanied him. After reaching Jack's Landing near Richmond, he and his father traveled about forty miles on foot to Far West. They purchased 120 acres of land in Caldwell County but needed more for Mormon converts

---

84. Joseph Smith, "Extract, from the Private Journal of Joseph Smith Jr.," *Times and Seasons* 1 (July 1839): 2–9 (*JSP*, H1:466).

85. "Elder Kimball's Journal," *Times and Seasons* 6 (15 Jan. 1845): 771–73; 6 (1 Feb. 1845): 787–90; Stanley B. Kimball, *On the Potters Wheel: The Diaries of Heber C. Kimball* (Salt Lake City: Signature Books, 1987), 177.

86. See *Deseret News* 6 (7 Jan. 1857): 345–55, 348 (DHC 5:478).

87. See Woodruff, Journal, vol. 7, 29 Apr. 1855. See also discussion in Vogel, *History of Joseph Smith and The Church of Jesus Christ of Latter-day Saints*, 5:574n27; 7:262n659.

soon to arrive with Almon W. Babbitt from Canada. At this point, Cyril left Anson to help other family members in Ohio migrate to Missouri. Meanwhile, Anson purchased a large tract of land near Three Forks of the Grand River, located about thirty miles northwest of Adam-ondi-Ahman, which, in turn, was located thirty miles north of Far West. Anson states that on the 5 July he "started back to meet my family" and met them on the road about 125 miles east of Far West with Babbitt and his company from Canada. According to Smith's journal, the Canadian company arrived at Far West on 28 July.[88] In his autobiography, Call mentions that his wife's sister, Hannah Flint, had joined the company and then states, "I travelled with the same company and my family to Far West. After resting about one week at Far West, I proceeded to the three forks of the Grand River to my farm in company with Phineas Young, John Schnider, Joel Terrill and some others."[89]

It is at this point that Call's 1879 reminiscence adds that during the week at Far West he heard Cowdery and Marsh read the Book of Abraham, which would have been 28 July to about 4 August 1838. However, it is possible that Call was mistaken about the sequence of events and that he had actually heard the Book of Abraham read during an earlier visit to Far West. In an 1885 interview with Mormons B. H. Roberts and John M. Whitaker, Call said that he shipped $2,400 of goods in boxes from Kirtland and that the church also sent boxes at the same time. When they arrived at the church's Missouri store, John Corrill and Vinson Knight discovered that $400 worth of goods were missing. Leaving Far West, Call opened a farm in Ray County and then visited Far West on his way north to Three Forks of the Grand River in Daviess County. According to Call,

> While there I received word from Vincent [Vinson] Knight that he had made a discovery of some of my goods and recognized some of them on the wives of David Whitmer, John Whitmer and Oliver Cowdery's families. There was a search warrant taken out and put in the hands of Dimmick Huntington, he being the sheriff. ... I then went and swore out warrents for the arrest of these men before the

88. Smith, Journal, 28 July 1838 (*JSP*, J1:294).
89. Anson Call, Autobiography, 6, typescript, BYU.

justice of the Peace whose name I have now forgotten. They took a change of Venue to Clay County. It was about this time that Sidney Rigdon preached "The Salt Sermon."[90]

Rigdon delivered his Salt Sermon—directed at Mormon apostates—on 17 June 1838, which led to the expulsion of Cowdery, the Whitmers, and other dissenters from Far West. Perhaps the boxes containing the Book of Abraham materials arrived at or near the same time as Call's boxes. Under 24 May 1838, William Swartzel wrote that he saw Smith's "box of mummys" at Richmond landing.[91] Cowdery's reading of the Book of Abraham may have occurred after 24 May and before his expulsion on 19 June 1838, although it is difficult to imagine Smith and Cowdery in the same room after Cowdery's excommunication on 12 April.

Nevertheless, it is possible to explain Call's reminiscence without concluding there was more of the Book of Abraham than we now have. It may be that Smith presented readers with the two ledger books, one with the longest finalized translation of the Book of Abraham and the other with the Grammar and Alphabet of the Egyptian Language, which included a translation of characters from the beginning of the scroll containing the Book of Abraham. In this regard, it is interesting that Call used the plural "translations"—"we will read to you from the Translations of the Book of Abraham."

If Smith possessed more of the Book of Abraham translation beyond chapter 5, it seems inconceivable that he would not have included it when he published Facsimile 3 in the May 1842 issue of the *Times and Seasons*. Although he resigned as editor of the *Times and Seasons* in the 15 November 1842 issue, Smith promised more text of the Book of Abraham in the 1 February 1843 issue.[92] There is no reason for him not to publish more text if he had it. Smith's journal entry for 8 March 1842 is clear that what was

90. Anson Call, Interview by B. H. Roberts and John M. Whitaker, 6 Dec. 1885, MS 4875, CHL.

91. William Swartzel, *Mormonism Exposed* (Perkin, Ohio: By the Author, 1840), 9.

92. See "Valedictory," *Times and Seasons* 4 (15 Nov. 1842): 8. "We would further state that we had the promise of Br. Joseph, to furnish us with further extracts from the Book of Abraham" (*Times and Seasons* 4 [1 Feb. 1843]: 95).

being translated was for the next issue of the periodical and would accompany the large illustration of Facsimile 2.[93]

Conclusion

There is no good reason to believe that Abraham 3–5 were first dictated in Kirtland in 1835. The presence of numerous Hebrew terms and Hebrew-inspired substitutions date these chapters to after, not before, Smith's lessons with Seixas in early 1836. Smith's journal clearly states that he was "translating" in March 1842 (for the tenth number of the *Times and Seasons*). The presence of the Hebrew terms is problematic for defenders, and no one has yet provided compelling evidence that Hebrew was added to an 1835 manuscript. The only reason to offer such suppositions is to argue for a reverse-translation theory.

---

93. Smith, Journal, 8 Mar. 1842 (*JSP*, J2:42).

7 The Lost Papyrus and Catalyst Theories

Despite the fact that the hieratic characters in the margins of the three Kirtland-era manuscripts of the Book of Abraham were taken from Hôr's Book of Breathings, one approach in arguing for the ancient historicity of the Book of Abraham has been to claim that its true source remains lost to this day and was perhaps destroyed in the 1871 Chicago fire. In this chapter, I analyze claims that the English text of Abraham did not come from the Breathing Permit of Hôr but from a now-lost portion of papyrus.

Red Ink

Shortly after the papyri fragments were discovered in the mid-1960s, BYU religion professor Hugh Nibley speculated that the fragments of the Book of Breathings were not the true source of the Book of Abraham. In 1975, he suggested:

> the Prophet Joseph [Smith] himself has supplied us with the conclusive evidence that the manuscript today identified as the Book of Breathings, J.S. Papyri X and XI, was *not* in his opinion the source of the Book of Abraham. For he has furnished a clear and specific description of the latter: "The record of Abraham and Joseph, found with the mummies, is (1) beautifully written on papyrus, with black, and (2) a small part red, ink or paint, (3) in perfect preservation."[1]

Because the Book of Breathings did not have red ink and was badly damaged, Nibley proposed that it was not the source for the Book of Abraham. Nibley quoted the *History of the Church* (2:348), which made it appear that Smith was speaking when actually the

---

1. Hugh W. Nibley, *The Message of the Joseph Smith Papyri: An Egyptian Endowment* (Salt Lake City: Deseret Book Co., 1975), 2.

History quoted, without attribution, Oliver Cowdery's description of the papyri from the December 1835 issue of the *Messenger and Advocate*, in which Cowdery stated, in a letter to William Frye: "Upon the subject of the Egyptian records, or rather the writings of Abraham and Joseph, I may say a few words. This record is beautifully written on papyrus with black, and a small part, red ink or paint, in perfect preservation."[2]

Cowdery was giving a general description of both papyri scrolls, one purportedly containing the record of Abraham, the other the record of Joseph son of Jacob/Israel, which does contain some writing in red ink. In describing the papyri, Cowdery was influenced by an affidavit that Michael Chandler had obtained from several medical doctors in Philadelphia: "The features of some of these Mummies are in perfect expression. The papyrus, covered with black or red ink, or paint, in excellent preservation, are very interesting."[3]

In 1975, H. Michael Marquardt, a scholar of early Mormon history, observed in regards to Nibley's assertion:

> Oliver Cowdery mentioned in his letter two rolls of papyri (Abraham and Joseph) plus two or three small pieces of papyri. The two rolls of papyri that were in Joseph Smith's possession ... were the Ta-sherit-Min Papyrus (beautifully written for a woman with [some] red ink) and the Book of Breathings Papyrus written for a man named Hor with black [ink] only. Oliver Cowdery wrote in terms of both records and not the record of Abraham alone. The statement used by Dr. Nibley does not disqualify Joseph Smith Papyrus XI as a candidate for the source of the Book of Abraham as he would like us to believe. ... The idea that Joseph Smith and/or Oliver Cowdery were describing another papyrus which has since been lost is certainly not correct.[4]

Nibley did not respond.

---

2. "Egyptian Mummies—Ancient Records," *LDS Messenger and Advocate* 2 (Dec. 1835): 234. See also Oliver Cowdery, Letter, Kirtland, Ohio, to William Frye, Lebanon, Calhoun County, Illinois, 22 Dec. 1835, Oliver Cowdery Letterbook, 68–74, Henry E. Huntington Library, San Marino, California.

3. "Egyptian Mummies," 235.

4. H. Michael Marquardt, *The Book of Abraham Papyrus Found: An Answer to Dr. Hugh Nibley's Book "The Message of the Joseph Smith Papyri: An Egyptian Endowment" as It Relates to the Source of the Book of Abraham* (Sandy, Utah: the author, 1975), 2; wording adjusted slightly for readability.

Glass Slides and Long Scrolls

John Gee and Kerry Muhlestein have advocated, post Nibley, a new version of the missing papyrus theory. According to them, the Book of Abraham text did not come from the fragments of the Book of Breathings but from a text that immediately followed the Book of Breathings on what they postulate was an extra-long papyri scroll that was sold to the Woods Museum in Chicago and was subsequently destroyed in the great Chicago fire of 1871. To support this theory, they refer to eyewitness testimony that identifies a long scroll as the source for the Book of Abraham, not the fragments which Joseph Smith had mounted on large pieces of paper about 1837 to help preserve them. These fragments mounted on pieces of paper, some of which featured on one or both sides plans for the Kirtland Temple and a map of northern Ohio, were at some point cut into smaller pieces and placed under glass in picture frames. In 2017, Gee asserted:

> The nineteenth-century eyewitnesses, both Mormon and non-Mormon, favorable and hostile to the Church, agree that the Book of Abraham was translated from a long roll of papyrus that was still a long roll in the 1840s and 1850s. The current fragments of the Joseph Smith Papyri, however, were all mounted on heavy paper and placed in glass frames in 1837. None of them can be the long roll described in the 1840s and 1850s. So these fragments are specifically not the source of the Book of Abraham according to the eyewitnesses.[5]

Four years earlier, Muhlestein had similarly explained:

> As we look through all the accounts, people who knew Joseph Smith and saw the papyri fragments and the rolls while he was alive and heard him or his mother talk about them … he had two rolls one of them a long roll and that's the one that Joseph and others refer to as the source of the Book of Abraham. That roll was destroyed

---

5. John Gee, *An Introduction to the Book of Abraham* (Provo, Utah: Religious Studies Center, Brigham Young Universities; Salt Lake City: Deseret Book Co., 2017), 84–85. See also John Gee, "Some Puzzles from the Joseph Smith Papyri," *FARMS Review* 20/1 (2008): 119, where Gee states: "Both Mormon and non-Mormon eyewitnesses from the nineteenth century agree that it was a 'roll of papyrus from which [Joseph Smith] translated the Book of Abraham,' meaning the 'long roll of manuscript,' and not one of the mounted fragments that eventually ended up in the Metropolitan Museum of Art."

in the Chicago fire. And what we can document is that he had already mounted some under glass before people were saying that he's translating from the long roll; so that the fragments that we have they're not what others were saying and what Joseph Smith was saying he was translating from. Anyone who tells you that Joseph Smith is translating from the text around Facsimile 1 on the small fragment that we have is just flying in the face of the historical accounts that tell us that the source is the long scroll.[6]

In 2016, Muhlestein discussed the sources upon which his long-scroll theory is based and stated: "While most of the accounts do not paint a fully clear picture, taken together the only scenario that can reconcile all of the accounts is that the long scroll was the source for the Book of Abraham. ... Differentiating between the mounted fragments and the longer rolls is an important component to understanding what eyewitnesses were referring to when they spoke of the source of the Book of Abraham."[7]

A problem with Muhlestein's method is that none of the eyewitnesses possessed the knowledge necessary to verify a long-scroll theory. Most witnesses simply expressed an assumption based on Smith's identification of one scroll as containing the writings of Abraham and the other scroll as containing the writings of Joseph. No one distinguished between the mounted fragments under glass and the scroll as the source for the Book of Abraham. Thus Muhlestein assigns to these casual observers a knowledge they most certainly did not have.

Condition and Length of the Breathing Permit

Before considering the eyewitnesses, we need to understand that the long-scroll theory requires several improbable assumptions. The main assumption is that the text of the record of Abraham followed the text of the Book of Breathings on the same papyrus roll. Gee believes that Book of Abraham Facsimile 3 "came from

---

6. FAIR Mormon, www.youtube.com/watch?v=HMVX-Km_G6Y. Accessed 26 May 2019.

7. Kerry Muhlestein, "Papyri and Presumptions: A Careful Examination of the Eyewitness Accounts Associated with the Joseph Smith Papyri," *Journal of Mormon History* 42 (Oct. 2016): 35, 37.

the middle of a long roll,"[8] instead of at the end, and that the Hôr scroll was originally "320 cm ([or] about 10 feet) [long]."[9] In 2000, he asserted that the

> Scroll of Hor ... was a roll of some size (estimated original dimen-sions ... 320 x 11 cm [or about ten feet]). The outer leaves, separated and mounted in Kirtland in 1836(?), remain as JSP I, XI, and X (in that order, from right to left). This roll contains the so-called "Book of Breathings Made by Isis" and at least one other text. The relation-ship of this roll to P. Louvre 3284 ... seems to be that JSP XI–X is an abridged copy of the same text as P. Louvre 3284 to the extent that a one-to-one correspondence exists between the columns of the text, which leads us to expect that there would have been two other col-umns [of text] on the roll of Hor's papyrus in addition to the vignette preserved as Facsimile 3 in the Book of Abraham. ... This argues for more than one text on the roll; thus we would expect more to have remained on the roll than the two columns of text from the Book of Breathings and the vignette (Facsimile 3).[10]

After giving examples of papyrus scrolls containing more than one record, Gee argued: "Just because the preserved sections of the Joseph Smith Papyri are funerary in nature does not mean that they could not have had other texts, either on the verso or on missing sections of the rolls."[11]

Gee believes the "one other text" on the scroll following Hôr's Book of Breathings was the Book of Abraham. University of Chi-cago Egyptologist Robert K. Ritner responded to Gee in 2011, explaining: "'320 cm' ... is the average length of a blank papyrus roll as manufactured in the Ptolemaic era—not the length of the known Books of Breathing copied on sections cut from such rolls."[12] Ritner further stated that Books of Breathings are of a

---

8. John Gee, "Facsimile 3 and Book of the Dead 125," in John Gee and Brian M. Hauglid, *Astronomy, Papyrus, and Covenant* (Provo, Utah: FARMS, 2005), 96.

9. John Gee, *A Guide to the Joseph Smith Papyri* (Provo, Utah: Foundation for Ancient Research and Mormon Studies, 2000), 10, 12–13.

10. John Gee, "Eyewitness, Hearsay, and Physical Evidence of the Joseph Smith Papyri," in *The Disciple as Witness*, Stephen D. Ricks, Donald W. Parry, and Andrew H. Hedges, eds. (Provo, Utah: FARMS, 2000), 188–89.

11. Ibid., 192.

12. Robert K. Ritner, *The Joseph Smith Egyptian Papyri: A Complete Edition* (Salt Lake City: Smith–Pettit Foundation, 2011), 87n27.

"uniform pattern" and "As a result of this uniformity, the original size of the papyrus is not in doubt. With textual restorations and the now lost Facsimile 3, the papyrus will have measured about 150–155 cm [or 59–61 inches long]."[13] In 2000, Ritner noted:

> The most that is missing from this text is simply two columns worth of Egyptian hieratic text and possibly a small vignette, but other than that there would be nothing more that would inflate its length beyond its current size. It is both unprecedented and unreasonable to assume that an intrusive text about a completely different matter, a narrative history of Abraham and his descendants, would have been inserted into a document whose beginning, middle, and end is devoted specifically to the resurrection of an Egyptian priest.[14]

Like Gee, Muhlestein believes that "large scrolls could contain several texts with several different original authors."[15] However, the fact that some Egyptian papyri contain more than one book cannot be reasonably used as proof, without additional documentation, to conclude that the Breathing Permit of Hôr *may have* included an alien text such as the Book of Abraham. As historian David Hackett Fischer explains: "Valid empirical proof requires not merely the establishment of possibility, but an estimate of probability."[16]

In this instance, the probability that Smith's Book of Breathings preceded another, unrelated text from a foreign author, such

---

13. Ibid., 7.

14. Robert K. Ritner interview in *The Lost Book of Abraham: Investigating a Remarkable Mormon Claim*" (Video/DVD; Grand Rapids, Michigan: Institute for Religious Research, 2002). Ritner more recently stated at the end of his translation of the Hôr papyrus: "This marks the end of the preserved text. Paragraphs XI–XIV are lost, comprising approximately two columns (Cols. VI–VII)" (Ritner, *Joseph Smith Papyri*, 137). In an essay published in *Dialogue: A Journal of Mormon Thought* in 2000 and again in the *Journal of Near Eastern Studies* in 2003, Ritner further responded: "The number of vignettes varies in Books of Breathings, but introductory and concluding vignettes are common. At most, the [Joseph Smith] papyrus might have been expanded by the inclusion of a further, middle vignette, as found in Papyrus Tübingen 2016, but there is no reasonable expectation of any further text, and certainly nothing even vaguely resembling the alien narrative of The Book of Abraham" (Robert K. Ritner, "The 'Breathing Permit of Hôr' Thirty-four Years Later," *Dialogue: A Journal of Mormon Thought* 33/4 [Winter 2000]: 101; "The 'Breathing Permit of Hôr' among the Joseph Smith Papyri," *Journal of Near Eastern Studies* 62/3 [2003]: 166).

15. Muhlestein, "Papyri and Presumptions," 35.

16. David Hackett Fischer, *Historians' Fallacies: Toward a Logic of Historical Thought* (New York: Harper & Row, 1970), 53.

as the Book of Abraham, is so remote as to be non-existent. Egyptologist Marc Coenen, an expert on Egyptian funerary texts, also responded to the long-scroll theory:

> Unquestionably, JSP I, X, and XI were originally longer. A comparison with Papyrus Louvre N 3158, which contains the most complete version extant of the Document of Breathing Made by Isis, indicates that as many as three to four columns of hieratic text may be missing between the end of PJS X and the segment [Joseph] Smith identified as "Book of Abraham" Facsimile 3. ... Finally, some writers have rightly pointed out that papyri from Greco-Roman Egypt are sometimes inscribed with more than one text. No one denies that other funerary and/or ritual compositions were sometimes appended to a Book of the Dead or other funerary compositions. However, concluding that a record of Abraham or any other text foreign to Ptolemaic Egyptian funerary and/or liturgical practice was once attached to the Smith papyri is an assertion not based upon widely accepted Egyptological analysis.[17]

Ritner and Gee agree that the Hôr papyrus originally included at least two additional columns of hieratic text and possibly another vignette between JSP X and the missing Facsimile 3, while Coenen thinks that "three or four columns of hieratic text" may be missing. As early as 1968, Klaus Baer used other Books of Breathings to estimate that the original length of the Hôr scroll was 150 to 155 cm, or 59 to 61 inches with about 59 cm or 23.2 inches missing.[18] In 2010, researchers Andrew W. Cook and Christopher C. Smith estimated the length of the missing papyrus by measuring the diminishing distance between the repeated patterns of damage along the top edge of the remaining fragments of the Hôr scroll, which were taken from the outer winds of the scroll when rolled up. They determined that the missing interior section was

---

17. Marc Coenen, "The Ownership and Dating of Certain Joseph Smith Papyri," in Ritner, *Joseph Smith Egyptian Papyri*, 67.

18. Klaus Baer, "The Breathing Permit of Hôr: A Translation of the Apparent Source of the Book of Abraham," *Dialogue: A Journal of Mormon Thought* 3/3 (Autumn 1968): 112n17, 127n113. Mormon Egyptologist Michael D. Rhodes estimates the total length of the Hôr scroll at 156 cm with 89.5 cm extant and 66.5 cm (26.1 inches) missing (Michael D. Rhodes, *The Hor Book of Breathings: A Translation and Commentary* [Provo, Utah: FARMS, 2002], 4).

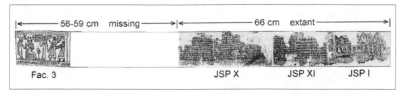

Figure 7.1. Approximate measurements for the Hôr Book of Breathings.

about 56 cm, or about twenty-two inches, long.[19] This means that there was an intact roll of about four inches wide and about two feet long that Gee's and Muhlestein's eyewitnesses saw and identified with the Book of Abraham.

This approximately two-foot roll was no doubt among the Egyptian relics sold on 26 May 1856 to Able Combs,[20] who immediately sold a portion of the collection to the St. Louis Museum, where they were placed on display. Later the same year, Gustaf Seyffarth, a visiting professor at nearby Concordia Seminary, described the contents of the Smith collection for the museum's catalogue and found that the purported Abraham "papyrus roll" was "not a record," as Joseph Smith had stated, but "an invocation to the Deity Osiris in which occurs the name of the person (Horus), and a picture of the attendant spirits introducing the dead to the Judge, Osiris."[21]

19. Andrew W. Cook and Christopher C. Smith. "The Original Length of the Scroll of Hôr." *Dialogue: A Journal of Mormon Thought* 43/4 (Winter 2010): 1–42. Gee had previously used the formula developed by Friedhelm Hoffman for calculating the length of incomplete scrolls and decided that Hôr's Book of Breathings was originally 41 feet long (John Gee, "Some Puzzles from the Joseph Smith Papyri," *FARMS Review* 20/1 [2008]: 120–21). After Cook and Smith's article appeared, Gee criticized their methodology as "anything but accurate" and "glaringly underestimates the length of the scroll" (John Gee, "Formulas and Faith," *Journal of the Book of Mormon and Other Restoration Scripture* 21/1 [2012]: 63). Gee was unaware that Cook and Smith's methodology was essentially the same as Hoffman's and that Gee had misapplied Hoffman's formula (Andrew W. Cook, "Formulas and Facts: A Response to John Gee," *Dialogue: A Journal of Mormon Thought* 45/3 [Fall 2012]: 1–10).

20. L[ouis]. C. Bidamon and Emma Smith Bidamon, Bill of Sale, Nauvoo, Illinois, to A[bel]. Combs, 26 May 1856, CHL. See also Jay M. Todd, *The Saga of the Book of Abraham* (Salt Lake City: Deseret Book Co., 1969), 290.

21. J. P. Bates, *Catalogue of Birds, Quadrupeds, Reptiles, &c.* (St. Louis: Democrat Book and Job Office, 1856), 31. See also Todd, *Saga*, 298; Stanley B. Kimball, "New Light on Old Egyptian Mummies, 1848–71," *Dialogue: A Journal of Mormon Thought* 16 (Winter 1983): 73–74.

Seyffarth was describing Facsimile 3 of the Book of Abraham, which only survives through "a poorly rendered engraving."[22] According to Smith, the image represents "Abraham sitting upon Pharaoh's throne ... reasoning upon the principles of Astronomy." The female figure standing behind the throne is Pharaoh, Smith continued, while the other female figure is a prince, followed by a waiter and a slave. Smith's interpretation was wrong. The vignette actually depicts the owner of the scroll, Hôr, being presented by Maat and Anubis to Osiris, who sits on the throne with Isis standing behind him. Smith thought that the figure between Maat and Anubis is "Shulem, one of the King's principal waiters, as represented by the characters above his hand." Ritner translates the characters as "The Osiris Hôr, justified forever."[23] Part of the invocation below the scene reads, according to Ritner, "Grant salvation to the Osiris Hôr, the justified."[24]

There is no doubt that the "papyrus roll" Seyffarth described in 1856 as containing a judgment scene and the name "Horus"— the Latin equivalent of Hôr—was the approximately two-foot roll that ended with Facsimile 3. This roll was evidently sold to the Woods Museum in Chicago along with the other Egyptian artifacts and destroyed in the fire in 1871.

The theory that this lost scroll was close to eight feet long— instead of two feet—and contained an alien text that defended the Hebrew belief in Yahweh and condemned the Egyptian religion and rituals found throughout the preceding text is, at the very least, improbable. Are to we to believe an actual Book of Joseph (son of Jacob/Israel) was similarly attached to the end of the scroll containing Ta-sherit-Min's Book of the Dead? The implications of the long-scroll theory are, in my opinion, ludicrous.

To bolster the long-scroll theory, Gee appeals to hearsay evidence based on Hugh Nibley's 1968 reminiscence of his uncle's account of LDS Church President Joseph F. Smith's 1906 reminiscence of an event that occurred more than sixty years earlier (when Smith was about five years old) of seeing his uncle Joseph

---

22. Ritner, *Joseph Smith Egyptian Papyri*, 137.
23. Ibid., 139.
24. Ibid., 140.

Smith working on the Egyptian papyri and that one of the rolls "when unrolled on the floor extended through two rooms of the Mansion House."[25] Earlier in 1968, Nibley had only represented Joseph F. Smith as saying he had seen his uncle Joseph Smith seated on the floor of his home in Nauvoo with "Egyptian manuscripts spread out all around him."[26] Muhlestein chooses not to mention Nibley's problematic reminiscence in his 2016 essay defending the long-roll theory.

Facsimile 1

Another problem the long-scroll theory has to overcome is that the text of the Book of Abraham twice refers to the accompanying vignette depicting Abraham upon an altar and an idolatrous priest attempting to sacrifice him. Egyptologists know that this actually describes the reanimation of Osiris. Abraham 1:12 reads: "and that you may have a knowledge of this altar, I will refer you to the representation at the commencement of this record." And this statement in verse 14: "That you may have an understanding of these gods, I have given you the fashion of them in the figures at the beginning."

These statements regarding Facsimile 1 create a serious problem for the long-scroll theory. Indeed, it is difficult to explain how the Book of Abraham can refer to the opening vignette of the Book of Breathings as "the commencement of this record." Another problem is that the vignette is associated with Books of Breathing from the Ptolemaic era (238–153 BCE),[27] not from Abraham's day (ca. 2000 BCE). In 2017, Gee acknowledged this problem but countered:

> Since the papyri come from the Ptolemaic period, 1,500 years after Abraham, the style of the pictures will not have been the same style as was current in Abraham's day. Abraham may not have included any

---

25. John Gee, "A Tragedy of Errors," *FARMS Review of Books* 4/1 (1992): 106n36. Hugh W. Nibley, "Phase I," *Dialogue: A Journal of Mormon Thought* 3/2 (Summer 1968): 101.

26. Hugh W. Nibley, "A New Look at the Pearl of Great Price: Part I. Challenge and Response," *Improvement Era* 71/3 (Mar. 1968): 17.

27. On dating of the Breathing Permit of Hôr, see Coenen, "The Ownership and Dating of Certain Joseph Smith Papyri," 57–71.

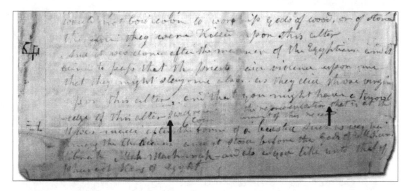

Figure 7.2. Page 1 of Book of Abraham Manuscript-A in the handwriting of Frederick G. Williams, showing where the line begins to curve upwards (left arrow) and the probable point where text was subsequently inserted (right arrow) explaining the location of the "representation."

illustrations in his original account. The references to the facsimiles within the text of the Book of Abraham seem to have been nine-teenth-century editorial insertions. The earliest manuscript we have shows that the phrase "I will refer you to the representation that is at the commencement of this record" from Abraham 1:12 was squished in two lines of smaller handwriting in the space at the end of the paragraph between Abraham 1:12 and 1:13.[28]

As discussed in chapter one, the Frederick G. Williams document is not the "earliest manuscript" but was created simul-taneously with Warren Parrish's manuscript as Smith dictated in November 1835. Although there was some hesitation about the wording, the reference to Facsimile 1 was not a later insertion. The characterization that the text is "squished in two lines of smaller handwriting in the space at the end of the paragraph" is inaccu-rate. Because this sheet of paper was unlined, there is a general upward slant to all of Williams's lines, especially at the end of paragraphs. The only thing that is apparent is that the last line of the paragraph signals an insertion since the text does not start at the left margin but was inserted into the space created by the up-ward angle of the previous line. The question is *where* the insertion begins. Cutting out the entire reference to the sacrificial altar does

---

28. Gee, *Introduction to the Book of Abraham*, 143–44.

not work, because doing so would create too much space between paragraphs, which was not Williams's practice.

Gee, as well as Jensen and Hauglid, have suggested that Williams inserted the phrase "I will refer you to the representation that is at the commencement of this record" because the line starts to curve upward at that point.[29] However, since other paragraphs in the Williams document also end with a similar upward angle, this suggestion provides no clue as to where the insertion begins. Moreover, the suggestion does not make grammatical sense, leaving the sentence incomplete: "and that you may have a knowledge of this altar."

To maintain coherence, the text probably originally ended at the word "representation," so that it read: "and that you may have a knowledge of this alter I will refer you to the representation," which would have been obvious to those in the room with Smith. At the same time, Parrish wrote the same words at the bottom of page 2 of his manuscript.[30] Later, Williams added, for clarification, the phrase "that is at the commencement of this record." Parrish's document demonstrates that there was some hesitation about the wording of this clarification. He first wrote: "that is lying before you." While this was true for Smith and his scribes, it would not be true for readers of the published text. Parrish therefore cancelled these words and added in the bottom margin of the page: "<at the commencement of this record.>"[31] Williams evidently made his insertion after the wording had been decided.

Gee's explanation for the reference in Abraham 1:14, which appears at the top of page 2 in the Williams document, also fails for similar reasons. Concerning this passage, Gee asserted: "Abraham 1:14 was added in a smaller hand squeezed into the margin at the top of the page above the header, ignoring the ruled left margin."[32]

There is no reason to believe these lines were inserted later. This page, like the previous one, is unruled; so there is no top margin that would have been left blank. Williams, in fact, began all of his

---

29. Ibid., 143; Book of Abraham Manuscript, 1 (*JSP*, R4:195).

30. Book of Abraham Manuscript, 2 (*JSP*, R4:207).

31. This text in the Jensen-Hauglid transcription should have been placed within angled brackets (*JSP*, R4:207).

32. Gee, *Introduction to the Book of Abraham*, 144.

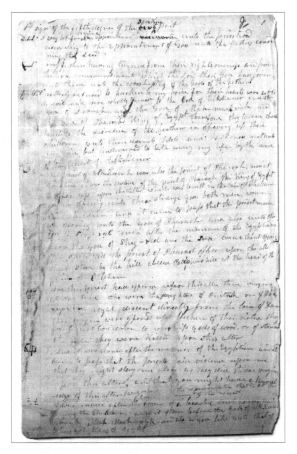

Figure 7.3. Page 1 of Book of Abraham Manuscript-A, showing upward angle of writing, especially at the end of paragraphs.

pages of text at the top. The left margin line is hand drawn in pencil and does not extend above the first character, indicating that it was drawn after the text. Page 4 also begins without observing the right margin, and each successive line of text moves a little to the right, making room for the first character that begins the fifth line. The handwriting of the passage in question is not smaller or cramped in any way. Most importantly, Parrish, who was writing at the same time, recorded the passage in the middle of his page 3 without any disturbance. Gee concludes: "The Book of Abraham actually reads smoothly without these additions. Thus these statements in the text seem to be nineteenth-century additions approved by, if not made by, Joseph Smith."[33] This could only be true if the first reference to Facsimile 1 were completely gone, which, as we saw, would leave too much space between paragraphs.

The Joseph Smith Papers editors in volume 5 of the documents series as well as in volume 4 of the revelations and translations series follow Gee's interpretation of the two passages in the Williams document, marking them as insertions.[34] In the latter volume, editors Robin Scott Jensen and Brian Hauglid incorrectly state, in introducing the Williams document, that the two insertions were "silently incorporated" in Parrish's shorter document and that "at least some parts of the [two] manuscripts were not created simultaneously."[35] However, in neither document are the two references to Facsimile 1 insertions, and there is no reason to believe that Parrish and Williams did not write simultaneously up to Abraham 2:2.

Mounting of the Fragments

To set up his argument that witnesses identified the "long roll" as the source of the Book of Abraham rather than the mounted fragments which contained the Breathing Permit, Muhlestein had to establish a probable time for when the fragments were mounted. For this, he relied heavily on the late reminiscence of Luman Shurtliff, who said that he toured the Kirtland, Ohio, temple in 1837 and that he "looked at the parchment or Papyrus," which he apparently described as "sheets ... about eight by 12 inches."[36] Although not clearly stated, Muhlestein believes Shurtliff described the mounted fragments.

---

33. Ibid.

34. *JSP*, D5:78; and *JSP*, R4:195, 239n57. Regarding the first insertion in the Williams document corresponding to Abraham 1:12, Jensen and Hauglid assert: "While the ink looks uniform, both the content and cramped nature of the final lines indicate that this text was inserted" (R4:239n57). Concerning Abraham 1:14, which appears at the top of page 2 in the Williams document, Jensen and Hauglid state: "The content and spacing of this paragraph, along with similar revisions to the line at the bottom of the previous page, suggest that this paragraph was inserted" (see R4:239n64). In his transcription of the Williams document, Brian Hauglid for some reason did not indicate the beginning of the insertion in his 2010 book (Brian Hauglid, *A Textual History of the Book of Abraham: Manuscripts and Editions* [Provo, Utah: Neal A. Maxwell Institute for Religious Scholarship, Brigham Young University, 2010], 69).

35. Historical Introduction, *JSP*, R4:193.

36. Luman A. Shurtliff, "Biographical Sketch of the Life of Luman Andros Shurtliff," 27, typescript, BYU.

The clearest reference to the fragments being mounted dates to 1840 and was published close to the time of reporting. Muhlestein avoids quoting it. An unnamed reporter visited Joseph Smith in Commerce (later Nauvoo), Illinois, in April 1840 and saw the Egyptian artifacts. After viewing the mummies, this reporter stated that Smith

> walked to a secretary, on the opposite side of the room, and drew out several frames, covered with glass, under which were numerous fragments of Egyptian papyrus, on which, as usual, a great variety of hieroglyphical characters had been imprinted. ... They have been unrolled and preserved with great labor and care. [Joseph Smith said:] My time has hitherto been too much taken up to translate the whole of them, but I will show you how I interpret certain parts. *There*, said he, pointing to a particular character, that is the signature of the patriarch Abraham.[37]

While this early source verifies the preservation of fragments under glass, it also challenges the Muhlestein–Gee theory in locating Abraham's signature on one of the mounted fragments. Smith may have pointed to the second character in the right-hand column of JSP XI as the signature of Abraham. The first two characters have since flaked off, but W. W. Phelps copied them in the margin of his translation manuscript and keyed the first to "In the land of the Chaldeans" and the second to "Abraham."[38] The same two characters appeared at the end of the three Alphabets, where the second character was also identified with Abraham.[39] A similar account was given by future mayor of Boston Josiah Quincy, who visited Smith in Nauvoo in 1844 and later reported: "Some parchments inscribed with hieroglyphics were then offered us. They were preserved under glass and handled with great respect. 'That is the handwriting of Abraham, the Father of the Faithful,' said the prophet."[40]

---

37. "A Glance at the Mormons," *The Friend; a Religious and Literary Journal* 13/43 (25 July 1840): 342–43. Reprinted in "A Glance at the Mormons," *Quincy [Illinois] Whig* 3 (17 Oct. 1840); "A Glance at the Mormons," *The [New York] Sun*, 28 July 1840.

38. Book of Abraham Manuscript-C, ca. July–Nov. 1835, 1 (*JSP,* R4:219).

39. See, e.g., Egyptian Alphabet-A, ca. July–Nov. 1835, 4 (*JSP,* R4:68, 83, 93).

40. Josiah Quincy, *Figures of the Past: From the Leaves of Old Journals* (Boston: Roberts Brothers, 1883), 386.

In 2016, Muhlestein undermined his own thesis when he tried to head off criticism by mentioning that many of his witnesses made unwarranted assumptions about the scrolls, often assigning the penmanship to Abraham and Joseph, and assuming that "an entire scroll contained just one text authored by just one person."[41] Muhlestein evidently included Smith among those making incorrect assumptions about the papyri, which renders any argument resting on a distinction between the scroll and the mounted fragments effectively meaningless.

Sidestepping these challenging sources, Muhlestein instead quoted Luman Shurtliff's 1850s reminiscence for evidence that "a number of fragments had been cut and mounted already by the end of 1837."[42] However, as previously mentioned, Shurtliff is unclear about what he saw. "The parchment," he said, "appeared to be made of fine linnen cloth, starched or sized with some kind of gum, then ironed smooth." At this point, Shurtliff's account switches to the plural: "These sheets were about eight by twelve inches. They were rolled, put in a gum case and laid on the breast of the leading men of the Egyptians."[43]

The use of the plural "sheets" appears to be a general statement about the practice of the Egyptians, not specifically about Smith's papyrus. Shurtliff then switches back to the singular: "When the mummies were found this record was on his breast"—evidently referring to the one male mummy among the four that Smith procured in July 1835. Shurtliff then stated: "It was from this record that the Pearl of Great Price was translated by the Prophet."[44] Apparently Shurtliff thought the 8 inches x 12 inches sheet was the complete record of Abraham, which is the opposite of what Muhlestein hoped to establish.

It is uncertain which fragments Shurtliff was shown, but he may have seen JSP I and XI, which were originally glued to the same sheet of paper before being cut apart; together, when glued

---

41. Muhlestein, "Papyri and Presumptions," 35.
42. Ibid.
43. Shurtliff, "Biographical Sketch," 27. The manuscript version reads differently: "these sheets were about as large as the face of this book when opened" (Luman A. Shurtliff, "History of Luman Andros Shirtliff," ca. 1852–76, 88, CHL).
44. Ibid.

to their backing paper, they measured about 14¼ inches by 4¾ inches.[45] Apparently, the beginning portion of the Breathing Permit was torn from the papyrus scroll before Smith purchased the Egyptian relics. On 25 March 1835, the *Cleveland Whig* reported on Michael Chandler's exhibition of the Egyptian artifacts in that city: "There was found deposited in the arms of the old man ... a book of ancient form and construction, which, to us, was by far the most interesting part of the exhibition. Its leaves were of bark, in length some 10 or 12 inches, and 3 or 4 in width. The ends are somewhat decayed, but at the centre the leaves are in a state of perfect preservation."[46]

Although Shurtliff called the pieces of papyrus "sheets," it is unclear if they were mounted at the time he saw them. Muhlestein argues that Shurtliff "does not discuss whether long rolls or sheets of papyrus were the source of the Book of Abraham, but rather associates the whole of the papyrus that came with the mummies as the source."[47] However, Shurtliff never mentioned the "long scroll" only that the 8 inches x 12 inches sheet was rolled up and placed on the breast of the male mummy. Shurtliff connected one of the fragments, whether mounted or not, with the Book of Abraham, which tends to refute the long-scroll theory.

The "Eyewitnesses"

As I discuss Muhlestein's sources, it is important to keep in mind that Muhlestein offers a two-part argument. First, he hopes to establish that his sources refer to the long roll as the source of the Book of Abraham. Second, he contends that the sources sometimes refer to images or drawings that appeared in vignettes that are no longer extant. This last argument is significant if the vignettes can be reasonably shown as relating to the long roll. However, since Smith also possessed the Book of the Dead for Ta-sherit-Min, some of which is missing, as well as other pieces of papyrus from Amenhotep's Book of the Dead—both of which are heavily illustrated—it is unnecessary to attempt to assign any

---

45. See Historical Introduction, *JSP,* R4:8.
46. "A Rare Exhibition," *Cleveland Whig,* 25 Mar. 1835.
47. Muhlestein, "Papyri and Presumptions," 40.

image to a hypothetical missing Book of Abraham text when the Ta-sherit-Min and Amenhotep texts are the much more likely, and available, sources.

1. Henry Tressler, 1838 (1897)

The first of Muhlestein's accounts is an 1897 secondhand report that while in Missouri in 1838, Henry Tressler (1810–1901) "saw the rolls of Papyrus from which the Pearl of Great Price was translated, and procured a piece of the bandage that was wrapped around one of the mummies exhibited by Mr. Chandler."[48] While nothing specific can be reasonably concluded from such a source, Muhlestein argues: "While Tressler's biographer does not appear to be trying to distinguish between the papyrus fragments and rolls, he is specific that, after having spoke with Joseph Smith about the antiquities, Tressler recounted that the rolls (or scrolls) were the source of the Book of Abraham."[49]

Who knows what eighty-six-year-old Tressler told Mormon missionary Foster W. Jones during a three-hour interview that Jones briefly summarized? For example, it is unclear if it was Tressler or Jones who connected the "scrolls" (plural) with the Mormon scripture. We do not know what Tressler may have seen or have been told about the Egyptian documents. Perhaps he saw Facsimile 3 on the intact two-foot Hôr scroll and made assumptions. He does not distinguish between the mounted fragments and the scrolls as the source of Abraham. Tressler must be more accurately described as a non-witness.

2. William I. Appleby, 1841 (1848)

In 1848, William I. Appleby recorded in his journal under the date of 5 May 1841 that he visited Joseph Smith in Nauvoo and "saw the Rolls of Papyrus and the writings thereon, taken from off the bosom of the Male Mummy, having some of the writings of ancient Abraham and of Joseph that was sold into Egypt."[50] Appleby described the two scrolls from memory:

---

48. Henry Tressler, Interview, 1897, in Foster W. Jones, Letter, Greenwood, Indiana, 16 June 1897, to Editor, "The Work in Indiana," *Deseret News* (31 July 1897): 209.

49. Muhlestein, "Papyri and Presumptions," 40.

50. William I. Appleby, Autobiography and Journal, 5 May 1841, 71, CHL.

The writings are chiefly in the Egyptian language, with the exception of a little Hebrew. I believe they give a description of some of the scenes in Ancient Egypt, of their worship, their Idol gods, etc. The writings are beautiful and plain, composed of red, and black inks. There is a perceptible difference, between the writings. Joseph, appears to have been the best scribe. There are also representations of men, beasts, Birds, Idols and oxen attached to a kind of plough, a female guiding it. Also the serpent when he beguiled Eve. He appears with two legs, erect in [the] form and appearance of [a] man. But his head in the form, and representing the Serpent, with his forked tongue extended.[51]

Muhlestein realizes that much of what Appleby describes as being on the scrolls was actually on the fragments under glass, which creates a problem for the long-scroll theory, so he suggests that Appleby may have been describing something else. Muhlestein, for example, points to Appleby's description of the walking serpent having his forked tongue extended, whereas on the fragment attributed to Joseph son of Jacob/Israel the serpent's tongue is not extended. Muhlestein argues: "While the papyri fragments we now have match some of those descriptions, such as a plowing scene in JSP II, many of these scenes are not found on any of the extant fragments."[52]

However, if we grant that Appleby was not looking at the papyri when he wrote his account, his descriptions of the extant documents are reasonably accurate. Another problem is that while Appleby's journal entry is dated 5 May 1841, it was actually written in 1848 from an earlier version edited and supplemented by the text of the Book of Abraham published in the *Times and Seasons* in 1842. The earlier version of Appleby's account of his seeing the Egyptian papyri was published on 10 September 1841 in the *Christian Observer* in London, England, under the title "Journal of a Mormon." In the published version, the part about the snake with a forked tongue is missing. Given the lapse of time, the reference to a snake's forked tongue is just the detail an imperfect memory might supply.

Muhlestein concedes that Appleby describes things on the

---

51. Ibid., 71–72.
52. Muhlestein, "Papyri and Presumptions," 42.

papyri that are actually on the surviving fragments, such as "birds" and "beasts," but undermines his analysis when he argues that "we cannot tell" for sure what Appleby saw or he objects that the word "beast" is "not the most obvious description" of a lion or ox. In fact, there are many birds and beasts that more than satisfy Appleby's description. Appleby also describes Abraham on the altar "with a dove over the person," and there are several obvious hawks. In the middle of JSP III, there is a large crouching lion and four human-shaped figures with heads of animals. No doubt, these and similar figures reminded Appleby and others of strange-looking "beasts" described in Revelation (Rev. 4:7–8; comp. Ezk. 1:5–10), especially since Oliver Cowdery had earlier described the vignette on JSP III as the last judgment.

Muhlestein claims that "none of the figures [in the extant papyri] are likely to be described as idols though it is difficult to know what Appleby would have given that label." Yet Appleby (and Joseph Smith for that matter) described Abraham "bound on the Altar with several Idol gods standing around it"—which we know are actually canopic jars, not idol gods. These same four "idol gods" appear on JSP III.

While Appleby may have described parts of the papyri which we no longer have, there is no compelling reason to conclude that he did. On the contrary, it is clear that he describes scenes that we know were contained among the mounted fragments as if they were on the intact scrolls. Thus Appleby only mentions that he saw the "Rolls of Papyrus and the writings thereon," including "the Idolatrous Priest 'Elkenah' [who] attempted to offer up Abraham as a sacrifice to their Idol Gods in Egypt, (as represented by the Altar &c. before refered to.)"[53]

Appleby is yet another witness who does not distinguish between the scrolls and the mounted fragments as the source of Abraham.

3. Charlotte Haven, 1843

Shortly after visiting Smith's mother, Lucy, and viewing the mummies and papyri in Nauvoo in 1843, Charlotte Haven wrote to her own mother and described her experience. She said that

---

53. Appleby, Autobiography and Journal, 5 May 1841, 72–73.

Mother Smith "opened a long roll of manuscript saying it was 'the writing of Abraham and Isaac, written in Hebrew and Sanscrit.'"[54] Muhlestein does not quote the next sentence, but it seems equally exaggerated, if not fanciful, "she read several minutes from it as if it were English." Lucy Smith could not read Hebrew, Sanskrit, or Egyptian. Nevertheless, Muhlestein argues, "This is after the fragments we now have were mounted, indicating that the scroll, rather than the fragments, were being designated as containing the writings of Abraham."[55]

This conclusion does not necessarily follow since it is possible for Lucy Smith to have made the statement about the scroll, as Haven reported, without excluding the fragments as the source for Abraham. She only identified the roll as the "writing of Abraham," not the source of the published Book of Abraham. There is nothing to indicate that the "long roll" was anything more than the approximately two-foot scroll containing the end section of Hôr's Book of Breathings, which included Book of Abraham Facsimile 3. As mentioned, Muhlestein conceded that many of his witnesses made unwarranted assumptions about the scrolls, often assigning the penmanship to Abraham and Joseph, and assumed that "an entire scroll contained just one text authored by just one person."[56]

Haven did not mention the fragments, but she may have seen them. According to Haven, Lucy began interpreting the images on "another roll":

> One was Mother Eve being tempted by the serpent, who—the serpent, I mean—was standing on the tip of his tail, which with his two legs formed a tripod, and had his head in Eve's ear. I said, "But serpents don't have legs."
>
> "They did before the fall," she asserted with perfect confidence.[57]

Haven is describing the walking snake on one of the mounted fragments of the Ta-sherit-Min papyrus (JSP V), although she

---

54. Charlotte Haven, Letter, Nauvoo, Illinois, to her mother, 19 Feb. 1843, in "A Girl's Letters from Nauvoo," *Overland Monthly* (Dec. 1890): 624.

55. Muhlestein, "Papyri and Presumptions," 43.

56. Ibid., 35.

57. Haven, Letter to her mother, 19 Feb. 1843, 624.

Figure 7.4. Baboon Adoring the Sun and Walking Snake. Copies of Egyptian Characters, ca. July 1835 (left), shows a tripod-looking baboon adoring/worshipping the rising sun. Fragment of the Book of the Dead for Ta-sherit-Min, ca. 300–100 BCE (top right); and Notebook of Copied Egyptian Characters, ca. July 1835 (bottom right), show a walking snake.

said it was from "another roll."[58] This creates a problem for Muhlestein, who contends that Haven "is describing scenes that are not on any of the extant papyri."[59] However, Haven evidently combined in her memory the image of the walking snake with the tripod-looking baboon adoring the rising sun, which someone copied onto a folded sheet about July 1835 from a badly damaged portion of Ta-sherit-Min's Book of the Dead (Chap. 16), which now can be seen as fragments glued in the upper left corner of JSP IX.[60] This raises the question as to what Haven actually saw and the reliability of her memory. Regardless, Haven provides us with

---

58. See *JSP*, R4:15.

59. Muhlestein, "Papyri and Presumptions," 35.

60. For the glued fragments, see Miscellaneous Scraps of Book of the Dead for Semminis [Ta-sherit-Min], ca. 300–100 BC, in *JSP*, R4:19. For the hand drawings, see Copies of Egyptian Characters, ca. Summer 1835, in R4:45; and Ritner, *Joseph Smith Egyptian Papyri*, 165.

another example of a witness describing the fragments as if they were complete scrolls.

4. Benjamin Ashby, 1843

Benjamin Ashby (1828–1907) was fifteen years old when he saw the papyri in November 1843. He later recalled that he and his mother visited Lucy Smith and that "she exhibited the mummies from which the Book of Abraham was taken as well as the original papyrus on which it was written."[61] Muhlestein argues: "It is not fully clear but it appears that his reference to 'the original papyrus' refers to the long roll as the source, since he does not mention frames or slides as is typical when they were exhibited."[62]

Besides being an argument from silence, Muhlestein's statement is surprising given that Ashby's account was made many decades later and is vague. Ashby wrote "papyrus," not "roll" or "scroll." Nothing in his statement can be reasonably construed to mean, as Muhlestein represents, that Ashby "seems to indicate that the long roll, rather than the mounted fragments, was the original source."[63] Ashby is another non-witness.

5. Unnamed Observer, 1846

An observer identified only as "M." visited Lucy Smith in 1846 and soon after reported, "She produced a black looking roll (which she told us was papyrus) found on the breast of the King, part of which the prophet had unrolled and read; and she had pasted the deciphered sheets on the leaves of a book which she showed us." This was likely a contemporary mid-nineteenth-century scrapbook with a copy of the published Book of Abraham from the *Times and Seasons* pasted inside. The anonymous reporter continues: "The roll was as dark as the bones of the Mummies, and bore very much the same appearance; but the opened sheets were exceedingly like thin parchment, and of quite a light color. There were birds, fishes, and fantastic looking people, interspersed amidst hyeroglyphics."[64]

---

61. Benjamin Ashby, Autobiography, typescript, 40, BYU.
62. Muhlestein, "Papyri and Presumptions," 44.
63. Ibid.
64. M., Letter to Editor, Sept. 1846, in *Friends' Weekly Intelligencer* 3/27 (3 Oct.

From this interview conducted more than a year after Joseph Smith's death, Muhlestein writes: "we learn that the Prophet had only unrolled and deciphered part of the roll. The fact that Lucy Mack Smith had a translation of what was on the scroll indicates that she thought the Book of Abraham came from that scroll, not the mounted fragments, though the account is not completely clear on this."[65]

Muhlestein offers an interpretation that is not based on a "careful" reading. Unrolling and reading "part" of the papyrus is a description of what Joseph Smith did in the past, not a comment about the current location of what he read. Smith's unrolling the first "part" of the papyrus and reading it occurred at least two years before the opening portions of the papyri were mounted. In this source, the "part" of the papyrus that was "unrolled" is parallel with "opened sheets," which Muhlestein presumes refers to the mounted fragments. Therefore, according to this source, the "part" of the papyrus that Smith read and translated became the mounted fragments, which contradicts the long-scroll theory.[66]

Muhlestein also notes that the anonymous observer described "birds, fishes, and fantastic looking people" and that "we have no depictions of fish," from which Muhlestein infers that the Book of Abraham was on a long scroll, not mounted fragments. However, this source describes what was seen on the "opened sheets," not on the papyrus roll, and it is possible that the observer was mistaken since he was describing from memory what he had seen.

6. Jerusha Blanchard, 1852-56 (1922)

Muhlestein next refers to the 1922 reminiscence of Hyrum Smith's granddaughter, Jerusha W. Blanchard, who said she used to hide in the old cabinet that held the mummies in the early 1850s when she was about five years of age. In recounting her

---

1846): 211–12. From this source, Gee asserts: "The main manuscript [of the Book of Abraham] seems to have been part of a book that was kept by Lucy Mack Smith until her death in 1856" (Gee, *Introduction to the Book of Abraham*, 31.) Gee speculates that the actual manuscript was glued into Lucy Smith's notebook and that it contained the entire Book of Abraham, possibly more.

65. Muhlestein, "Papyri and Presumptions," 45.

66. Ibid., 44.

childhood, she described the mummies: "There were three mummies: The old Egyptian king, the queen and their daughter. The bodies were wrapped in seven layers of linen cut in thin strips. In the arms of the Old King, lay the roll of papyrus from which our prophet translated the Book of Abraham."[67]

It is doubtful that the papyrus roll was still in the arms of the male mummy in the 1850s, so Blanchard probably meant that the roll containing the Book of Abraham once lay in his arms. Still, we do not know if her statement was based on an assumption or if she was imperfectly repeating what her great-grandmother Lucy Mack Smith had told her—which would have been the same as what Lucy told Charlotte Haven—namely, the scroll contained the "writing of Abraham." Regardless, because Blanchard was six years old in 1856, when Lucy Smith died and the mummies and papyri were sold to Abel Combs, and her statement was given sixty-six years later, her account provides no support for the missing-papyrus theory.

7. Joseph Smith III, 1898

In 1898 Joseph Smith III, Joseph and Emma Smith's son born in 1832 and president of the Reorganized Church of Jesus Christ of Latter Day Saints (now Community of Christ), related what he knew about the mummies and papyri. Among other things, he said:

> The papyrus from which the Book of Abraham was said to have been translated by Father, was with other portions found in a roll with some Egyptian mummies, pasted on either paper or linen and put into a small case of flat drawers, some dozen or sixteen in number. ...
>
> Part of the stock, one case of mummies and part or all the cases of drawers, found their way to Wood's Museum, [in] Chicago, and a part to St. Louis, where, we never learned. I personally, in company with Elder Elijah Banta, of Sandwich, Illinois, saw the mummies in Chicago before the great fire in 1871; in which they undoubtedly perished with the rest of the accumulated relics and curiosities.[68]

---

67. Jerusha W. Blanchard, "Reminisce of the Granddaughter of Hyrum Smith," *Relief Society Magazine* 9 (Jan. 1922): 9.

68. Joseph Smith III, Letter, Lamoni, Iowa, to Heman C. Smith, Lamoni, Iowa, 24 Oct. 1898, in *Saints Herald* 46 (11 Jan. 1899); Heman C. Smith, Letter, Lamoni, Iowa, to R. B. Neal, Grayson, Kentucky, 24 Oct. 1898, which included the text of an earlier

According to Muhlestein, "Joseph Smith III considered the papyri that burned in the Great Chicago Fire to be the source of the Book of Abraham, not the papyri that remains. … Joseph Smith III does not specify that the long roll was the source of the Book of Abraham but does indicate that it was papyrus that we no longer have."[69]

Joseph Smith III never mentions an intact scroll going to any museum or seeing one in Chicago, but clearly states that the papyrus that produced the Book of Abraham was glued to paper or linen and kept in a "small case of flat drawers." He assumed "part or all the cases of drawers" containing the source of Abraham followed the mummies to the Chicago Museum and were destroyed in the fire, as did everyone else. Joseph III's statement does not support the long-scroll theory, but rather refutes it.

Catalyst Theory

While some writers attempt to disconnect the Book of Abraham from Hôr's Book of Breathings to support a long-scroll theory, others do the same thing but for a different reason, proposing that the papyri functioned not as a translatable text, but as a catalyst for revelation. In 2002, Glen M. Leonard, in a book published by Mormon Church-owned Deseret Book, referred to the Book of Abraham as a "revelation" and not as a translation. "The messages triggered by the Egyptian sources that Joseph Smith had purchased in Kirtland," Leonard explained, "prompted him to seek a deeper understanding of the meaning of the cosmos and its origins."[70] Sixteen years later, Robin Scott Jensen, co-editor of a study of the Book of Abraham published by the LDS Church Historian's Press, stated: "Joseph Smith received revelation for the text of the Book of Abraham. He may have through that revelation, made assumptions about where that text came from. It could be that Joseph Smith assumed that he was translating from the papyri when he was not, in fact, translating from the papyri. We do not know in

---

letter from Joseph Smith III to Herman C. Smith, as published in "President Smith's Statement," Robert B. Neal, *Anti-Mormon Tracts, No. 4: Smithianity; or Mormonism Refuted by Mormons,* Part II [Salem, Kentucky: Church of Christ, 1899], 16–17.

69. Muhlestein, "Papyri and Presumptions," 47, 48.

70. Glen M. Leonard, *Nauvoo: A Place of Peace, A People of Promise* (Salt Lake City: Deseret Book Co./Provo, Utah: Brigham Young University Press, 2002), 210–12.

the revelatory process how much of this is Joseph Smith and how much of it is the divine."[71]

Recently, Terryl Givens, Emeritus Professor of Literature and Religion at the University of Richmond, Virginia, and Senior Research Fellow at BYU's Neal A. Maxwell Institute, defended both the catalyst theory and the long-scroll theory, while also drawing on different models of translation proposed by David Bokovoy and Blake Ostler. Bokovoy suggests the Book of Abraham is "inspired pseudepigrapha"; Ostler that the Book of Mormon is an inspired expansion of an ancient source.[72] Like advocates of the catalyst theory, Givens hopes to absolve Smith from allegations of deception, agreeing with the LDS Church that it is possible that "prophetic misunderstanding and prophetic inspiration may coexist in the same person even at the same moment."[73] Givens admits that "Smith certainly believed that he was successfully rendering the actual Egyptian symbols into their English counterparts," but "in the case of the facsimiles he was apparently wrong, and in the case of the Book of Abraham narrative he may have been as well"[74]—meaning that Smith thought he was translating the Hôr scroll when he was actually receiving independent revelation.

Givens defines "translation" as broadly as possible, even to the point that the word loses any significant meaning.[75] Such an approach to translation makes it difficult if not impossible to identify an original source document, because it would bear little resemblance to a conventional translation of the same document. Rather than elucidating Smith's concept of translation, Givens's redefinition allows him to propose comparisons between Hôr's Book of Breathings and Smith's temple endowment ceremony that see Smith "reconstituting [translating] a source document into an

71. Robin Scott Jensen, Interview with Stephen Smoot, 7 Nov. 2018, www. ldsperspectives.com, Episode 97, 45:50–46:20.

72. Terryl Givens with Brian M. Hauglid, *The Pearl of Greatest Price: Mormonism's Most Controversial Scripture* (New York: Oxford University Press, 2019), 193, 201.

73. Ibid., 180. See "Translation and Historicity of the Book of Abraham," www.churchofjesuschrist.org/study/manual/gospel-topics-essays/translation-and-historicity-of-the-book-of-abraham?lang=eng; accessed 3 Dec. 2019.

74. Givens, *Pearl of Greatest Price,* 180.

75. Ibid., 180–202.

inspired and inspiring temple text, of which the original would then appear as a pale reflection."[76]

While stating his intention to "broaden or complicate reductive ways of thinking about translation," Givens cautions that his redefinition may not be the way Smith understood the process of translation. Nevertheless, he thinks Smith was translating as he, Givens, redefines it without knowing it. The problem is that the redefinition of translation that Givens and other advocates of the catalyst theory formulate is circular. Such approaches do not "broaden or complicate reductive ways of thinking about translation" as performed by Smith. Instead, they make a conclusion true by definition, "by subtly importing a highly questionable definition of a key word into one of the premises."[77] In other words, they redefine translation solely to explain away problems and disconfirming evidence.

In redefining translation, Givens employs four lines of argument. First, he discusses a pre-Champollion belief that hieroglyphics carried multi-layered esoteric meanings available only to prophets, priests, and kings. Chief among the proponents of this metaphysical school of interpretation was seventeenth-century Jesuit scholar Athanasius Kircher, who produced three volumes of translations titled *Oedipus Aegyptiacus* described by historian Frank Manuel as "one of the most learned monstrosities of all times."[78] Egyptologist E. A. Wallis Budge wrote of Kircher's work:

> Many writers pretended to have found the key to the hieroglyphics, and many more professed, with a shameless impudence which is hard to understand in these days, to translate the contents of the texts into a modern tongue. Foremost among such pretenders must be mentioned Athanasius Kircher, who, in the 17th century, declared that he had found the key to the hieroglyphic inscriptions; the translations which he prints in his *Oedipus Aegyptiacus* are utter nonsense, but

76. Ibid., 196.
77. T. Edward Damer, *Attacking Faulty Reasoning: A Practical Guide to Fallacy-Free Arguments,* 4th ed. (Belmont, California: Wadsworth, 2001), 106.
78. Frank Manuel, *Eighteenth Century Confronts the Gods* (Cambridge, Massachusetts: Harvard University Press, 1959), 190–91.

as they were put forth in a learned tongue many people at the time believed they were correct.[79]

This school of interpretation did not disappear with Champollion's decipherment of the Rosetta Stone, but persisted into the nineteenth century.[80] While this may provide some background for the five-degree system Smith used in his bound Grammar, it has nothing to do with actually translating Egyptian. There is little to gain by comparing Smith's attempt to translate Egyptian against the mistaken beliefs of those who preceded him. At best, it can only tell us how Smith's "translations" may have made sense to some of his more educated followers such as W. W. Phelps.

Second, Givens likens translation to the principle of *bricolage* espoused by twentieth-century French anthropologist Claude Levi-Strauss to denote the process of mythmaking, which Levi-Strauss described as recombining disparate pieces of one's culture in improvisational ways to create new mythologies. The *bricoleur* or mythmaker, according to Strauss, makes do with whatever pieces are available to "the task in hand because it has nothing else at its disposal."[81] *Bricolage* is a French word that means "tinkering" and is associated with do-it-yourself projects or similar kinds of makeshift repairs. Givens applies this term to translation and revelation to explain how Smith's revelatory texts could be "simple echoes of the many instances of appropriation and adaptation." Specifically, Givens theorizes, Smith's "Book of Abraham texts may reflect a practice of scriptural fluidity, versatility, adaptability, and malleability that constituted one key facet of his self-conception as translator."[82] What Givens means is made clear when he references Bokovoy's hypothesis that Abraham is "inspired pseudepigrapha," whereby Smith "took theological constructs that were in chaos and

---

79. E. A. Wallis Budge, *Egyptian Language: Easy Lessons in Egyptian Hieroglyphics* (Mineola, New York: Dover, [1910] 1983), 15.

80. John T. Irwin, *American Hieroglyphics: The Symbol of the Egyptian Hieroglyphics in the American Renaissance* (New Haven, Connecticut: Yale University Press, 1980), 6, 8–9; R. B. Parkinson, Whitfield Diffie, Mary Fischer, and R. S. Simpson, *Cracking Codes: The Rosetta Stone and Decipherment* (Berkeley: University of California Press, 1999), 41.

81. Claude Levi-Strauss, *The Savage Mind* (Chicago: University of Chicago Press, 1966), 16–17, as quoted in Givens, *Pearl of Greatest Price*, 189.

82. Givens, *Pearl of Greatest Price*, 191.

provided them with an inspired structure."[83] Used this way, translation has nothing to do with an underlying ancient source.

Givens connects *bricolage* to Smith's translation of Egyptian papyri by adopting the argument that the Breathing Permit of Hôr served as a catalyst for Smith's temple theology.[84] According to Givens, Smith "may have repurposed Egyptian funerary texts in such a way as to constitute a new narrative that places fragmentary images and passages of death and resurrection into a fuller cosmic scheme."[85] However, washing, anointings, and sealing powers—all present in Smith's Nauvoo temple theology/liturgy—were actually part of Smith's practice before he acquired the papyri, and the substance of the temple endowment owes more historically to Smith's 1832 vision of three heavens and to the three introductory degrees of Masonry than to an Egyptian Book of Breathings. The only connection between the papyri and Smith's temple theology is his 1842 explanations of Facsimile 2, which mention "the grand Key-words of the Priesthood" and an item that "cannot be revealed unto the world; but is to be had in the Holy Temple of God." Apologists have tended to use these 1842 explanations to justify broader comparisons between the Book of Breathings and Smith's temple endowment ceremony. In fact, Smith never connected his temple theology to the Hôr papyrus because he regarded the papyrus as the source of the Book of Abraham. Smith himself acknowledged his principal source of inspiration for the temple endowment ceremony when he stated that Masonry was an "apostate endowment" and that "Masonry was taken from the preasthood but has become degenerated."[86]

Comparison between the Hôr papyrus and Smith's temple endowment is an exercise in "parallelomania," which is well known in biblical criticism and comparative mythology as an overemphasis

83. David Bokovoy, *Authoring the Old Testament: Genesis–Deuteronomy* (Salt Lake City: Kofford Books, 2014), 171, as quoted in Givens, *Pearl of Greatest Price*, 193.

84. Givens, *Pearl of Greatest Price*, 121–40, 189–93. See Hugh W. Nibley, *The Message of the Joseph Smith Papyri: An Egyptian Endowment* (Salt Lake City: Deseret Book Co., 1975).

85. Givens, *Pearl of Greatest Price*, 190.

86. Benjamin F. Johnson, *My Life's Review* (Independence, Missouri: Zion's Printing and Publishing Co., 1947), 96; and Heber C. Kimball, Letter to Parley P. Pratt, 17 June 1842, Parley P. Pratt Papers, CHL.

or exaggeration of the similarities between texts or cultures to prove a connection without any apparent historical support.[87] The use of *bricolage* does nothing to "broaden or complicate reductive ways of thinking about translation" as it pertains to Smith, and instead creates a circular definition that only serves to justify an improper use of the comparative method.

Third, Givens explores the theory of translation discussed by Friedrich Schleiermacher, an early nineteenth-century German theologian who described the translator's job as either moving the reader closer to the foreign source text and remaining as close to the source as possible or bringing the foreign source text closer to the reader, not only translating the words but also the culture of the foreign text, thus minimizing its strangeness.[88] This latter method is more akin to paraphrase and is known in linguistics as the *domestication* of the text, whereas the former is referred to as the *foreignization* method—approaches to translation that are still debated.[89] Givens believes that Smith's texts could be a combination of both approaches. On the one hand, Givens argues, Smith might use the foreignizing element of the King James Bible diction, and, on the other, he could domesticate the text of the Book of Breathings by "reconstituting" it as the Mormon temple endowment.[90]

Similar to Ostler's theory that the Book of Mormon is a modern expansion of an ancient source, Givens fashions an apologetic tool to highlight the perceived "Egypticity" of the text as the result of foreignization, while at the same time explaining away problems and anachronisms in Abraham as inspired domestication. Egyptologist Robert Ritner, for example, observes that "the text

---

87. See the classic discussion of this phenomenon in Samuel Sandmel, "Parallelomania," *Journal of Biblical Literature* 81 (Mar. 1962): 1–13, which defines parallelomania "as that extravagance among scholars which first overdoes the supposed similarity in passages and then proceeds to describe source and derivation as if implying literary connection flowing in an inevitable or predetermined direction" (p. 1). For a critical analysis of Nibley's attempt to connect Smith's temple endowment with the Book of Breathings, see Edward H. Ashment, "The LDS Temple Ceremony: Historical Origins and Religious Value," *Dialogue: A Journal of Mormon Thought* 27/3 (Fall 1994): 289–98.

88. Givens, *Pearl of Greatest Price*, 194–96. See Friedrich Schleiermacher, "On the Different Methods of Translating," trans. Susan Bernofsky, in *The Translation Studies Reader*, ed. Lawrence Venuti, 3rd ed. (New York: Routledge, 2012), 43, 46, 49.

89. See Lawrence Venuti, *The Translator's Invisibility* (New York: Routledge, 1995).

90. Givens, *Pearl of Greatest Price,* 196.

itself includes anachronistic and impossible expressions ... and situations." More specifically,

> Wherever one locates Ur of the Chaldees, human sacrifice dictated there by "priests of Pharaoh" is unbelievable to credible scholars of the Ancient Near East. Nor was there any "Pharaoh, the eldest son of Egyptus, the daughter of Ham" (Abraham 1:25). As previously noted, "Pharaoh" is a title, not a name. Neither is "Egyptus" ("Egypt") an ancient Egyptian personal name, but the name for the primary temple in Memphis that became generalized *outside of Egypt* as a designation for the country. Accurate translation or revelation would not produce such basic errors.[91]

Like *bricolage*, foreignization and domestication tell us nothing about Smith's claimed method of translation and more about the need to neutralize counter evidence.

Finally, Givens argues that the nineteenth century was marked by "rampant destabilization of narrative authority" as well as "genre anarchy." Consequently, he observes, "many of the era's works grounded their appeal to authority in ways that today would be seen as dishonest, irresponsible, implausible, and self-contradictory. ... Given the complex linguistic and literary environment of the early nineteenth century, a word with the potency and high stakes of 'translation' cannot be adequately circumscribed within the confines of Noah Webster's 1828 definition: 'to render into another language.'"[92] In other words, Smith was not deceptive when he received a revelation about Abraham and represented it as a translation of the Egyptian papyri in his possession, even if he knew he was not actually translating Egyptian. However, the Book of Abraham was not publicized by Smith and others as a "translation of some ancient Records that have fallen into our hands, from the catacombs of Egypt" as a way of participating in the "genre anarchy." Smith went through very elaborate motions of "translating" them as the Joseph Smith Egyptian papers demonstrate.

---

91. See Robert K. Ritner, "'Translation and Historicity of the Book of Abraham'—A Response," www.uchicago.edu/sites/oi.uchicago.edu/files/uploads/shared/docs/Research_Archives/Translation%20and%20Historicity%20of%20the%20Book%20of%20Abraham%20final-2.pdf; accessed 27 Mar. 2019.

92. Givens, *Pearl of Greatest Price*, 196–97, 199.

Did Smith truly believe—mistakenly—that his inspired dictation of the Abraham text came from the papyrus? The text itself references Facsimile 1 twice, which suggests that Smith believed he was translating, in the conventional sense, and not receiving revelation. Smith himself was responsible for the translations of specific characters in the "Valuable Discovery" notebooks, the Egyptian Alphabets, the bound Grammar, as well as in the margins of the three Book of Abraham manuscripts. This cannot easily be brushed aside as Smith's working things out in his mind à la a form of revelation (see D&C 9). Some of the ideas Smith developed in the Alphabets and bound Grammar, such as the discovery of Egypt while still underwater, made their way into the Book of Abraham text as translations of characters Smith invented to fill in the gap in the damaged Hôr scroll. In my opinion, without seriously considering the possibility of deception, Abraham apologetics will remain mired in convoluted, incoherent theories.

Givens's endeavor to expand the definition of translation diverges from how Smith represented his method of translation. The Joseph Smith Egyptian papers tell us Smith's definition of translation was conventional and straightforward. The production of an Egyptian alphabet and explanation of their principles of grammar imply such an understanding of translation. It is also present in Oliver Cowdery's December 1835 report that Smith had given Michael Chandler "the interpretation of some few [characters] for his satisfaction" and that Chandler immediately supplied an affidavit affirming that he found Smith's decipherment of the Egyptian characters "to correspond in the most minute matters" to that which he had obtained from "the most learned" men "in many eminent cities" in the East.[93] Cowdery's use of intepretation/translation implies that there would be little difference between Smith's translation and that of the learned (assuming the learned had an accurate knowledge of Egyptian).

Cowdery was also careful to frame his report as indirect support from the learned for Smith's translation of the Book of Mormon, stating that on the morning that Chandler showed Smith

---

93. "Egyptian Mummies," 235.

the papyri, Smith showed Chandler "a number of characters like those upon the writings of Mr. C[handler]. which were previously copied from the plates, containing the history of the Nephites, or book of Mormon."[94] On 19 July 1835, W. W. Phelps reported to his wife that the papyri when translated and published "will make a good witness for the Book of Mormon."[95]

To the world, Smith represented his translations as literal renditions of original texts. In an early portion of Smith's official history published in October 1842 in the *Times and Seasons*, then under his editorship, Smith explained that "the title page of the Book of Mormon is a literal translation, taken from the very last leaf, on the left hand side of the collection or book of plates, which contained the record which has been translated; the language of the whole running the same as all Hebrew writing in general."[96] This description comports with eye-witness testimonies that describe Smith reading the translation from the stone. David Whitmer, for instance, repeatedly described what Smith told him about how the seer stone operated when placed in the bottom of his hat, stating in 1879 that in the darkness "a spiritual light would shine forth, and parchment would appear before Joseph, upon which was a line of characters from the plates, and under it, the translation in English; at least, so Joseph said."[97] This

---

94. Ibid.

95. William W. Phelps, Letter, Kirtland, Ohio, to Sally Waterman Phelps, Liberty, Missouri, 19 July 1835, partial transcription in Historian's Office, Journal History of the Church, 20 July 1835, CHL. Another partial transcription with some variant readings also available in Leah Y. Phelps, "Letters of Faith from Kirtland," *Improvement Era* 45 (Aug. 1942): 529. The concern for secular validation shows up again in the early portion of Smith's official 1838–39 history, which recounts Martin Harris's 1828 visit to Columbia University Professor Charles Anthon. Upon being shown a facsimile of characters purportedly copied from the golden plates as well as Smith's translation, Anthon supposedly declared that "the translation was correct, more so than any he had before seen translated from the Egyptian." Anthon's words were crafted to bolster Smith's claims to translate ancient writings and imply that Smith's translations were superior to those of professional linguists but were still recognizable by them. Joseph Smith, History, 1838–1857, vol. A-1, 9, quoted in Dan Vogel, *Early Mormon Documents*, 5 vols. (Salt Lake City: Signature Books, 1996–2003) 1:70.

96. "History of Joseph Smith," *Times and Seasons* 3 (15 Oct. 1842): 943.

97. J. L. Traughber, Letter to the Editor, 13 Oct. 1879, *Saints Herald* 26 (15 Nov. 1879): 341, quoted in Dan Vogel, *Early Mormon Documents*, 5 vols. (Salt Lake City: Signature Books, 1996–2003) 5:61.

description, which sounds as though one is reading from an interlinear edition of the Bible, is problematic for appeals to the pre-Champollion metaphysical school of fake translation, the concept of *bricolage*, Schleiermacher's discussion of the *domestication* of the text, as well as Ostler's expansion theory and Bokovoy's "inspired pseudepigrapha" theory.

Some writers point to the lack of manuscript support for Smith's Bible Revision (1830–33) and also called a "translation" as evidence that Smith, in fact, used a non-standard definition of translation.[98] However, while the reality of what Smith was doing is apparent to us, there is no indication that he used "translation" in any sense different from the conventional sense. In 1843, Smith declared: "I believe the bible, as it ought to be, as it came from the pen of the original writers." He then gave an example from his revision of the Old Testament, implying that he had corrected the text to its original reading.[99] Rather than redefining "translation" to address problems, the problems should tell us that Smith was not translating as he claimed.

Conclusion

There is no reasonable or compelling evidence to support the theory that the Book of Abraham English text came from a long roll of papyrus—now missing—and not from the surviving mounted papyrus fragments. The so-called "eyewitnesses" to a lost scroll turn out to be problematic, unreliable, or non-witnesses. The only people who could have known for certain from where on the papyrus scroll Smith translated the Book of Abraham are W. W. Phelps,

---

98. Kerry Muhlestein, for example, described Smith's "translation" of the Bible as an instance where Smith was inspired to emend and expand the English text without reference to a foreign text. "That's not how we usually think of translation," Muhlestein argues, "but that's what Joseph Smith calls it" (Kerry Muhlestein, "The Book of Abraham and Unnoticed Assumptions," FairMormon Conference, 7 Aug. 2014, www.fairmormon.org/conference/august-2014/book-abraham-unnoticed-assumptions; accessed 15 Dec. 2019). See also *JSP*, R4:xxiii; Brant A. Gardner, *The Gift and Power: Translating the Book of Mormon* (Salt Lake City: Greg Kofford Books, 2011), 243.

99. Joseph Smith, Journal, 15 Oct. 1843 (*JSP*, J3:113). The text Smith used as an example was Genesis 6:6, which states that "it repented the LORD that he had made man on the earth, and it grieved him at his heart," which he changed to read: "it repented Noah, and his heart was pained that the Lord had made man on the earth, and it grieved him at the heart" (Moses 8:25).

Warren Parrish, and Frederick G. Williams, and the documents they produced or helped to produce all use characters from the Breathing Permit of Hôr. Furthermore, appeals to a catalyst theory of the Book of Abraham, including attempts to redefine the term translate, fail to account satisfactorily for the text's own references to Facsimile 1 and to Smith's own use of the term "translate" in its conventional meaning.

8 Nineteenth-Century Sources

Throughout this study, I occasionally discuss possible nineteenth-century sources for the English text of the Book of Abraham. In chapter five, I deal with the cosmos and pre-mortal intelligences in Abraham 3 and Facsimile 2; in chapter six, I discuss the influence of Joseph Smith's Hebrew lessons on the account of the Creation in Abraham 4–5.

In this chapter, I examine the text of Abraham 1–2, which Smith dictated in Ohio in 1835, and focus on places where the Book of Abraham text differs from the Genesis (KJV) text. I also discuss Smith's interpretation of Facsimile 1, which informs the text of Abraham 1. In my analysis, I deal with defensive attempts to support the Book of Abraham's antiquity that draw parallels between unique/non-biblical aspects of Abraham's narrative and genuinely ancient Egyptian, Jewish, Christian, and Muslim sources. In my opinion, these parallels are invariably weak, misrepresented, or irrelevant, and arguments for ancient historicity overestimate the significance of the evidence and underestimate what Smith's contemporaries knew about non-biblical legends involving Abraham.

Evidences of Antiquity

In 2001 the Foundation for Ancient Research and Mormon Studies (FARMS), based at Mormon-owned Brigham Young University in Provo, Utah, published a 553-page tome titled *Traditions about the Early Life of Abraham*, a compilation of late Jewish, Christian, and Muslim sources said to support the antiquity of the Book of Abraham. This collection was created by three scholars associated with BYU: John A. Tvedtnes, a specialist in Hebrew; Brian M. Hauglid, a PhD in Middle Eastern studies and Arabic; and John Gee, an Egyptologist. Included in the volume is a 10-page index titled "Unique Elements of the Book of Abraham Supported by Extrabiblical Traditions."[1] The index is arranged into eight categories, including "Idolatry in Abraham's Day," "Sacrifice of Abraham and Others," "Famine in Chaldea," and so on. These eight categories are divided into forty subcategories. The apologetic nature of this work is clearly announced at the beginning of the volume:

> Because the Book of Abraham parallels so many nonbiblical stories, it is clearly of the same tradition. One might dismiss a single element found in a nonbiblical tradition that parallels the Book of Abraham as mere coincidence. However, when a large number of such elements come together from diverse times and places, they overwhelmingly support the Book of Abraham as an ancient text. There are far too many references to Terah as an idolator, Abraham as a sacrificial victim, Abraham as an astronomer, and Abraham as a missionary to lightly dismiss their antiquity. ... The majority of these nonbiblical traditions were not available to the Prophet Joseph Smith during his lifetime. ... While we think these traditions provide substantial evidence that the Book of Abraham is an ancient text, we realize that others may not find the evidence convincing.[2]

This claim was made as early as 1981 by Hugh Nibley, who asserted: "Going through a list of Abraham sources with their dates of publication is one way of showing how recent most of the stuff is and how highly improbable it is that Joseph Smith could have made use of any of it."[3] BYU professor Andrew Hedges conducted his own survey of nineteenth-century sources and concluded: "[The] Critics' charges that Joseph Smith borrowed and adapted popular ideas in the production of Latter-day Saint scripture and doctrine are unfounded in the case of the Book of Abraham."[4] On the Mormon apologetic website FAIR Mormon, researchers state: "The stories and worldviews we find in the translated text of our

---

1. John Tvedtnes, Brian Hauglid, and John Gee, *Traditions about the Early Life of Abraham* (Provo, Utah: Neal A. Maxwell Institute, Brigham Young University, 2001), 537–47.

2. Tvedtnes, Hauglid, and Gee, *Traditions about the Early Life of Abraham,* xxxv.

3. Hugh W. Nibley, *Abraham in Egypt* (Salt Lake City: Deseret Book Co., 1981), 47.

4. Andrew H. Hedges, "A Wanderer in a Strange Land: Abraham in America, 1800–1850," in *Astronomy, Papyrus, and Covenant,* ed. John Gee and Brian M. Hauglid (Provo, Utah: FARMS, 2005), 187.

Book of Abraham coincide nicely with what we find from ancient Abrahamic lore. … He [Joseph Smith] could only have received this information through revelation, since there were no resources available to him on many of these traditions."[5]

I contend that the so-called unique elements in the Book of Abraham—that Abraham's father, Terah, was an idolater; that Abraham was a victim of an attempted sacrifice; that Abraham was an astronomer; that Abraham made converts in Haran—were all known to Joseph Smith's contemporaries. That said, I am not arguing that Smith knowingly plagiarized these sources. Rather, I believe that Smith arrived at a similar narrative but through a different process. The realization that Smith's contemporaries had access to the same Jewish, Christian, and Muslim traditions about Abraham and that these traditions were widely known in Smith's day stands, I believe, as a corrective to claims of antiquity.

Delay and Creation

In the previous chapters, I discussed Smith's identification of the four Egyptian mummies in his possession, two of which he said were King Onitas and Princess Katumin. Smith obtained this information by "translating" characters from a papyrus owned by a man named Amenhotep (and which no longer survives). In July 1835, Smith started to dictate the English text of the Book of Abraham from a copy of the Egyptian funerary manual Book of Breathings once owned by an Egytptian priest named Hôr but soon interrupted his dictation to compile an Alphabet and then a Grammar and Alphabet of Egyptian, in which he gave "translations" of random hieratic-looking characters. In November 1835, Smith returned to the Book of Abraham. Thus there was a delay of four-plus months during his dictation of Abraham, during which Smith was able to brainstorm some of the material which he used in his subsequent dictation of the Book of Abraham.

During this time, Smith may have also consulted Bible commentaries such as Methodist Adam Clarke's well-known volumes and other theological works. By the end of November 1835, Smith

---

5. At www.fairmormon.org/answers/Question:_What_evidence_does_the_Book_of_Abraham_demonstrate_to_support_its_own_antiquity%3F; accessed 2 Apr. 2019.

had dictated to Abraham 2:18. The remainder of Abraham would not be dictated until March 1842, giving Smith even more time to consider the text. There is evidence that Smith was thinking about Abraham prior to his 1842 resumption of the dictation. On 9 March 1841—a year before dictating Abraham 3–5—Smith preached on the Godhead, explaining that "these personages, according to Abraham's record, are called God the first, the Creator; God the second, the Redeemer, and God the third, the witnesses or Testator."[6] While this information does not appear in the Book of Abraham, it shows that Smith had time to think about his pseudepigraphic text and that he thought of it much as pseudepigraphists did: as a means of lending ancient authority to his own ideas.

One or Two Calls?

I begin with Abraham 2 because it parallels Genesis 11–12, and there is much to learn about Smith's methodology from the ways in which the text of Abraham reads differently from that of Genesis. The first thing to notice about Abraham 2 is that Abraham receives two revelations in which God commands him to depart: one from Ur, in Chaldea, the other from Haran, in northern Mesopotamia. Genesis mentions only Haran (Gen. 12:1). However, according to Stephen in Acts 7, God's appearance to Abraham and the command to depart occurred in Ur, not Haran: "The God of glory appeared unto our father Abraham, when he was in Mesopotamia, before he dwelt in Charran [Haran], And said unto him, Get thee out of thy country, and from thy kindred, and come into the land which I shall shew thee" (vv. 2–3).

The difference between Genesis and Acts evidently caused a controversy in Smith's day over whether Abraham received one or two calls. According to Adam Clarke, "There is great dissension between commentators concerning the call of Abram; some supposing he had *two* distinct calls, others that he had but *one*." Clarke conjectured that when Terah, Abraham, Lot, and their

---

6. Joseph Smith, Discourse, [9 Mar. 1841], Joseph Smith Collection, CHL. See also "Extracts from Wm Clayton's Private Journal, 10–11, in Andrew F. Ehat and Lyndon W. Cook, *Words of Joseph Smith: The Contemporary Accounts of the Nauvoo Discourses of the Prophet Joseph* (Provo, Utah: Religious Studies Center, Brigham Young University, 1980), 87–88n5.

new wives left Ur, "This was, no doubt, in consequence of some Divine admonition."[7] Under Acts 7:2, Clarke wrote: "It seems most probable that Abraham had *two* calls, one in *Ur*, and the other in *Haran*."[8]

In Abraham 2, Smith attempts to resolve this conflict by creating two calls. In creating the first call in Ur, Smith borrows wording from Genesis 12:1, a later command to leave Haran:

ABRAHAM 2:3–4	GENESIS 12:1	ACTS 7:3
Now the Lord had said unto me: Abraham,	NOW the LORD had said unto Abram,	And said unto him,
get thee out of thy country,	Get thee out of thy country,	Get thee out of thy country,
and from thy kindred,	and from thy kindred,	and from thy kindred,
and from thy father's house, unto a land that	and from thy father's house, unto a land that	and come into the land which
I will show thee.	I will shew thee:	I shall shew thee.

For the second calling, Smith creates three new verses to replace Genesis 12:1 instead of repeating it:

ABRAHAM 2:6–8	GENESIS 12
6 But I, Abraham, and Lot, my brother's son, prayed unto the Lord, and the Lord appeared unto me, and said unto me: Arise, and take Lot with thee; for I have purposed to take thee away out of Haran, and to make of thee a minister to bear my name in a strange land which I will give unto thy seed after thee for an everlasting possession, when they hearken to my voice.	

---

7. Adam Clarke, *The Holy Bible ... With a Commentary and Critical Notes*, vol. 1 (New York: N. Bangs and J. Emory, for the Methodist Episcopal Church, 1825), 90; s.v. Gen. 12:1.

8. Adam Clarke, *The New Testament ... With a Commentary and Critical Notes*, vol. 1 (New York: N. Bangs and J. Emory, for the Methodist Episcopal Church, 1825), 690; s.v. Acts 7:2.

ABRAHAM 2:6–8

7 For I am the Lord thy God;
I dwell in heaven; the earth is
my footstool; I stretch my hand
over the sea, and it obeys my
voice; I cause the wind and the
fire to be my chariot; I say to the
mountains—Depart hence—and
behold, they are taken away by a
whirlwind, in an instant, suddenly.

8 My name is Jehovah, and I know
the end from the beginning; therefore my hand shall be over thee.

GENESIS 12

Then Smith continues with the remainder of Abraham's call
in Genesis 12:2–3, expanding them in much the same way he did
when revising the King James Bible in 1830–33:

ABRAHAM 2:9–11

9 And I will make of thee a
great nation, and I will bless
thee *above measure*, and make
thy name great *among all nations*,
and thou shalt be a blessing *unto
thy seed after thee, that in their
hands they shall bear this ministry
and Priesthood unto all nations*;

10 *And I will bless them through
thy name; for as many as receive
this Gospel shall be called after thy
name, and shall be accounted thy
seed, and shall rise up and bless
thee, as their father;*

11 And I will bless them that
bless thee, and curse them that
curse thee; and in thee *(that is,
in thy Priesthood) and in thy seed
(that is, thy Priesthood), for I give
unto thee a promise that this right
shall continue in thee, and in thy*

GENESIS 12:2–3

2 And I will make of thee a great
nation, and I will bless thee, and
make thy name great; and thou
shalt be a blessing:

3 And I will bless them that
bless thee, and curse him that
curseth thee: and in thee *shall all
families of the earth be blessed.*

*seed after thee (that is to say, the
literal seed, or the seed of the body)
shall all the families of the earth be
blessed, even with the blessings of
the Gospel, which are the blessings
of salvation, even of life eternal.*

In attempting to resolve the problem of two Abrahamic
callings, Smith has to make additional adjustments to Genesis.
Compare Abraham 2:4 and Genesis 11:31:

ABRAHAM 2:4	GENESIS 11:31
4 Therefore *I left* the land of Ur, of the Chaldees, to go into the land of Canaan; and *I took* Lot, my brother's son, and his wife, and Sarai my wife; *and also my father followed after me*, unto the land which we denominated Haran.	31 And *Terah took Abram* his son, and Lot the son of Haran his son's son, and Sarai his daughter in law, his son Abram's wife; *and they went* forth with them from Ur of the Chaldees, to go into the land of Canaan; and they came unto Haran, and dwelt there.

The statement in Genesis 11:31 that Terah "took" Abraham,
Lot, and their wives to Haran could no longer stand since in
Smith's version God commands Abraham to leave Ur. So instead
of saying "Terah took Abraham" and the others, Smith's text reads:
"I left the land of Ur" and "I took Lot" and the others "and also my
father followed after me."

This created a problem of explaining Terah's motivation for
following Abraham, given the fact that in Abraham 1 Terah is
an idolater and seeks to kill Abraham. So Smith's Terah repents,
at least long enough to get him to Haran, as Genesis requires.
The reason for Terah's repentance is a famine, apparently the same
one mentioned in Genesis 12:10 when Abraham is in Canaan,
which forces him to move farther south into Egypt. Smith's text
expands both the duration and the location of the famine to include Chaldea and northern Mesopotamia and has it begin much
earlier when Abraham was still in Ur. The famine appears in
Abraham 1 as God's retribution for Terah's attempting to sacrifice
Abraham (vv. 29–30). Smith uses it to explain the death of Abraham's brother Haran, whereas Genesis gives no cause (Abr. 2:1;

Gen. 11:28). In Abraham, the famine causes Terah to repent, but when the famine "abated" in Haran, Terah returned to his former idolatrous practices (Abr. 1:30; 2:5). When the Book of Abraham mentions the famine in Canaan, it becomes a "continuation" of the famine (2:21). Smith's text maintains one long famine that briefly abates rather than creates a second famine to harmonize with Genesis 26:1, which mentions a famine in the days of Isaac ("there was a famine in the land, beside the first famine that was in the days of Abraham").

These changes do not appear in Smith's 1831 revision of the early chapters of Genesis (which Smith called the Book of Moses), but are nevertheless the kinds of changes that fit comfortably with the revisions he made in his KJV translation.

Assessing Ancient Parallels for Abraham 2

There are larger issues and more immediate concerns in Smith's environment that helped to shape the English text of the Book of Abraham to consider before we assess the value of the isolated parallels to the ancient world. As I have mentioned, Abraham's use of Genesis is little different from Smith's Bible revision, which clearly responded to problems in the English translation of the KJV rather than to restoring original or ancient texts. Of the parallels defenders have offered for Book of Abraham 2, I examine the most significant.

- There is a famine in Abraham's homeland of Chaldea (Abr. 1:29–30; 2:1, 5).

Of the eleven sources Tvedtnes, Hauglid, and Gee offer as parallels to the Book of Abraham, all but one date between the first and fourteenth centuries CE; one, the Book of Jubilees, dates to the second century BCE. One has nothing to do with Abraham and another only mentions the famine in Canaan.[9] Two sources deal with a problematic legend about Abraham and Nimrod competing to feed the people during a famine, with Nimrod drawing

---

9. Philo of Alexandria, dating to the first century CE, is irrelevant because he describes the famine just before Abraham goes into Egypt, and one Muslim tradition is about Noah, not Abraham, and the crows (Tvedtnes, Hauglid, and Gee, *Traditions about the Early Life of Abraham*, 40, 459).

on his many storehouses and Abraham providing grain by a miracle.[10] Six sources deal with another legend about Abraham praying for ravens (crows/birds) to stop eating the seeds that the farmers threw on the ground, causing a scarcity of food. Abraham then teaches the people how to plow and plant the seeds in the soil. In these stories, Abraham is an adolescent between fourteen and fifteen years old.[11] Three references in the Midrash, dating to the fourth and fifth centuries CE, state that there were "two famines" in Abraham's day.[12]

One commentator in Joseph Smith's day noted that there was a chronological problem with the legends describing Abraham and Nimrod as contemporaries. In 1828, Algernon Hebert, in his book titled *Nimrod: A Discourse on Certain Passages of History and Fable*, wrote:

> Although Nimrod was only the fourth in descent from Noah inclusive, and though it is not insinuated that he was ever an old man, and although Abraham was the eleventh in descent from Noah, the Jews have harboured the strange notion of their having been cotemporaries, and describe victories of Abraham over Nimrod, and persecutions of him by the same tyrant.[13]

Herbert speculated that the Nimrod of these fables must be "Tidal king of Nations," who was Abraham's contemporary. Regardless, the famine happens in these legends (dating to the thirteenth and fourteenth centuries CE) before Nimrod attempts to execute Abraham by casting him into a furnace, whereas in the Book of Abraham the reverse is the case since the famine is God's punishment of the Chaldeans for attempting to kill Abraham. Likewise, the raven story happens when Abraham is fourteen or fifteen years old, which is before the attempted execution of Abraham and creates two famines in Abraham's day, contrary to Genesis 26:1. The Midrash states three times that there were

---

10. Tvedtnes, Hauglid, and Gee, *Traditions about the Early Life of Abraham*, 391, 441, 445.

11. Ibid., 15, 211, 230, 241, 263, 275.

12. Ibid., 90, 94, 102.

13. Algernon Hebert, *Nimrod: A Discourse on Certain Passages of History and Fable*, vol. 1 (London: Richard Priestley, 1828), 405–06.

"two famines in the days of Abraham,"[14] probably based on the crow story in Jubilees which takes place before Abraham burns the idols. Clearly, none of these legends mentioning a famine in Chaldea supports the Book of Abraham's account of a famine appearing in retribution for the attempted sacrifice of Abraham.

- Abraham prays God to end the famine in Chaldea (Abr. 2:17).

Abraham's praying to end the famine in Abraham 2:17 does not happen while Abraham is in Ur, as all of the ancient sources state, but rather years later after Abraham has left Haran and is about to enter into Canaan. There he builds an altar and prays that the "famine might be turned away from my father's house," which is located in Haran (Abr. 2:5).

- Haran dies in the famine (Abr. 2:1).

Tvedtnes et al. give only one source for Abraham's brother Haran dying in the famine, but it is actually a fourteenth-century-CE source about Haran dying in a fire.[15] Their choice of this one source is unclear as there are several accounts of Haran dying accidentally in the fire that Abraham builds in which to burn the idols. Still, they have provided no support for Abraham's account of Haran dying in the famine.

- Terah, after repenting, returns to his idols (Abr. 1:30; 2:5).

Of the eleven sources listed, only two clearly state Abraham's father, Terah, turned from idolatry, but for different reasons than given in the Book of Abraham. Instead of Terah being humbled by the famine, as Abraham 1:30 states, it is because in one source he sees Abraham miraculously delivered from Nimrod's furnace and in another because Noah and Shem (chronologically impossible) persuade him to do so.[16]

As mentioned, in Genesis, Terah takes Abraham and the others to Haran for no specific reason. When the Book of Abraham created two callings and two departures by divine command,

---

14. Tvedtnes, Hauglid, and Gee, *Traditions about the Early Life of Abraham,* 90, 94, 102.

15. Ibid., 445–46.

16. Ibid., 133, 149.

Abraham, not his father, was made to lead his family out of Ur. Having Terah repent temporarily is a way of explaining why Terah followed Abraham to Haran.

• Abraham makes converts in Haran (Abr. 2:15).

Genesis 12:5 states that when Abraham left Haran for Canaan, among other things he "took … the souls that they had gotten in Haran." Abraham 2:15 changes this to read: "the souls we had won in Haran"—evidently those whom Abraham had converted. Commenting on Genesis 12:5, Adam Clarke stated: "This may apply either to the persons who were employed in the service of Abram, or to the persons he had been the instrument of converting to the knowledge of the true God; and in this latter sense the Chaldee paraphrasts understood the passage, translating it, *The souls of those whom they proselyted in Haran*."[17] Tvedtnes et al. include, among the sources they quote, the same paraphrasts referred to by Clarke. Abraham merely makes the passage in Genesis less ambiguous.

• Abraham is sixty-two years of age when he leaves Haran, not seventy-five as Genesis says (Abr. 2:14).

Genesis 12:4 states that Abraham is seventy-five when he leaves Haran. The Book of Abraham changes this to sixty-two (Abr. 2:14). Tvedtnes et al. stress the change as important, but it is surprisingly unremarkable as Smith also changed the ages of the patriarchs in his Bible revision without any reason.[18] None of the sources Tvedtnes et al. cite say Abraham was sixty-two when he left Haran, but rather give ages that vary from thirty-seven to eighty.[19] Summarizing the work of Tvedtnes et al., the recent Gospel Topics essay at the LDS Church's website incorrectly asserts that the Book of Abraham is supported by "ancient traditions

---

17. Clarke, *Holy Bible*, 1:90; s.v. Gen. 12:5.

18. Old Testament Manuscript 1, 11–12, 19, in Scott H. Faulring, Kent P. Jackson, and Robert J. Matthews, eds., *Joseph Smith's New Translation of the Bible: Original Manuscripts* (Provo, Utah: Religious Studies Center, Brigham Young University, 2004), 97–98, 110. This portion of the manuscript was composed before 7 Mar. 1831 (ibid., 57).

19. Tvedtnes, Hauglid, and Gee, *Traditions about the Early Life of Abraham*, 31, 81, 122, 246, 270, 324, 353.

located across the Near East," including "Abraham's being 62 years old when he left Haran, not 75 as the biblical account states."[20]

Assessing Ancient Parallels for Abraham 1

I now turn to Book of Abraham 1 which features a story inspired by Facsimile 1. In fact, Facsimile 1 is mentioned twice in the English text, once for the likeness of the bedstead or altar upon which Abraham is placed for sacrifice and once for the representation of the gods who appear under the altar (Abr. 1:12, 14). To Smith, this partly intact vignette looked like human sacrifice, and no doubt the attempted sacrifice of Isaac by Abraham came to mind—where "Abraham stretched forth his hand, and took the knife to slay his son," but God called to him to stop (Gen. 22:10). At some point after the original of Facsimile 1 was mounted on thick paper, someone drew a knife in the priest's right hand. Later in Nauvoo, in consultation with Smith, engraver Reuben Headlock made a printing plate with the knife in the left hand.[21]

Regarding the possible sacrifice of Abraham, Tvedtnes et al. point to fifty-eight early Jewish, Christian, and Muslim sources where Abraham is thrown into a furnace or onto a pyre, most often at the order of Nimrod.[22] Their index subheading reads: "Abraham was brought to be killed or sacrificed because he would

---

20. "Translation and Historicity of the Book of Abraham," www.churchofjesus-christ.org/study/manual/gospel-topics-essays/translation-and-historicity-of-the-book-of-abraham. One of the sources cited in the footnote is probably the source for their statement about Abraham's age: E. Douglas Clark, review of Michael E. Stone, *Armenian Apocrypha Relating to Abraham* (2012), in *BYU Studies Quarterly* 53/2 (2014): 176, which gives an often misleading summary of the parallels between the Book of Abraham and non-biblical Abrahamic traditions. Clark mentions that in a footnote that Stone commented that a difficult reading in one of the texts "may be construed to mean Abraham went forth [from Haran] in his sixtieth year." To use this to make it seem as if the Book of Abraham's 62 was confirmed in ancient sources is disingenuous.

21. On 23 February 1842, Willard Richards recorded in Joseph Smith's journal: "Gave R. Hadlock [Hedlock] instructions concerning the cut for the altar & Gods in the Records of Abraham. As designed for the Times and Seasons" (Joseph Smith, Journal, 23 Feb. 1842, in *JSP*, J2:36). On 1 March 1842, Richards recorded: "During the fore-noon at his office. & printing office correcting the first plate or cut. of the Records of father Abraham, prepared by Reuben Hadlock for the Times & Seasons" (Smith, Journal, 1 Mar. 1842, in *JSP*, J2:39).

22. Tvedtnes, Hauglid, and Gee, *Traditions about the Early Life of Abraham*, index, 539–40.

not worship idols (Abraham 1:7, 12, 15; Facsimile 1, figure 3)." Muhlestein observes that "most non-canonical, ancient traditions held that Abraham was to be burned, while the Book of Abraham spoke of an altar—though it never specifies how he was to be killed on the altar. Facsimile 1 indicates a knife was being used. What I found in the few cases of Egyptian sacrifice (human or not) about which we have details is that typically the sacrificial victim was struck with a blade and then burned. ... This is likely what was intended for Abraham as well."[23] In fact, none of the non-canonical sources has Abraham stabbed or slashed with a knife before being thrown into the fire. He is simply thrown into the fire alive and a miraculous power preserves him until he emerges. More importantly, in these sources Abraham is literally thrown into the fire; this does not happen in the Book of Abraham. None of these sources provide support for the account in the Book of Abraham.

Besides, these stories were well known to Smith's contemporaries. The story is much like the three Hebrews—Shadrach, Meshach, and Abednego—in Daniel 3, where Nebuchadnezzar, king of Babylon, has them thrown into a furnace for refusing to worship a golden image. Adam Clarke commented that the furnace was "an ancient mode of punishment among the Chaldeans, if we may credit the tradition that Abram was cast into such a fire by this idolatrous people because he would not worship their idols."[24] Eighteenth-century English poet and scholar Abraham Cowley noted: "Some of the *Jews* ... tell a ridiculous Fable, that *Abraham* and *Haran* his Brother were cast by the *Chaldeans* into a burning Furnace for opposing their *Idolatry*, in which *Haran* was consumed, but *Abraham* was preserved."[25] This information was readily available to Smith's contemporaries through various

---

23. Kerry Muhlestein, "Egyptian Papyri and the Book of Abraham: A Faithful, Egyptological Point of View," in *No Weapon Shall Prosper*, ed. Robert L. Millet (Salt Lake City: Deseret Book Co., 2011), 220–21.

24. Adam Clarke, *The Holy Bible ... With a Commentary and Critical Notes*, vol. 4 (New York: J. Emory and B. Waugh, for the Methodist Episcopal Church, 1829), 315; s.v. Dan. 3:6.

25. *The Works of Mr. Abraham Cowley: In Two Volumes* (11th ed.; London: J. Tonson, 1710), 1:380. See also Anon., *A View of the Late Momentous Events as Connected with the Latter Days* (London: E. Palmer & R. Baynes, 1830), 9.

dictionaries and encyclopedias in Europe and America.[26] *A New Complete English Dictionary* published in London in 1760, for example, recounted the story of Abraham destroying his father's idols, and continued that "Terah, being angry thereat, brought Abraham before Nimrod, to be punished; that Nimrod, who was one of the Magi, commanded Abraham to worship the fire, and upon his refusal ordered him to be thrown into a burning furnace, but that Abraham came out unhurt."[27] Andrew Hedges is mistaken when he asserts that "none of these [Bible] commentators mentioned the available traditions concerning attempts to sacrifice Abraham himself."[28]

When we understand that Tvedtnes et al. want to support the Book of Abraham by comparing it to legends about the attempted burning of Abraham, the other elements they cite in association with that execution become irrelevant. Consider the following elements when "fire" is included in the descriptions:

- Children are sacrificed [in fire] (Abr. 1:7–8, 10–11).

- Those who do not worship idols are killed [by fire] (Abr. 1:11).

- Abraham is fastened or bound [before being thrown into fire] (Abr. 1:15; Fac. 1, fig. 2).

- When his life is in danger, Abraham prays [not to be burned] (Abr. 1:15).

- An angel comes to rescue Abraham [in fire] (Abr. 1:15; 2:13; Fac. 1, fig. 1).

- God rescues Abraham from death [by fire] (Abr. 1:16; 3:20).

- The altar (furnace) and the idols are destroyed [in fire] (Abr. 1:20).

This last one may require additional comment. The Book of Abraham states that as a result of the attempted sacrifice of Abraham, "the Lord broke down the alter of Elkenah, and of the gods of the land, and utterly destroyed them" (1:20). In the legends that

---

26. See Thomas Stackhouse, *An History of the Holy Bible: From the Beginning of the World to the Establishment of Christianity*, vol. 1 (London: I. Garner, 1787), 192; *Calmet's Dictionary of the Holy Bible*, 5 vols. (London: Holdsworth and Ball, 1830), 1:27.

27. D. Bellamy et al., *A New Complete English Dictionary* (London: J. Fuller, 1760), s.v. Abraham.

28. Andrew H. Hedges, "A Wanderer in a Strange Land," 186.

supposedly support the Book of Abraham, Abraham is the one who either throws the idols into the fire or smashes them, which is why he is being executed. Other so-called parallels are likewise irrelevant or misrepresented:

- The priest (or leader) is smitten and dies (Abr. 1:20, 29).

The Book of Abraham states that in retribution for the attempted sacrifice of Abraham, the Lord not only destroys the altar and gods but also "smote the priest that he died" (1:20). The legends to which Tvedtnes et al. refer either describe the flames of the furnace/pyre rising up into the face of the executioner (sometimes Nimrod) or subsequently a bug flying up Nimrod's nose and slowly eating his brain, causing madness until someone splits Nimrod's head open and the bug flies out. In the Book of Abraham, it is the priest of Pharaoh who dies, not Pharaoh, and not from the fires of the furnace, and there is no mention of Nimrod and a bug. None of Tvedtnes et al.'s sources support the Book of Abraham's account.

- Terah is behind the attempt to kill Abraham (Abr. 1:7, 30).

Tvedtnes et al. cite seven sources to support Tehah's wanting to kill Abraham for destroying his gods. The Book of Abraham does not say that Abraham destroyed Terah's idols, only that Abraham's life was sought because he preached against idolatry, adding that his father, Tehah, was among those who "hearkened not unto my voice, but endeavored to take away my life by the hand of the priest of Elkenah" (Abr. 1:7). There is no account of Terah's dragging Abraham before Pharaoh and demanding his execution for destroying his idols (the penalty for such an act). Rather, in the Book of Abraham, Abraham is silenced by his own family by being offered up as a sacrifice, not executed.

- Terah, Abraham's father, worships idols (Abr. 1:16–17, 27).

It is surprising that these authors list Terah's idolatry as one of the evidences in favor of ancient historicity since Terah's story was well known in Smith's day. For example, *A New Complete English Dictionary*, published in London in 1760, under "A'Bram," reads:

He [Abraham] spent the first years of his life in his father's house, where they adored idols. Many are of opinion, that he himself was at first engaged in this way of worship; but that God giving him better understanding he renounced it; and for this reason, as some believe, suffered a severe persecution from the Chaldeans, who threw him into a fiery furnace; from which God miraculously rescued him. ... Jewish writers tell us, that Terah, Abraham's father, made and sold images, or representations of sun, moon, and stars to worship; and that Abraham being well skilled in the Astronomy of those times, learned from thence, that the heavenly bodies could neither make nor move themselves by their own power; but that there was one only God, who created, preserved, and governed all things, and that therefore they ought to worship him alone.[29]

The published minutes of an anti-Masonic convention held in Massachusetts in 1829 include the following statement about Abraham and his father:

Those who did not emigrate with their venerable ancestor, Shem, fell under the tyranny and idolatry of Nimrod; for the Bible informs us, that Nahor, Terah, and perhaps Serug, bowed to idols. Indeed, ancient story informs us, Terah was a manufacturer of idols. This gave offence to Abraham; and in the absence of Terah, one day, Abraham broke up his father's idols. This so enraged Terah, that he accused Abraham before Nimrod, to have him punished for condemning his gods.[30]

Finally, Terah's idolatry has long been assumed based on Joshua 24:2, which states that "Terah, the father of Abraham ... served other gods."[31] This passage along with the Jewish legends available to Smith and his contemporaries render evidence for the uniquely ancient historicity of Abraham very weak.

---

29. John Marchant et al., *A New Complete English Dictionary* ... (London: J. Fuller, 1760), s.v. "A'Bram." See also Thomas Stackhouse, *An History of the Holy Bible: From the Beginning of the World* ..., vol. 1 (London: I. Garner, 1787), 192.

30. P[eter] Sanborn, *Minutes of an Address, Delivered before the Anti-Masonic Convention of Reading, Mass. January 15, 1829* (Boston: The Free Press, 1829), 11.

31. Andrew H. Hedges agrees that knowledge of "Abraham's father's idolatry," based on Joshua 24:2 and nonbiblical traditions, was readily available to Joseph Smith's contemporaries ("A Wanderer in a Strange Land," 185–86).

Human Sacrifice

Muhlestein has long contended that the Egyptians in Abraham's day practiced human sacrifice, although as a result of challenges from other Egyptologists and scholars of the Near East, he has since equivocated somewhat when addressing the historicity of the Book of Abraham. His 2003 dissertation at UCLA, for example, is titled: "Violence in the Service of Order: The Religious Framework for Sanctioned Killing."[32] The term "sanctioned killing" is ambiguous and may be applied to human sacrifice or capital punishment. In 2011, Muhlestein admitted the lack of evidence for human sacrifice in Egypt but still seemed to hold out hope for a kind of ritual execution: "While the Egyptians *may* have had some kind of regular program of human sacrifice (slight bits of evidence suggest this but there is no conclusive evidence), at the same time they certainly *did* believe there were certain circumstances in which the only appropriate response was to ritually slay someone."[33] The Book of Abraham explicitly describes human sacrifices as being performed "after the manner of the Egyptians" (1:9, 11) "in the land of the Chaldeans" (1:1), specifically in "the land of Ur, of the Chaldees" (2:1), by "the priest of Elkenah [who] was also the priest of Pharaoh" (1:7). As University of Chicago Egyptologist Robert Ritner noted, "Wherever one locates Ur of Chaldees, human sacrifice dictated there by 'priests of Pharaoh' is unbelievable to credible scholars of the Ancient Near East."[34] Christopher Woods, Associate Professor of Sumerology in the Oriental Institute at the University of Chicago, responded to the Book of Abraham's assertions:

> One of the more remarkable claims encountered in the Book of Abraham is the attestation of Egyptian religious and cultic practices at Ur. ... If we are correct in identifying Abraham's Ur, this poses grave

---

32. Kerry Muhlestein, "Violence in the Service of Order: The Religious Framework for Sanctioned Killing in Ancient Egypt" (PhD dissertation, University of California, Los Angeles, 2003).

33. Muhlestein, "Egyptian Papyri and the Book of Abraham," 220–21.

34. Robert K. Ritner, "'Translation and Historicity of the Book of Abraham'—A Response," www.uchicago.edu/sites/oi.uchicago.edu/files/uploads/shared/docs/Research_Archives/Translation%20and%20Historicity%20of%20the%20Book%20of%20Abraham%20final-2.pdf. Accessed 27 Mar. 2019.

difficulties for the account given in the Book of Abraham, as there is no evidence whatsoever for the cults of the purported Egyptian gods described in the narrative or for established Egyptian religious practices more generally in the city. ... If we assume a northern location for Abraham's Ur ... the prospects hardly improve. ... There is no evidence for the regular worship of Egyptian gods at Haran or, for that matter, at any other location in northern Mesopotamia.[35]

Despite such difficulties, defenders of the Book of Abraham not only persist but overstate their case.[36] There is, of course, a simpler explanation: Joseph Smith assumed from Abraham's attempted sacrifice of Isaac that human sacrifice was common in Abraham's time.

Smith's Interpretation of Facsimile 1

When Smith studied the Book of Breathings vignette that became Facsimile 1 (fig. 8.1), he was no doubt reminded of Abraham's attempted sacrifice of Isaac in Genesis (Gen. 22:1–14). In fact, Smith's English text of Abraham refers the reader to Facsimile 1—with its four canopic jars under the lion couch—as an illustration of the altar and four gods named in his text. He also referred specifically to "a god like unto that of Pharaoh, king of Egypt" (Abr. 1:13), which, in 1842, he tied to the crocodile at the bottom of the vignette. Commenting on the reference to Pharaoh in Exodus 1:11, Adam Clarke said:

> It may be necessary to observe that all the Egyptian kings, whatever their *own* name was, took the surname *Pharaoh* when they came to the throne; a name which, in its general acceptation, signified the same as king or monarch, but in its literal meaning, as Bochart has amply proved, it signifies a *crocodile*, which being a *sacred animal* among the Egyptians, the word might be added to their *kings* in order to procure them the greater reverence and respect.[37]

Most Egyptologists, recognizing Facsimile 1 as a depiction of the reanimation of Osiris, restore it in ways contrary to Smith's

---

35. Christopher Woods, "The Practice of Egyptian Religion at 'UR of the Chaldees'?" in Robert K. Ritner, *The Joseph Smith Egyptian Papyri: A Complete Edition* (Salt Lake City: Smith–Petit Foundation, 2011), 73–74.

36. See Muhlestein, "Egyptian Papyri and the Book of Abraham," 221.

37. Clarke, *Holy Bible,* 1:281; s.v. Ex. 1:11.

Figure 8.1. Mounted fragment of the Book of Breathings for Hôr, circa 238–153 BCE (top). "A Fac-Simile from the Book of Abraham, No. 1," Times and Seasons 3 (1 Mar. 1842): 703 (bottom).

reconstruction. While there are many examples of Osiris's reanimation, no two are precisely alike. In some, Osiris is mummified; in others, he is animated. If we draw from other surviving examples of this scene, the missing parts in Smith's vignette should be restored more accurately as follows: The priest's head should be that of a jackal, representing Anubis, the god of the dead. In fact, part of Anubis's headdress is still visible in the area of the right shoulder. The color and clothing are also consistent with Anubis. The knife would not be in the left hand, but, if anything, it would be a small

233

urn. The upper fingers of two hands raised to Osiris's face are more probably the tips of the wing of another bird representing Isis hovering over Osiris, as seen in other similar vignettes.[38]

Muhlestein argues that Smith's Facsimile 1 is different from what one might expect in a scene depicting the reanimation of Osiris. He notes that the person on the altar is neither mummified nor naked as is typically the case with Osiris. More importantly, he states, "The figure on the couch has two hands raised, in a position that almost certainly denotes a struggle."[39] Whether or not the upper fingers are actually a hand or the tips of Isis's wings, Muhlestein's assertion that two hands represent a defensive mode is unlikely given the fact that there are many depictions of Osiris having one hand raised. How does two hands change what is being depicted? In other examples of this scene, other figures surrounding the couch have two hands raised in prayer, supplication, or praise. Note also that the person on the couch is not bound, although Smith's 1842 description says the image represents "Abraham fastened upon an altar" and the Book of Abraham itself says the angel "unloosed my bands" (Abr. 1:15).

Muhlestein also claims: "we have found a papyrus depicting a person on a lion couch whom the Egyptians labeled as Abraham."[40] This is incorrect. This papyrus Muhlestein refers to is a magical text dating to the second century CE written in demotic and Greek accompanying a drawing of a mummy—not identified as Abraham—attended by Anubis. As Ritner explains, "the text is a love compulsion spell intended to force a woman to submit to a male's sexual lust, not a reflection of the Book of Abraham." While the spell includes a string of names, including "Abraham," the names are "no more relevant to the image" than the other names in the "string of magical names." Ritner concludes, "there is no intent

---

38. See, e.g., Edward H. Ashment, "The Facsimiles of the Book of Abraham: A Reappraisal," *Sunstone* 4 (Dec. 1979): 33–46; Ritner, *Joseph Smith Egyptian Papyri*, 91.

39. Muhlestein, "Egyptian Papyri and the Book of Abraham," 234.

40. Ibid. The papyrus Muhlestein refers to is P. Leiden I 384 (PGM XII), in Tvedtnes, Hauglid, and Gee, *Traditions about the Early Life of Abraham*, 501–02, 523. See also John Gee, "References to Abraham Found in Two Egyptian Texts," *Insights: An Ancient Window* (Sept. 1991): 1, 3; John Gee, "Research and Perspectives: Abraham in Ancient Egyptian Texts," *Ensign* (July 1992): 60–62.

here to represent a sacrifice, just Osiris tended by Anubis. ... The body on the lion bed is certainly that of the deceased Osiris ... not a threatened Abraham."[41] Without mentioning Ritner, Muhlestein subsequently admitted that he had misrepresented the magical papyrus, stating: "I have misstated that the text of a particular papyrus said that it was Abraham on top of a lion couch, a scene that is similar to that on Facsimile One. However, the text did not say it was Abraham on top of the lion couch." Yet Muhlestein persists in using this source as evidence for the Book of Abraham. In 2016, he mentioned that Abraham's name appears below the vignette but did not discuss the context. "This means," he stated, "that, while we cannot be sure what the association between Abraham and the lion couch scene was, there was an intended association. The association of a lion couch with Abraham, whatever the nature of the association, is the point here."[42] Muhlestein seems to assume that the reader will make the connection he does not.

"Plain of Olishem"

Muhlestein also discusses one of the names in the Book of Abraham that he and other Mormon scholars believe supports its antiquity. Abraham 1:10 mentions "the altar which stood by the hill called Potiphar's Hill, at the head of the plain of Olishem." When the place name Ulishim was discovered in two texts dating to about Abraham's time, apologists began pointing to it as evidence for the Book of Abraham, although making this argument requires moving Ur from Chaldea in the south to an unlikely location in northern Mesopotamia near Haran. In 2011, Muhlestein mentioned the discovery of Ulishim and stated: "The chances that Joseph Smith would make up a fictional, outlandish place that turned out to be accurate in name, time, and location

---

41. Ritner, "'Translation and Historicity of the Book of Abraham'—A Response," [3]. Ritner gives a transliteration of the words as: "aydyo oryx thambyto abraam o epy ... planoyegxybyoth" etc. (p. [3]). Gee's transliteration and translation reads: "Aidiō ōrich thambitō Abraham who is upon ... anoienchibiōth bind them" (Tvedtnes, Hauglid, and Gee, *Traditions about the Early Life of Abraham*, 502).

42. Kerry Muhlestein, "Assessing the Joseph Smith Papyri: An Introduction to the Historiography of their Acquisitions, Translations, and Interpretations," *Interpreter: A Journal of Latter-day Saint Faith and Scholarship* 22 (2016): 47–48.

are too astronomical even to be considered."[43] Professor Christopher Woods, who specializes in the Ancient Near East, was less impressed, writing in 2011:

> Certainly, Ulishim could be superficially linked on phonetic grounds to the Olishem mentioned in the Book of Abraham in connection with the location of "Ur of Chaldea," where Abraham's kin are said to have turned to the worship of Egyptian gods and Egyptian sacrificial rites. But convincing identification would have to be based on much more substantial evidence. ... [E]verything we know about the region during the period in question—not to mention the likely location of Biblical Ur in southern Mesopotamia—speaks strongly against it. That the phonetic similarity is accidental (and here it should be pointed out that cuneiform sources attest thousands of place names) is again suggested by its coupling to the place "Potiphar's Hill," which likewise is said to be in the land of Ur. Potiphar, of course, is the Egyptian official to whom Joseph is sold in Genesis (37:36, 39:1)—the name Potiphar is Egyptian in derivation ("He-whom-[the sun god]-Re-has-given") and has no place linguistically or culturally in the toponymy of southern or northern Mesopotamia. Finally, it must be observed that the identification of Ulishim with an Olishem alleged to be in the area of Ur makes little geographic sense within the context of Abraham's travels from Ur to Haran and subsequently to Canaan as described in Genesis and the Book of Abraham itself—for Ulishim no doubt lay west of Haran and so the latter could in no way be considered to be en route from Ulishim to Canaan, Haran being diametrically in the wrong direction.[44]

Patriarchal Priesthood

Another point of comparison between ancient and nineteenth-century texts deals with priesthood before Moses. Tvedtnes et al. parallel non-canonical writings mentioning Abraham as a holder of the priesthood and the Book of Abraham's claim that Abraham had a right to the priesthood through his father's lineage. Their index lists:

• Abraham is heir to the priesthood of his fathers (Abr. 1:2–3, 18).

---

43. Muhlestein, "Egyptian Papyri and the Book of Abraham," 222.
44. Woods, "The Practice of Egyptian Religion at 'UR of the Chaldees'?" 74.

- Abraham holds the priesthood (Abr. 1:2; 2:9, 11; Fac. 2, fig. 3; Fac. 3, fig. 1).

In the opening lines of the Book of Abraham, Abraham declares: "I sought for the blessings of the fathers, and the right whereunto I should be ordained to administer the same; ... I became a rightful heir, a High Priest, holding the right belonging to the fathers" (1:2).

As discussed in chapter three, Smith tried to establish the handing down of the high priesthood through the patriarchs, including Abraham, as early as September 1832 (D&C 84:6–16), when he dictated a revelation that included the following: "Abraham received the priesthood from Melchizedek, who received it through the lineage of his fathers, even till Noah; And from Noah till Enoch, through the lineage of their fathers" (vv. 14–15). In the months prior to the arrival of the papyri in 1835, Smith expanded the text of a revelation originally dictated in 1831, in which he declared that the patriarchal priesthood was "instituted in the days of Adam, and came down by lineage" from father to son until Noah, the details of which were "written in the book of Enoch," which "are to be testified of in due time" (D&C 107:40–57).

This Book of Enoch never appeared. Instead, Smith made his case in the Book of Abraham, which had the advantage of being physically accessible. It is no accident that Abraham 1 deals with Abraham's right to the priesthood through the patriarchs, which contrasts with the illegitimate claim by the Pharaohs to the patriarchal priesthood through Ham's daughter Egyptus. Thus one nineteenth-century source of inspiration for the text of the Book of Abraham was Smith's own revelations. This means that some of the ideas in Abraham had their trajectory in Smith's theological development apart from any supposed parallels from the ancient world. As a pseudepigraphist, Smith had a purpose for dictating the text.

Most of the non-canonical sources that Tvedtnes et al. cite have a different reasoning for asserting that Abraham held the priesthood. Later Jews struggled to explain how the patriarchs could build altars and offer sacrifice before Moses instituted the priesthood. They speculated that the patriarchs had authority, but did not actually hold the priesthood. As *Midrash Rabbah*, a rabbinic commentary on the five books of Moses and a few other books dating to at least the fifth century CE, explained: "The priesthood, surely, was not given to any man until Aaron arose. What then is the meaning of the statement here, "*and he [Melchizedek] was priest*"? [Gen. 14:18] Because he offered sacrifices like priests. Shem [who was identified as Melchizedek in Jewish tradition] died and handed it on to Abraham. But was Abraham a firstborn? The fact is that because he was a righteous man the birthright was transferred to him, and he offered sacrifices."[45] According to this source, Abraham acted as a priest but was not a priest. Elsewhere, the same source reports: "R[abbi]. Ishmael holds that Abraham was a High Priest."[46] This was based on an idiosyncratic reading of Psalms 110:4: "The Lord hath sworn, and will not repent, Thou art a priest for ever after the order of Melchizedek." Based on Hebrews 7, Christian commentators interpreted the passage as a reference to Christ's priesthood, whereas the rabbis interpreted it as a reference to Abraham's receiving the priesthood from Melchizedek. Commenting on Psalm 110, Adam Clarke wrote: "The *Jews*, aware of the advantage which the Christian religion must derive from this Psalm, have laboured hard and in vain to give it a contrary sense. Some have attributed it [Psalms 110] to *Eliezer*, the servant or steward of Abraham; and state that he composed it on the occasion of his mater's victory over the *four* kings at the valley of Shaveh, Gen. xiv."[47]

Christian scholars also struggled to explain animal sacrifice before Moses. Eighteenth-century English theologian Joseph Story, in his book *An Essay Concerning the Nature of the Priesthood*, wrote:

> After the Flood, Noah ministered as a Priest when he went out of the Ark. ... Abraham also exercised the same Office, although the youngest Brother: He built an Altar, erected Groves, and called on the Name of the Lord the everlasting God, and offered a Ram for a Burnt-offering. And yet Abraham is no where called a Priest. ... Jacob also, the younger Brother, in the Life-time of his Father Isaac,

---

45. Quoted in Tvedtnes, Hauglid, and Gee, *Traditions about the Early Life of Abraham*, 109.

46. Ibid., 105; see also 100, 101, 120–21.

47. Clarke, *Holy Bible* (1829), 3:360; s.v. Ps. 110.

offered Sacrifice. ... Before Aaron was appointed, Moses performed the Part of a Priest.[48]

Such statements by rabbis and Christian theologians were merely speculations to overcome problems they perceived in the biblical text and have no historical relevance. Smith merely took these speculations a step farther by inserting them into his pseudepigraphic works.

Abraham's Records

The final item I address is the claim in the Book of Abraham that Abraham possessed records containing "the chronology running back from myself to the beginning of the creation, for the records have come into my hands, which I hold unto this present time," and that "the records of the fathers, even the patriarchs, concerning the right of Priesthood, the Lord my God preserved in mine own hands" (Abr. 1:28, 31). These records would certainly include the Book of Enoch mentioned in Smith's expansion of his 1831 revelation (D&C 107:57). In their index, Tvedtnes et al. list as parallels with ancient sources:

- Abraham possessed records from the fathers (Abr. 1:28, 31).
- Abraham left a record of his own (Abr. 1:31).

They cite several sources that mention multiple books of Abraham as well as writings of Enoch and Noah. Of course, the prophecy of Enoch is mentioned in Jude 1:14, and other missing books and writings are mentioned in various other places in the Bible.[49] The handing down of records from one prophet to the next is an early claim of Smith, beginning with the Book of Mormon. Smith chose Abraham for his pseudepigraphic work because the Egyptian setting gave him limited options. Nevertheless, Smith's contemporaries discussed Abraham's writings. As early as 1760, *A New Complete English Dictionary* noted under "Abraham":

---

48. Joseph Story, *An Essay Concerning the Nature of the Priesthood* (London, J. Noon, 1752), 6, 9.

49. See, e.g., Ex. 24:7; Num. 21:14; Josh. 10:13; 1 Sam. 10:25; 1 Kings 11:41; 1 Chron. 29:29; 2 Chron. 12:15; 2 Chron. 20:34; 26:22; 33:19.

He [Abraham] is also said to be author of several works; ... He is said to be the author of that famous book, mentioned in the Talmud, and highly valued by the Rabbins, called *Jetzirah*, or the *Creation*, of which it treats. There is also an apocalypse attributed to him by the Sethians. His assumption is mentioned by St. Athanasius; and Origen tells us of an apocryphal book, said to be written by him, wherein two angels, a good and bad one, are introduced disputing about his salvation, or damnation. The Jews make him also the composer of some prayers, and of the 19th Psalm; and a treatise against idolatry.[50]

This statement about Abraham is repeated in other dictionaries in Europe and America.[51] The first source is *Sefer Yetzirah* or "Book of Creation" (sixth century CE), which Tvedtnes et al. include in their compilation, stating that "many early commentators and other books of kabbalah ... attribute its authorship to Abraham."[52] The next source is probably the *Apocalypse of Abraham* (first or second century CE), also included in Tvedtnes et al.[53] The apocryphal book mentioned by Origen is probably the *Testament of Abraham* (first or second century CE), which is not in Tvedtnes et al. but is discussed by Hugh Nibley. The "assumption" of Abraham mentioned by Athansius is also probably the *Testament of Abraham* but is considered here as a separate work.

According to Charles Buck's well-known *Theological Dictionary* published in Philadelphia in 1826, the Muslims believed there were 104 sacred books, and that "ten were given to Adam, fifty to Seth, thirty to Edris or Enoch, ten to Abraham."[54] In his 1829 debate with skeptic Robert Owen, Alexander Campbell, the founder of the Disciples of Christ, said, "But Dr. Hyde, and the

---

50. D. Bellamy et al., *A New Complete English Dictionary* (London: J. Fuller, 1760), s.v. Abraham. See also *An Universal History, from the Earliest Account of Time* (London: T. Osborne, 1748), 3:271.

51. John Marchant et al., *A New Complete English Dictionary* ... (London: J. Fuller, 1760), s.v.; *An Universal History, from the Earliest Account of Time* (London: T. Osborne, 1748), 3:271; Abraham Rees, *The Cyclopaedia; or, Universal Dictionary of Arts, Sciences, and Literature* (London: Longman, Hurst, Rees, Orme, & Brown, 1819), vol. 1 under "Abraham."

52. Tvedtnes, Hauglid, and Gee, *Traditions about the Early Life of Abraham*, 86.

53. Ibid., 52–60.

54. Charles Buck, *A Theological Dictionary* (Philadelphia: Joseph J. Woodward, 1826), 330.

most learned antiquarians, present documental proof that the Persians retained the true history of the creation, of the antediluvian age; and so attached were the Persians to the religion of Abraham, that the sacred book which contained their religion is called *Sohi Ibrahim*, i.e., the Book of Abraham."[55]

The possibility that Abraham may have written books is less important than the fact that there is no evidence that he wrote the book translated by Smith.

Conclusion

Some of Smith's contemporaries knew the content of early Jewish, Christian, and Muslim traditions about Abraham. Whether or not Smith knew about these sources is debatable, but such a debate is unnecessary since the majority of those works would not have been helpful to him. Most of the ancient sources are, at best, only remotely similar to the text of the Book of Abraham or contain accounts that are completely different from what Abraham describes.

The sacrifice of Abraham, the central theme of Abraham 1, was inspired by Facsimile 1; Abraham 2 is a reworking of Genesis 11 and 12. Most importantly, the Book of Abraham served Smith's interests in documenting the establishment of the high priesthood among the ancient patriarchs. Later, in Nauvoo, Abraham is used to establish Smith's doctrine of a pre-mortal existence for humans and of a plurality of gods, which, ironically, conflicts with Abraham's monotheism.

In the previous chapters of this study, I provide what I believe is reliable, compelling evidence to show that Smith, who could not accurately translate Egyptian, nonetheless produced an Egyptian Alphabet and a Grammar and Alphabet of the Egyptian Language. He then "translated," as he stated unambiguously, the English text of a Book of Abraham from characters on the Breathing Permit of

---

55. *The Evidences of Christianity: A Debate between Robert Owen, of New Lanark, Scotland, and Alexander Campbell, President of Bethany College, Va. Containing an Examination of the "Social System" and All the Systems of Skepticism of Ancient and Modern Times Held in the City of Cincinnati, Ohio, in April, 1829* (Nashville: McQuiddy Printing Co., 1912), 388.

Hôr. Defenders of Smith's Abraham try to overcome this evidence by proposing demonstrably implausible, factually erroneous theories. Weak, nonsensical parallels should never be used to justify patently incorrect conclusions. History deserves better.

■ Conclusion

None of the leading theories of Book of Abraham historicity exhibits an accurate understanding of the Joseph Smith Egyptian papers. Attempts to explain the creation of the three Egyptian Alphabets and the bound Grammar and Alphabet of the Egyptian Language as an effort by W. W. Phelps to reverse engineer Joseph Smith's English translation of the Book of Abraham are simply not sustainable. Part 1 of these works deals with Princess Katumin and her mother, who lived centuries after Abraham. The information regarding Katumin was based on Smith's translation of characters from fragments of Amenhotep's Book of the Dead and possibly the Ta-sherit-Min scroll, the latter of which Smith identified with Joseph son of Jacob/Israel. Part 2 of these works begins with the "pure language" characters and definitions, which Smith talked openly about before he procured the Egyptian papyri. The themes of the pure language continue with characters copied from column 3 of JSP I, which is immediately to the right of the vignette that is identified today as Abraham Facsimile 1. The translation of these characters evolves into a factually incorrect explanation of Egyptian astronomy. The English translation of Abraham begins with characters from JSP XI, the first two of which appear at the end of the Alphabets, at the beginning of the bound Grammar, and in the margin of the longest manuscript of the English Book of Abraham. These documents represent a movement through the Egyptian papyri that ended with an English translation of the Book of Abraham, not a reverse engineering of Abraham's contents.

Apologetic theories also ignore Smith's official history, which not only dates the beginning of the creation of the Alphabets and bound Grammar to July 1835 but explicitly assigns primary authorship to Smith. This portion of Smith's official history was composed in 1843 by Willard Richards and W. W. Phelps, the latter of who was the main scribe during the creation of these documents. Understanding that Richards and Phelps worked under Smith's supervision corrects attempts to date the Alphabets and bound Grammar to October 1835 or to the beginning of 1836, after Smith's translation of the Book of Abraham. It also corrects speculation that Phelps was responsible for the content of the Alphabets and bound Grammar.

The Kirtland documents, together with entries in Smith's journal, show the general order in which the documents were created. The identification of the Michael Chandler mummies and papyri came first. Phelps and Oliver Cowdery copied fragments of the Amenhotep Book of the Dead into two small notebooks, the latter of which bears the title "Valuable Discovery of hiden reccords that have been obtained from the ancient buring place of the Egiyptians," followed by Smith's holographic signature. Some of the hieratic characters were translated as an epitaph for Princess Katumin, supposedly one of the mummies, which also identified the male mummy as her father, King Onitas.

This material evolved into part 1 of the three Alphabets, which were created simultaneously by Smith, Phelps, and Cowdery. The "translation" of characters in this section pertains to the founding of Egypt and to various aspects of the Egyptian dynasty, particularly the female royal line of the Kah-tou-mun family. Part 2 deals with characters from the pure language project which preceded the arrival in Kirtland of the Egyptian papyri. These characters pertain to grades of heavenly beings, humans, and priesthood. This section is followed by characters copied from the vertical columns flanking Facsimile 1 on JSP I and mixed with derivative or invented hieratic-looking characters, which continues with priesthood lineage and levels of paradise leading to a Celestial Kingdom, "the greatest place of hapiness where God resides." About two-thirds of the characters in part 2 have no definitions, but Cowdery later added names to eighteen characters in Smith's Alphabet. Parts 3, 4, and 5 of the Alphabets were sequentially copied from the columns flanking Facsimile 1. Only two of these characters received names: Ki-ah-bram Ki-ah-bra-oam Zub-zool-oan and Iota nitah veh ah que. At the end of the Alphabets appear two characters, which were copied from JSP XI (once attached to JSP I) and given English definitions that relate to the beginning of the Book of Abraham.

At this point Phelps began entering material into two bound volumes: one for the finalized English translation and another titled "Grammar and A[l]phabet of the Egyptian Language." In the translation book, Phelps drew the two characters from the beginning of JSP XI and a third that coincided with an empty space on the damaged papyrus, but which actually came from column 2 on JSP I, corresponding with Ki-ah-bram Ki-ah-bra-oam Zub-zool-oan in the Alphabets. To the right of these, Phelps entered a rough translation of the first three verses of the Book of Abraham. At the same time, Phelps used the same three characters at the beginning of the Grammar book to explain how each part of a character has meaning and how that meaning may be amplified and expanded through five degrees of English translation. Phelps organized the Grammar book with five sections or degrees with blank pages between each to allow for expansion. The characters in part 1 of the Alphabets were copied into the bound Grammar and developed—that is, translated into English—in each of the five degrees. In part 2, the method of copying changed so that the first character in the Alphabet was copied into the first degree of the Grammar, the second character into the second degree, and so on until the fifth. Then the sixth character was copied into the first degree, the seventh character into the second, and so on. However, the last seven characters, which pertain to Egyptian astronomy, were copied into the Grammar and developed in all five degrees. Smith's ideas on cosmology did not come from Facsimile 2 but from characters copied from column 3 on JSP I. This coincides with the entry in Smith's journal which mentions that Smith, Cowdery, and Phelps "labored on the Egyptian alphabet" and that "the system of astronomy was unfolded."[1] This work evidently continued on 7 October 1835, according to Smith's journal.[2]

The next mention in Smith's journal of working on the English translation is 19 November, after Smith inspected work on the Kirtland Temple/House of the Lord with scribes Frederick G.

---

1. Joseph Smith, Journal, 1 Oct. 1835, CHL (*JSP*, J1:67).
2. Smith, Journal, 7 Oct. 1835 (*JSP*, J1:71).

Williams and Warren Parrish and then "returned home and spent the day in translating the Egyptian records."[3] Evidence shows that the two Book of Abraham manuscripts, one in the handwriting of Williams and the other in that of Parrish, were composed simultaneously from Smith's dictation and that the hieratic and hieratic-looking characters were drawn in the margins as the men proceeded with the translation. This was accomplished on 19–20 November, two consecutive days of translating mentioned in Smith's journal.[4] Both manuscripts begin with Abraham 1:4, which is where Phelps ended his entry in the translation book. Williams's document includes four verses not recorded by Parrish, ending with Abraham 2:6.

At some point, Parrish copied this additional material into the translation book following Phelps's text. Then Parrish wrote Abraham 2:7–18 directly into the translation book as Smith dictated. This occurred on 24–25 November, the last two consecutive days in Smith's journal that record his working on the translation in Kirtland.

All three Kirtland-era Book of Abraham manuscripts bear the same hieratic Egyptian or invented hieratic-looking characters in the left margins. These characters were copied in order from the first four lines of JSP XI—that is, the Breathing Permit of Hôr—except where characters were invented to fill gaps in the damaged papyrus. Some writers have suggested that the characters served to organize the paragraphs on the documents or to provide decorations. Such explanations fail because the characters are integral to the English text, which is sometimes divided mid-sentence to line up with the characters. Nor do such explanations account for the invented hieratic-looking characters. The obvious relationship between the characters and the accompanying English text is that of a translation, and the source of that "translation" is the Breathing Permit of Hôr.

Despite efforts to resume his work on the Egyptian papyri and related manuscripts, Smith did not return to dictating more of the text until 8–9 March 1842 in Nauvoo, Illinois, at which

---

3. Smith, Journal, 19 Nov. 1835 (*JSP*, J1:107).

4. Smith, Journal, 19–20 Nov. 1835 (*JSP*, J1:107).

time he dictated Abraham 2:19–5:21 to Willard Richards. This text bears evidence of Smith's knowledge of Hebrew, which he had gained from his lessons with Joshua Seixas in January–March 1836. Attempts to explain away this evidence and force the last three chapters of the Book of Abraham into an 1835 context are not convincing.

Reversing the chronology of events seems essential to theories that seek to support the narrative that the Alphabets and bound Grammar were the work of Phelps who was attempting to reverse engineer Smith's English translation of Abraham—thus releasing Smith from responsibility for the creation of the Alphabets and Grammar and thereby preserving the historicity of the Book of Abraham as well as, presumably, Smith's prophetic reputation.

In their essay on Book of Abraham chronology, Kerry Muhlestein and Megan Hansen conclude that "there is no theory that accounts for all the evidence" and that "either we need to find more evidence or create another model." In my opinion, there is at least one more choice: Perhaps we should interpret the evidence we do have more accurately. Muhlestein and Hansen continue: "For the time being, the most we can do is say that it seems likely Joseph Smith translated all of the text of the Book of Abraham we now have, and perhaps even more, by 1835. While such a theory is plausible, it remains problematic because it is simultaneously incomplete *and* the most probable of the theories proposed thus far."[5]

On the contrary, the chronology they propose is neither plausible nor does it account for most of the evidence but requires the addition of problematic, improbable interpretations such as a long-scroll and a missing text containing more than the published Book of Abraham. The entire rationale for reversing the chronology is to sustain the claim that the Alphabets and bound Grammar derive from the text of the Book of Abraham. Once it is appreciated that they do not derive from Abraham, there is no reason to postulate a reverse-translation theory or a missing

---

5. Kerry Muhlestein and Megan Hansen, "'The Work of Translating': The Book of Abraham's Translation Chronology," in J. Spencer Fluhman and Brent L. Top, eds., *Let Us Reason Together: Essays in Honor of the Life's Work of Robert L. Millet* (Provo, Utah: Brigham Young University, 2016), 157.

proto-Abraham text. Likewise, once the true nature of the hieratic characters in the margins of the Book of Abraham manuscripts is understood, there is no need to look for a missing source and/or to speculate about the length of the Hôr scroll.

Some may think that expertise in Egyptology renders one qualified to comment on all aspects of the Smith papyri. Needless to say, I disagree. The meaning of Smith's Egyptian papers has little to do with Egyptology and much with what Smith claimed he was doing, which cannot be recovered without an accurate historical understanding of the documents and a true chronology of events.

In late 2018, Brian Hauglid announced that he has changed his mind about Book of Abraham apologetics:

> For the record, I no longer hold the views that have been quoted from my 2010 book [*A Textual History of the Book of Abraham*].[6] ... In fact, I'm no longer interested or involved in apologetics in any way. I wholeheartedly agree with Dan [Vogel]'s excellent assessment of the Abraham/Egyptian documents. ... I now reject a missing Abraham manuscript. I agree that two of the Abraham manuscripts were simultaneously dictated. I agree that the Egyptian papers were used to produce the BoA [Book of Abraham]. I agree that only Abr. 1:1– 2:18 were produced in 1835 and that Abr. 2:19–5:21 were produced in Nauvoo. And on and on. I no longer agree with [John] Gee or [Kerry] Muhlestein.[7]

Gee and Muhlestein may represent the last stand of one school of Abrahamic apologetics, which holds onto the claim that Smith translated an actual Egyptian document in his possession that is

---

6. Brian Hauglid, *A Textual History of the Book of Abraham: Manuscripts and Editions* (Provo, Utah: Neal A. Maxwell Institute for Religious Scholarship, Brigham Young University, 2010).

7. Brian Hauglid, Facebook post to Dan Vogel, 8 Nov. 2018 (www.facebook. com/dan.vogel.35/posts/1398006876998582?hc_location=ufi; accessed 12 Aug. 2019). Hauglid's statement has since been widely disseminated. See, for example, Jeff Lindsay, "A Precious Resource with Some Gaps," *Interpreter: A Journal of Latter-day Saint Faith and Scholarship* 33 [2019]: 19 (www.journal.interpreterfoundation.org/a-precious-resource-with-some-gaps/). See Brian M. Hauglid, "'Translating an Alphabet to the Book of Abraham': Joseph Smith's Study of the Egyptian Language and His Translation of the Book of Abraham," in *Producing Ancient Scripture: Joseph Smith's Translation Projects in the Development of Mormon Christianity*, eds. Michael Hubbard MacKay, Mark Ashurst-McGee, and Brian M. Hauglid (Salt Lake City: University of Utah Press, 2020), 363–89, where Hauglid argues precisely as he had previously stated to me.

no longer extant. Robin Scott Jensen and Terryl Givens represent a new school of apologetics which asserts that the Egyptian papyri served as a "catalyst" for Smith's dictation of the Book of Abraham, which was the result, not of translation, but of independent revelation. These scholars believe that Smith never had an actual Egyptian Book of Abraham in his possession, although he may have believed he did. Proponents of such a catalyst theory believe they can explain away—unsuccessfully, I believe—references to Facsimile 1 in Abraham 1:12 and 14 as later insertions.

While some scholars entertain the possibility that "prophetic misunderstanding and prophetic inspiration may coexist in the same person even at the same moment,"[8] can they conceive the possibility that Smith believed himself authorized by God to use misdirection/deception—claiming, for example, that his "inspired" text was a translation—to promote greater faith in his "inspired pseudepigrapha"? A revelation Smith dictated in 1830 says yes. According to this revelation, God sometimes uses misleading language about "eternal damnation," which the revelation denies as a literal truth, so that "it might work upon the hearts of the children of men, altogether for my name's glory" (D&C 19:7).[9] This theory is supported by the text of Abraham itself. At the end of the second chapter, which Smith dictated in 1842, the story of Abraham asking Sarah to tell the Egyptians that she is his sister instead of his wife in order to save his life is changed to God telling Abraham to tell Sarah to lie to the Egyptians (Abr. 2:22–25).[10]

The belief that God sometimes inspires the use of what we may

---

8. Terryl Givens with Brian M. Hauglid, *The Pearl of Greatest Price: Mormonism's Most Controversial Scripture* (New York: Oxford University Press, 2019), 180. See "Translation and Historicity of the Book of Abraham," www.churchofjesuschrist.org/study/manual/gospel-topics-essays/translation-and-historicity-of-the-book-of-abraham?lang=eng; accessed 3 Dec.2019.

9. For a discussion of the religious use of deception and its relevance to Smith, see Dan Vogel, "'The Prophet Puzzle' Revisited," *Dialogue: A Journal of Mormon Thought* 31 (Fall 1998): 125–40; Dan Vogel, *Joseph Smith: The Making of a Prophet* (Salt Lake City: Signature Books, 2004), x–xxi.

10. A Baptist newspaper accused Smith of publishing "a blundering imitation of the history of Abraham," which "represents the Lord as instructing Abraham to tell Sarai to lie to the Egyptians" ("Mormon Blasphemy," *Witness* [Pittsburgh] [July 1842]: 34).

deem to be questionable methods to accomplish a greater good is a useful belief for a pseudepigraphist. Those who write pseudepigrapha, explains New Testament scholar Bart D. Erhman, do so to give their own religious views—often deemed heretical by the dominant group of believers—respectability and authority.[11] Likewise, the Book of Abraham attempted to lend ancient support to several of Joseph Smith's doctrinal innovations not clearly discussed in the Bible, such as a line of high priests among the ancient patriarchs, origin of the Black race and preservation of the "curse" through the Flood, plurality of gods, and the preexistence of humankind.

In this work, I have shown that attempts to draw parallels between the Book of Abraham and the ancient world are flawed; that we have the source of the Book of Abraham; that the reverse-translation, long-scroll, and catalyst theories are untenable; and that attempts to redefine translation apart from what Joseph Smith represented amount to question-begging. For believers, perhaps a responsible way forward is *faith*, faith in Smith as a revelator who sometimes used what we today may define as questionable strategies to secure and strengthen that faith.

---

11. Bart D. Ehrman, *Forgery and Counter-Forgery: The Use of Literary Deceit in Early Christian Polemics* (2013), 150, and *Forged: Writing in the Name of God—Why the Bible's Authors Are Not Who We Think They Are* (2012), 8–9, which examine the motivation and function behind early Christian forgeries.

Index

Abraham (patriarch), ix–xii, xvi, xxiii, 1, 5, 10, 18, 25, 26, 33, 34, 133, 134n42, 135, 151–52, 160, 166, 221, 249; ancient traditions about, 215–42; and astronomy/cosmology, xxiii, 121, 123, 132, 143, 152–53, 216, 217; as human sacrifice, 188, 198; meaning of name, 4–5; one or two calls, 218–22; receives revelation through Urim and Thummim, 133; signature of, 193–94; *see also* Book of Abraham

Adamic language. *See* pure language

Amenhotep papyrus. *See* Joseph Smith Papyri

anti-Masonry, 113, 230. *See also* Masonry

apologetic arguments: characters in margins of English text do not imply translation, xvii, 8–9, 10–15; disproportion of English text to characters inconsistent with a translation scenario, 1–7; Egyptian Alphabets and Grammar not authored by Joseph Smith, xvii, 7–9, 33, 243–44; Book of Abraham translation preceded creation of Egyptian Alphabets and Grammar (reverse-translation theory), xvii, 8–9, 16, 20–21, 33, 40–42, 59, 60, 74, 80, 82, 147, 172, 177, 243–47, 250; entire Book of Abraham dictated in 1835, 15–16, 157–70; Egyptian Alphabets and Grammar created in 1836/1837, 36–40, 100–02, 125–27, 243; Book of Abraham translated

from a second record at end of Hôr papyrus (long scroll/lost papyrus theory), 8, 52, 179–205, 247–50; Parrish and Williams documents not orally dictated but copied from a no longer extant original dictated text of Abraham, 16–31; Joseph Smith translated more than the current text of Abraham, 16, 170–77; Joseph Smith dictated Abraham by revelation and mistakenly believed he translated from papyri (catalyst theory), 204–13, 249–50; evidence of antiquity in English text of Abraham, 215–42; attempts to redefine/problematize the term translation, 205–13

Appleby, William I., 196–98

Ashby, Benjamin, 201

Ashment, Edward, 23, 23n58

Baer, Klaus, 14, 60, 61, 74, 75n47, 185

Bennett, James Arlington, 98, 99, 124

Blanchard, Jerusha, 202–03

Bokovoy, David, 205, 207, 213

Book of Abraham: probable dictation chronology of, 140–42, 147–51, 157–58, 246–47; and high and patriarchal priesthoods, 67–74, 236–39; and race, 96, 105–11, 115–17; and the cosmos, 120, 132–40, 143–44; and nineteenth-century sources, 215–22. *See also* Scripture Index

Book of Abraham Translation Manuscripts. *See* Joseph Smith Egyptian Papers

Book of Breathings, xiv, xv, 1, 2, 8, 9, 35, 40–41, 46, 52, 57, 60, 74, 75, 82, 85, 104, 121, 127, 137, 164, 179, 180, 181, 188, 192, 195, 199, 204, 205, 208, 209, 214, 217, 232, 241, 246. *See also* Joseph Smith Papyri

Book of the Dead, xiv, xxiii, 40, 46, 51, 52, 57, 59, 104, 105, 142, 185, 187, 195, 200, 243, 244. *See also* Joseph Smith Papyri

Book of Enoch, 67–68, 69, 108, 161, 237, 239, 240

Book of Mormon, vii, viii, 5–6, 22, 23n57, 26, 63, 68, 77, 205, 209, 211, 212, 239

Book of Breathings. *See* Joseph Smith Papyri

Book of the Dead. *See* Joseph Smith Papyri

Brodie, Fawn M., 153

Brown, Samuel, 6, 66

Call, Anson, 172–77

Champollion, François, ix, 6, 66, 206, 213, 207

Chandler, Michael, vii–x, xv, xxiii, 46n37, 68, 180, 195, 196, 211, 212, 244

Clarke, Adam, 4, 48, 128, 139, 217–19, 225, 227, 232, 238

Coenen, Marc, 185

Combs, Abel, xiv, 186, 203

Cook, Andrew W., 185–86, 186n19

Cowdery, Oliver, 73, 107, 154, 161, 172, 173, 175, 176, 211; describes papyri, vii, 46n37, 51, 104, 180, 198; explains compressed nature of

Egyptian language, 2–3; recounts purchase of papyri, viii–ix; as scribe, xi, xii–xiii, xxiii, 24, 23n57, 33, 34, 37, 38, 45–49, 54–55, 69, 70–71, 72, 73–74, 80, 82n54, 84, 84n57, 88, 89, 89n69, 89n70, 90–91, 92, 93, 97, 115, 120, 121, 125, 127, 143, 244, 245

Dick, Thomas, 129, 129n28, 132, 138, 139, 144, 153, 154

Egypt, 109n39, 185, 197, 198, 210; Abraham in, xii, 69, 121, 152, 160, 166, 196, 222n9; Joseph in, 34, 69, 166, 196; and astronomy, ix, 111, 114, 121, 122, 126, 128, 132, 134n42, 138, 143, 152–53, 165, 243, 245; discovered and founded by Ham's daughter, 41, 43–45, 50–51, 53, 56–57, 60, 82, 105–106, 110, 211, 244; called Mestre by Josephus, 69, 166; called Ah-Mehstrah by Joseph Smith, 70, 166; and alleged human sacrifice, 231

Egyptian Alphabet(s). *See* Joseph Smith Egyptian Papers

Egyptus (daughter of Ham), 106, 107, 109, 210, 237; as a man's name in Josephus, 107. *See also* Zeptah

Facsimiles. *See* Joseph Smith Egyptian Papers

Freemasonry. *See* Masonry

Gee, John, xvi, 8, 11, 12, 14, 15, 16, 21, 28, 31, 33, 34, 37, 38, 40, 41, 42, 45, 52, 59, 81, 82, 83, 84, 85, 86, 88, 89, 92, 93, 97, 98, 99, 100, 101, 102, 125, 126, 127, 128, 133, 134, 135, 136, 137, 138, 142, 155, 157, 158, 159, 159n44, 164, 170, 171,

172, 174, 181–86, 186n19, 187–93, 202n64, 215, 222, 235n41, 248

Gibbs, Josiah W., 155, 156

Givens, Terryl, viii, 7, 205–11, 249

Grammar and Alphabet of the Egyptian Language (GAEL). *See* Joseph Smith Egyptian Papers

Hamblin, William J., 133, 135, 136

Hansen, Megan, 16, 39, 159, 160, 162–71, 173, 247

Harris, Martin, 6, 162, 212n95

Hauglid, Brian, ix, xvi–xvii, xviii, 9, 10, 19, 19n39, 20, 20n42, 21–28, 31, 39, 59, 60, 128, 141, 147, 148, 157, 158, 158n39, 159, 190, 192, 192n34, 215, 222, 248, 248n7

Haven, Charlotte, 49, 198–201, 203

Hebrew (language), 5, 6, 35, 66, 101, 102, 102n22, 143, 145–47, 154–57, 158n39, 160, 162–63, 167–69, 177, 197, 199, 212, 215, 247

Hedges, Andrew, 216

Hedlock, Reuben, 126n21, 149, 150, 226

Herschel, William, 130, 139, 123

Heusser, Edward and Alice, xiv

hieratic (characters), viii, xiv, xv, xxiii, xxiv, 1, 2, 4, 9, 10, 23, 28, 35, 40, 41, 46, 47, 48, 50, 55, 56, 61, 74, 75, 106, 111, 142, 179, 184, 185, 217, 244, 246, 248

Huggins, Ronald V., 102n22

hypocephalus. *See* Joseph Smith Egyptian Papers

Irwin, John, 6

Jensen, Robin Scott, ix, 19, 20, 20n42, 21, 23, 148, 158, 190, 192, 192n34, 204, 249

Joseph (son of Jacob/Israel), x, xi, xxiii, 33, 34, 51, 69, 72, 187

Joseph Smith Egyptian Papers (listed individually):

–"Valuable Discovery" notebooks, xi, xii, xv, xxiii, xxiv, 45–49, 54–55, 56, 59, 86, 105, 142, 142n66, 170, 211, 244

–Copies of Egyptian characters (single sheets), xii–xiii, 45

–Egyptian Alphabet(s), xi, xiii, xvii, xxiii, 3, 4, 7, 9, 16, 20, 21, 31, 33, 36–39, 40–45, 49–50, 52–57, 59–62, 65, 68, 70, 74–80, 81–84, 85, 86, 88, 89, 89n70, 92, 93, 96, 97, 100, 100n18, 101, 103, 104, 105, 110–14, 121, 124–28, 142, 157, 158, 165, 170–72, 193, 211, 241, 243–45, 247; dating of, 36–40; overview of, 40–41; part one of, 41–45, 49–54; source of characters in part one, 54–57; part two of, 59–67, 79–81; source of characters in part two, 74–79; and Abraham, 81–85; authorship of, 85–93

–Grammar and Alphabet of the Egyptian Language (GAEL), xi, xiii, xvii, xxiii, 3–9, 15, 16, 18, 20, 21, 31, 33, 36–38, 40, 42–45, 50, 52, 53, 56, 57, 59, 60, 65, 68, 70, 74, 76, 80, 83, 85, 86, 88, 89, 96–102, 103–105, 106, 110, 111, 112, 114, 120, 121, 125–27, 131, 133, 138, 140, 143, 153, 157, 158, 160, 164, 165, 170–72, 176, 207, 211, 217, 241, 243–45, 247; organized into a five-degree system, 7, 37, 40–41, 44–45, 50–53, 84–86, 88–89, 98, 102–103, 111, 127, 129, 165, 207, 245; compound nature of characters explained, 2–7; and race, 95–96, 115–17; authorship of, 96–102; date of, 100–102, 125–27; overview of, 102–105; part one of, 105–111; part two of, 111–15; and cosmology, 119–40, 143–44

–hypocephalus (Fac. 2), ix, xiii, xv

–Book of Abraham Translation Manuscripts, xiii, 1, 3; meaning of characters in margins, 10–15; some characters in margins invented (and correspond to lacunae in JSP XI), xv, 9, 14–15, 40, 41, 45, 56, 60, 86, 211, 244, 246

   –Translation Manuscript-A (F. G. Williams): composed from dictation (not copied from missing original), 15–31; dating of, 140–41

   –Translation Manuscript-B (W. Parrish): composed from dictation (not copied from missing original), 15–31; dating of, 140–41

   –Translation Manuscript-C (W. W. Phelps/W. Parrish): cut from translation book, 15, 23, 25, 26, 28–31, 34, 71, 84, 104, 105, 115, 140, 141, 147, 148, 158, 245, 246; Phelps's contribution possibly dates to July 1835, 36–40; dating of Parrish's contribution, 141

   –Book of Abraham Manuscript (copy) (W. Richards), xi–xii, xiii; copied from Book of Abraham Manuscript-C, 147–50

   –Translation Manuscript (Abraham 3, fragment) (W. Richards), xii, xiii; dictated 8–9 March 1842, 150, 157–58, 160

   –Facsimiles, xiv, 189, 205; No. 1, xii, xiii, xv, xxiv, 40, 47, 86, 87, 182, 188, 189, 192, 211, 214, 215, 226, 227, 232–35, 241, 243, 244, 249; fig. 1, 228; fig. 2, 228

   –No. 2, iv, xii, xiii, xxiv, 39, 46, 80, 119, 120, 126, 133, 136, 137, 138, 139, 140, 143, 147, 149, 150, 151, 153, 160, 163, 176, 177, 182, 183, 184, 185, 187, 196, 199, 208, 215, 245; fig. 3, 237; fig. 4, 160; fig. 5, 138n55, 160. See also hypocephalus

   –No. 3, xxiv; fig. 1, 237

Joseph Smith Papers (editors), 10, 21, 64n13, 87n63, 97, 146, 161, 174, 192

Joseph Smith Papyri (JSP) (listed individually): purchase of, vii, xv; fragments mounted under glass, 192–95; thought to have been destroyed in Great Chicago Fire of 1871, xiv, xvii, 10, 179, 181–82, 187, 203, 204; rediscovered, xiv, 1

   –Hôr papyrus (Book of Breathings), xiv, xv, 4, 8, 40–41, 46, 56, 57, 60, 74, 82, 106, 121, 164, 179, 180, 183–85, 187, 196, 205, 208, 211, 214, 217, 242, 246, 248; lacunae (gaps), xv, 1, 14, 56, 111, 211, 106, 246; length of, 182–88; JSP I, xiii, 3, 36, 40, 41, 47, 75, 78, 79, 82, 83, 85–88, 88n64, 104, 113, 127, 164, 183, 185, 194, 243, 244, 245; JSP XI, xv, 1–3, 7, 35, 83, 87, 88, 104, 105, 127, 164, 183, 193, 243, 245, 246. See also Book of Breathings

   –Ta-sherit-Min papyrus (Book of the Dead), xii–xiii, xiv, 40, 46, 47, 51, 52, 55, 56, 105, 180, 187, 195, 196, 199, 200, 200n60, 243. See also Book of the Dead

   –Amenhotep papyrus (missing) (Book of the Dead), xii–xiii, xxiii,

40, 46, 46n37, 47, 55, 57, 59, 86, 195, 196, 217, 243, 244. *See also* Book of the Dead

–Nefer-ir-nebu papyrus, xiv, 51

–Hypocephalus. *See* Joseph Smith Egyptian Papers

Joseph Smith Translation (JST/Bible Revision), 20, 109, 213, 222, 225

Josephus, 51, 69, 70, 107, 111, 121, 132, 143, 152

Katumin (princess), xxiii, 33, 45–49, 50, 52, 53, 54–57

Kircher, Athanasius, 65, 66, 206

Kirtland, Ohio, vii–ix, xi, xv, 1, 7, 8, 10, 15, 17, 20, 29, 31, 33, 35, 36, 48, 61n3, 63, 64, 64n13, 68n26, 87, 87n63, 96n2, 97, 101, 115, 121, 125, 141, 142, 145, 147–49, 151, 159, 159n44, 161, 162, 168, 169, 171, 174, 175, 177, 179, 181, 183, 192, 204, 210, 211, 243, 244, 245, 246, 248

Kirtland Egyptian Papers. *See* Joseph Smith Egyptian Papers

Kolob (ruling star/planet), 18, 78, 80, 120, 122, 124, 127, 131–33, 135, 139, 163, 164

Larson, Stan, 26

Latter Day Saints' Messenger and Advocate, 2, 33, 51, 115, 154, 180

Lebolo, Antonio, vii, viin2

Levi-Strauss, Claude, 207

Lindsay, Jeffrey Dean, 20n42, 23

Marquardt, H. Michael, 180

Masonry, 77; Masonic signs, 76–77, 113–14; and temple endowment, 208–209. *See also* anti-Masonry

Metcalfe, Brent Lee, 48n43

Morgan, William, 76, 113

Muhlestein, Kerry, xvi, 16, 33, 39, 52, 81, 82, 159, 160, 162–71, 173, 181, 182, 184, 186, 188, 192–202, 204, 213n98, 227, 231, 234, 235, 247, 248

mummies, vii, viii, xiv, xv–xvi, xxiii, 33, 47, 49, 51, 53, 68, 96, 105, 106, 179, 180, 193–96, 198, 201–04, 217, 244; purchase of, vii, xv, xxiii; sold to Abel Combs, xiv

Nauvoo, Illinois, xi, 49, 80, 99, 100n18, 131, 132, 147, 150, 151, 156, 163, 169, 171, 174, 188, 193, 196, 198, 208, 226, 241, 246, 248

New York Metropolitan Museum, xiv, xv, 1, 181n5

Nibley, Hugh, xvi, 1–2, 7–8, 10–11, 15, 23n58, 33, 40, 42, 47, 86, 179, 180, 181, 187, 188, 209n87, 216, 240

Olea(h) (earth/moon/plains of), 62, 81, 124n17, 160, 162, 162n52, 163

Olishem (plain of), 235–36

Onitas (Onitus) (King), 33, 48, 49, 53, 54, 186, 217, 244

Osiris (god), 4, 46, 187, 188, 232, 233, 234–35

Ostler, Blake T., 205, 209, 213

Parrish, Warren, xi, xiii, xxiii–xxiv, 9–12, 15–20, 20n42, 21–23, 23n58, 24–31, 35, 36, 45, 48, 80, 97, 98n8, 127, 128, 131, 140, 141, 142, 145n3, 147–49, 158, 164, 170, 171, 189–92, 214, 246

Peterson, Daniel C., 133, 135, 136

Pettengill, Amos, 119, 120

Phelps, William W., x–xi, 6, 68, 79, 95, 107–09, 111, 115, 161, 162, 173n83, 207, 212; as scribe, xi, xii–xiii, xxiii, 4, 10, 11, 15, 23n58, 29, 31, 33–40, 43, 44, 46–48, 50, 53, 55, 61, 61n3, 68, 71, 72, 82–84, 92, 93, 104, 105, 121, 125–27, 140–42, 147, 148, 171, 193, 213, 244, 245, 246; as supposed author of Egyptian Alphabets and Grammar, 7–9, 33, 34, 37–40, 42, 59, 85–93, 96–101, 137, 147, 243, 247

pure (Adamic) language, xiii, 40, 59–65, 68, 74, 79–81, 86, 111, 161, 243, 244

"Reformed Egyptian," vii, viii, 5

Richards, Willard, xi–xii, xiii, xxiv, 34, 34n4, 36–39, 39n20, 97, 99, 126, 147–50, 156–58, 160, 167, 173n83, 226n21, 243, 244, 247

Rigdon, Sidney, 67, 96n3, 120, 125, 161, 173, 176

Ritner, Robert K., xv, 46, 48, 50, 51, 183, 184, 184n14, 185, 187, 209, 231, 234, 235, 235n41

Schleiermacher, Friedrich, 209

Seixas, Joshua, 101, 102, 102n22, 145–47, 154–58, 160, 167–69, 177, 247

Seyffarth, Gustavus, 6, 186, 187

Shinehah, 124n17, 158–63

Shurtliff, Luman, 192, 194–95

Skousen, Royal, 24, 25n62

Smith, Emma, xiv, 203

Smith, Joseph, Jr.: compares papyri to Book of Mormon characters, viii; purchases mummies and papyri, vii, xiv, xv, xxiii; identifies patriarchs Abraham and Joseph as authors of two scrolls, x–xi, xxiii, 69, 170, 179, 180, 194, 199, 243; as scribe for one of the Alphabets, xi, xiii, 36–37, 40–45, 53, 89–93; as author of Egyptian Alphabets and Grammar, xvii, xxiii, 31–32, 40, 96–102; dictates translation of the papyri, vii–viii, ix, x–xii, xv–xvi, xxiii–xxiv, 9–10, 17–21, 31, 34–35, 57, 128, 140–41, 151–53, 170, 218–22; responsible for characters in margins of translation manuscripts, 9, 14; and pure language, 61–66; as student of Hebrew, 145–47, 154–58; and high and patriarchal priesthoods (including claims of angelic ordination), 67–74; and African slavery, 95–96, 107–11, 115–17; models Abrahamic cosmology after church organization, 124–25, 143–44; and plurality of gods, 167–69; use of delay and brainstorming, 217–18; publishes Book of Abraham (1842), 119, 147; translates in conventional sense with divine aid, 211–13; and pseudepigrapha, 68, 74, 85, 205, 207, 213, 218, 237, 239, 249–50; and pious fraud/deception, 249–50; and *History of the Church* account, 34, 36, 38, 93, 102, 126, 180; and Bible revision, 20, 109, 213, 222, 225

Smith, Joseph III, 203–04

Smith, Joseph F., 187–88

Smith, Lucy Mack, 14, 49, 198, 199, 201, 202, 202n64, 203

St. Louis Museum, xiv, 186, 203

Ta-sherit-Min papyrus. *See* Joseph Smith Papyri

Times and Seasons, xii, xxiv, 98, 119, 126, 147–51, 160, 168, 174, 176, 177, 197, 201, 212, 233

Tressler, Henry, 196

Tvedtnes, John, 86–88, 215, 222, 224–26, 228, 229, 236, 237, 239, 240

"Valuable Discovery." *See* Joseph Smith Egyptian Papers

West, William, 14

Whitmer, David, 6, 72, 175, 212

Whitmer, John, 33, 161, 175

Williams, Frederick G.: as scribe, xi, xiii, xxiii–xxiv, 10, 13, 15, 17–19, 19n39, 20, 20n42, 21–23, 23n57, 23n58, 24, 25, 27–31, 45, 48, 66, 87, 98n8, 115, 125, 128, 128n23, 140, 141, 148, 149, 162, 170, 171, 189, 190, 192, 192n34, 214, 246

Williams, R. John, 66

Woodruff, Wilford, 163, 164, 174

Woods, Christopher, 231

Woods Museum (Chicago), xiv, 72, 181, 187, 236

Young, Brigham, 63, 110

Zeptah (wife of Ham), 106, 107; changed to Egyptus, 106, 107n32, 109

237. *See also* Egyptus

Zomar, 64, 65

Zucker, Louis C., 154, 155

Scripture Index

Abraham

Abr. 1:1–3 — 34, 115, 171
Abr. 1:2 — 68, 83, 71, 237
Abr. 1:2–3 — 236
Abr. 1:4 — 17, 246
Abr. 1:7 — 227, 229
Abr. 1:7–8 — 228
Abr. 1:10 — 235
Abr. 1:10–11 — 228
Abr. 1:12 — 188, 189, 192n34, 227, 249
Abr. 1:13 — 232
Abr. 1:14 — 190, 192n34, 249
Abr. 1:15 — 227, 228, 234
Abr. 1:16 — 228
Abr. 1:16–17 — 229
Abr. 1:17 — 18
Abr. 1:18 — 27, 236
Abr. 1:20 — 228, 229
Abr. 1:21–22 — 53
Abr. 1:23 — 116
Abr. 1:23–24 — 45, 106
Abr. 1:23–28 — 9n23
Abr. 1:24 — 116
Abr. 1:25 — 210
Abr. 1:25–27 — 53
Abr. 1:26 — 17, 109, 110, 116
Abr. 1:27 — 109
Abr. 1:28 — 239
Abr. 1:29 — 229
Abr. 1:29–30 — 221, 222
Abr. 1:30 — 222, 224, 229
Abr. 1:31 — 69, 152, 239
Abr. 2:1 — 221, 222, 224
Abr. 2:2 — 192
Abr. 2:2–6 — 28
Abr. 2:3–4 — 219
Abr. 2:4 — 221
Abr. 2:5 — 222, 224
Abr. 2:6 — 25, 246
Abr. 2:6–8 — 219–20
Abr. 2:8 — 26

Abr. 2:9 — 237
Abr. 2:9–11 — 220
Abr. 2:11 — 237
Abr. 2:12 — 226
Abr. 2:13 — 228
Abr. 2:14 — 225, 226
Abr. 2:15 — 225
Abr. 2:17 — 224, 224
Abr. 2:18 — 140, 148, 158, 169, 218
Abr. 2:19 — 151–52
Abr. 2:22–25 — 249
Abr. 2:24 — 152
Abr. 3:1 — 152
Abr. 3:4 — 135, 139
Abr. 3:5 — 136, 138, 143
Abr. 3:8 — 136
Abr. 3:9 — 136
Abr. 3:13 — 124, 137, 155, 159, 159n44, 160, 162, 163
Abr. 3:15 — 152
Abr. 3:15–23 — 153
Abr. 3:17 — 136
Abr. 3:18 — 154
Abr. 3:18–19 — 136
Abr. 3:19 — 164
Abr. 3:20 — 228
Abr. 4 — 156
Abr. 4:1 — 156
Abr. 4:2 — 156, 157
Abr. 4:6 — 157
Abr. 4–5 — 167, 168, 170, 215
Abr. 5 — 173

Doctrine and Covenants

D&C 9 — 211
D&C 19:7 — 249
D&C 27:8 — 72
D&C 27:12 — 73
D&C 29:14 — 137n51
D&C 34:9 — 137n51
D&C 45:42 — 137n51
D&C 64:21–22 — 96

259

D&C 76 — 112
D&C 76:24 — 120
D&C 82:12 — 159n42
D&C 84:6–16 — 237
D&C 88:43 — 137n52
D&C 88:45 — 131, 137n51, 137n52
D&C 88:51–57 — 131
D&C 88:60–61 — 131
D&C 88:87 — 137n51
D&C 93:29 — 154
D&C 102:3 — 125
D&C 104:21 — 159n42
D&C 104:40 — 159n42
D&C 104:48 — 159n42
D&C 107:33 — 125
D&C 107:39–57 — 67
D&C 107:40–57 — 237
D&C 107:41–52 — 67
D&C 107:53–55 — 65, 73
D&C 107:56–57 — 67
D&C 107:57 — 239
D&C 116 — 64
D&C 117 — 162
D&C 121:87 — 137n51
D&C 128:23 — 137n51
D&C 133:49 — 137n51
D&C 134:12 — 116

Bible
Gen. 1 — 145, 155, 155n26, 170
Gen. 1:2 — 156, 157
Gen. 1:6 — 157
Gen. 2 — 155, 170
Gen. 6:6 — 213n99
Gen. 9:25 — 107
Gen. 9:25–26 — 116
Gen. 9:26 — 108n36
Gen. 11 — 218, 241
Gen. 11:1–9 — 61, 63n5
Gen. 11:28 — 222
Gen. 11:31 — 221
Gen. 12 — 151, 218, 241
Gen. 12:1 — 218, 219
Gen. 12:2 — 5n7, 219n7, 166
Gen. 12:2–3 — 83, 220
Gen. 12:4 — 225
Gen. 12:5 — 225, 225n17

Gen. 12:7 — 151
Gen. 12:7–13 — 170
Gen. 12:10 — 221
Gen. 12:14–20 — 152
Gen. 14:18 — 238
Gen. 17:5 — 5n7
Gen. 22:1–14 — 232
Gen. 22:10 — 226
Gen. 24:1–9 — 114
Gen. 26:1 — 222, 223
Gen. 37:36 — 236
Gen. 39:1 — 236
Ex. 1:6 — 48n45
Ex. 1:11 — 232, 232n37
Ex. 24:7 — 239n49
Num. 21:14 — 239n49
Deut. 10:14 — 128
Josh. 10:13 — 239n49
1 Sam. 10:25 — 239n49
1 Kings 11:41 — 239n49
1 Chron. 29:29 — 239n49
2 Chron. 12:15 — 239n49
2 Chron. 20:34 — 239n49
2 Chron. 26:22 — 239n49
2 Chron. 33:19 — 239n49
Ps. 19 — 240
Ps. 110 — 238, 238n47
Ezk. 1:5–10 — 198
Isa. 19:11 — 109
Isa. 45:18 — 119
Isa. 54:4 — 26
Dan. 3:6 — 227
Dan. 7:13–14 — 64
Acts 7:2 — 219, 219n8
Acts 7:2–3 — 218
Acts 7:3 — 219
Heb. 7 — 238
Rev. 4:7–8 — 198

Book of Moses
Moses 5:30–31 — 77
Moses 6:4 — 63
Moses 6:6 — 63
Moses 7:20 — 109
Moses 7:22 — 108
Moses 8:25 — 213n99

JST
Gen. 11:30 — 108n37

Book of Mormon
Alma 24:19 — 25n63
Alma 37:21 — 77
Alma 37:27 — 77
Alma 39:16 — 25n63
Alma 56:41 — 24
3 Ne. 22:4 — 26
Ether 1:33–37 — 63
Ether 8:15 — 77

About the Author

Dan Vogel is the author of *Joseph Smith: The Making of a Prophet*, which won the Best Book Award from the Mormon History Association, and editor of the five-volume series, *Early Mormon Documents*, recipient of Best Documentary awards from both the Mormon History Association and the John Whitmer Historical Association. His other works include, as author, *Indian Origins and the Book of Mormon, Religious Seekers and the Advent of Mormonism*; and, as editor, *The Word of God: Essays on Mormon Scripture*, a critical edition of Eber D. Howe's *Mormonism Unvailed*, and the eight-volume *History of Joseph Smith and The Church of Jesus Christ of Latter-day Saints: A Source- and Text-Critical Edition*. He is co-editor, with Brent Lee Metcalfe, of *American Apocrypha: Essays on the Book of Mormon*. He lives in Ohio.